A way to measure time

to Clark
Oct 28/92
from an
associate
of Finnish literature

[illegible]

A way to measure time

CONTEMPORARY FINNISH LITERATURE

SUOMALAISEN KIRJALLISUUDEN SEURA • HELSINKI
FINNISH LITERATURE SOCIETY

ISBN 951-717-695-3

Sisälähetysseuran kirjapaino Raamattutalo
Pieksämäki 1992

Contents

	To the reader	15
Pentti Haanpää	At his own graveside	19
	Translated by David Barrett	
Mika Waltari	Aton's kingdom*	35
	Translated by Naomi Walford	
Aaro Hellaakoski	*The last dinosaur*	46
	The nightingale	47
	Translated by Herbert Lomas	
P. Mustapää	*The yellow jackdaw*	57
	Drought	58
	Memory	60
	The fowler	60
	Thrace	60
	Translated by Herbert Lomas	
Gunnar Björling	*Tremble, hand*	64
	I have no birds' names	65
	And when day is not	65
	Your hunger your pain	65
	The leaves did not break	66
	We went not namelessly away	66
	One day the bells	67
	Now all boats glide away	67
	Now is not dead	68
	That yet in the night	68
	Translated by David McDuff	
Rabbe Enckell	*O Bridge of Interjections...*	69
	Translated by David McDuff	

Childhood

The house slowly — Bo Carpelan 85
Translated by Anne Born

The far journey* — Toivo Pekkanen 86
Translated by Hildi Hawkins

Leaving home* — Eila Pennanen 89
Translated by Hildi Hawkins

A farewell to the Rööperi of my childhood — Arvo Turtiainen 100
Translated by Anselm Hollo

The Ostrobothnian about the sea — Lars Huldén 102
Translated by David McDuff

Light's sound
5 o'clock
You do not see them
From the light — Peter Sandelin 103
Translated by Rika Lesser

An old cabin
In grandma's room
This is how it is — Viljo Kajava 105
Translated by Keith Bosley

Eila Kivikkaho
Shouted interjection 109
Raising the flag 109
Defiance 110
Victories and defeats 110
The generations 111
Long-playing record 113
Charcoal sketch 113
Translated by Herbert Lomas

Solveig von Schoultz
Dream 114
Heart 114
Translated by Lennart Bruce and Sonja Bruce
The birds 115

Sea in November 115
Gone away 116
The burning glass 116
A way to measure time 116
Translated by Anne Born

Eeva-Liisa Manner
Counterpoint 118
When shore and reflection 119
*Strontium** 120
Deep and clear 121
Boabdil, the defeated Arab 121
There are other worlds 123
Theorem 123
Story 124
I've walked 124
The sea-and-skyline 125
Translated by Herbert Lomas

Tove Jansson
The stone 126
Translated by Kingsley Hart

Veikko Huovinen
Hirri 130
Translated by Herbert Lomas

Home

Summer morning — Aale Tynni 139
Translated by Herbert Lomas

Stone god — Aila Meriluoto 140
Translated by Herbert Lomas

Concrete mixer — Lauri Viita 141
Translated by Herbert Lomas

Hymn to my homeland
From the interior — Pentti Holappa 145
Translated by Herbert Lomas

Tragedy, Finnish style — Matti Rossi 147
Translated by Keith Bosley

Bedrock — Helvi Juvonen 148
Translated by Herbert Lomas

Finnish winter dawn Elmer Diktonius 149
Translated by George C. Schoolfield

Poem of our land Juhani Peltonen 150
Translated by Anselm Hollo

In a letter you write to me Ralf Nordgren 151
Translated by David McDuff

From evening's ragged blue Viljo Kajava 152
In autumn the field grows old
The invincible
Translated by Keith Bosley

Tree of God* Christer Kihlman 153
Translated by Joan Tate

The spring Bo Carpelan 159
Translated by Anne Born

Paavo Haavikko
No forest no field 163
Outside, blind trees 163
I hear the rain wake up 164
Now, when on some night 164
Translated by Anselm Hollo
I like slow things 164
Translated by Keith Bosley
In praise of the tyrant 165
Very carefully, lingering 167
Conversations with Dante 167
Translated by Anselm Hollo

Tuomas Anhava
I've never made a book out of less 171
I look out 171
House, fir trees 171
The soul is in me 172
It's already dark 172
The wind is an eye 172
Whoever believes what he sees 172
The snow's turned 172
Translated by Herbert Lomas

War

Boxes of nails — Veijo Meri 175
Translated by Aili and Austin Flint

Soldiers' voices* — Paavo Rintala 182
Translated by Herbert Lomas

Before battle* — Väinö Linna 190
Translated by Herbert Lomas

Clock time* — Samuli Paronen 196
Translated by Hildi Hawkins

The unetched heart* — Eeva Joenpelto 200
Translated by Aili and Austin Flint

The funeral — Marja-Liisa Vartio 205
Translated by Aili and Austin Flint

A little old lady — Helena Anhava 214
Translated by Herbert Lomas

The villas of forgetfulness — Matti Paavilainen 215
Translated by Herbert Lomas

War's coming* — Eeva Kilpi 215
Translated by Hildi Hawkins

In the summer of 1941* — Oscar Parland 223
Translated by Joan Tate

Eight statements — Kari Aronpuro 227
Translated by Herbert Lomas

Antti Hyry — The dam 231
Translated by Herbert Lomas

Mirkka Rekola — *What is this* 238
You remember 238
One wouldn't want 239
It's here 239
I laid my pack lunch 239
Today they're so ideal 239

How could I 240
A peoplecloud 240
Before water 240
Translated by Herbert Lomas

Pentti Saarikoski
We were a people 241
The sea and forest 241
The men rowed 241
Life is given to man 242
Horse 242
One day a dog 242
*The Obscure dances** 243
Translated by Herbert Lomas

Väinö Kirstinä
If you come 250
Around you 250
One roof 251
Horse, hoofs 251
Above the blackening ground 251
Through my face 252
The bird lived 252
*The first of May** 252
Translated by Aili and Austin Flint

Jarkko Laine
The hotel Oblivion 255
Oh Mr Q., Death 257
Life, when you taste it 258
Picture post card 258
I know the scent 259
Translated by Anselm Hollo

Jyrki Pellinen
I think 260
Close to myself 260
The depiction 260
Tree 262
Spring days 262
It's as if 263
I was a quiet child 263
I almost wrote 263
Translated by Herbert Lomas

Martti Joenpolvi The guest of honour 265
Translated by Herbert Lomas

Alpo Ruuth Fury 274
Translated by Anselm Hollo

Lassi Nummi *Recitative* 278
As a ship gliding 281
Ballad of a heat-wave morning 282
A shallow ditch 284
Translated by Herbert Lomas

Antti Tuuri Melancholy tale 285
Translated by Herbert Lomas

Erno Paasilinna The advance of our troops 295
Translated by Hildi Hawkins

Intimacy

When the one Helena Anhava 309
Translated by Herbert Lomas

Our friendship Maila Pylkkönen 309
Translated by Herbert Lomas

Love song Inga-Britt Wik 310
Translated by David McDuff

Arctic journey Kirsti Simonsuuri 311
Translated by Kirsti Simonsuuri

The music has died away Kai Nieminen 311
Translated by Herbert Lomas

My old dad
Year by year Niilo Rauhala 312
Translated by Herbert Lomas

Come home Tua Forsström 313
Translated by David McDuff

The boat Henrik Tikkanen 314
Translated by Rika Lesser

And then
Circle
Translated by David McDuff — Gösta Ågren 314

At home* — Kerttu-Kaarina Suosalmi 316
Translated by Herbert Lomas

A family reunion* — Pentti Holappa 321
Translated by Hildi Hawkins

Vanumäki — Pertti Nieminen 325
Translated by Herbert Lomas

The days — Hannu Salakka 326
Translated by Herbert Lomas

Unlived life
Little children — Pentti Saaritsa 327
Translated by Herbert Lomas

Right in the center — Märta Tikkanen 328
Translated by Stina Katchadourian

An extra Christmas gift* — Annika Idström 329
Translated by Hildi Hawkins

My child, my mourning dress — Eira Stenberg 333
Translated by Herbert Lomas

Eat this message — Thomas Wulff 334
Translated by David McDuff

Midsummer eve — Jörn Donner 335
Translated by David McDuff

A town
I'm drinking tea
On every side — Hannu Mäkelä 338
Translated by Keith Bosley

When I was born
When a person — Claes Andersson 341
Translated by Rika Lesser

Deep south nights — Arto Melleri 342
Translated by Herbert Lomas

Europe's antechamber — Rosa Liksom 344
Translated by Hildi Hawkins

Very possible
When I was younger — Bo Carpelan 346
Translated by David McDuff

Winter
Birth and death — Veijo Meri 348
Translated by Aili and Austin Flint

Daniel Katz — A little night music 353
Translated by Anselm Hollo

Raija Siekkinen — The meal 361
Translated by Hildi Hawkins

Joni Skiftesvik — The black gull 368
Translated by Herbert Lomas

Johan Bargum — Canberra, can you hear me? 374
Translated by George Blecher and Lone Thygesen Blecher

Beyond reality

I speak and listen
Call these rooms
Keeping silence
Here I am — Tyyne Saastamoinen 387
Translated by Herbert Lomas

I'm thinking
When the Heavenly Host — Pertti Nieminen 388
Translated by Herbert Lomas

To the union's member country — Pekka Suhonen 389
Translated by Herbert Lomas

If a lady's hat *The crow* Translated by David McDuff	Håkon Påwals	389
A time's coming *As light on rock* Translated by Herbert Lomas	Caj Westerberg	391
Everything, everything! *Swimming instructions* Translated by Herbert Lomas	Risto Ahti	393
The aquarium Translated by Hildi Hawkins	Leena Krohn	394
The Old Water Rat Translated by Herbert Lomas	Kirsi Kunnas	396
Birds Translated by David McDuff	Thomas Wulff	397
Olli Jalonen	An ever-deepening sleep Translated by Herbert Lomas	403
Sirkka Turkka	*Before death itself comes*	412
	Impromptu to my grandfather that never was	414
	Inside the trees	419
	And I want you Translated by Herbert Lomas	420
Matti Klinge	A history of Finland in fourteen paragraphs	421
Acknowledgments		425
Authors		427

Texts marked with an asterisk are extracts from novels, longer prose pieces or poems.

Titles have been added to some prose extracts by the editors.

To the reader

This book presents an anthology of writing in Finland since the Second World War.

From the earliest item, a short story by Pentti Haanpää written in 1945, to the most recent poems of the late 1980s by Gösta Ågren and Sirkka Turkka, the texts trace their writers' individual preoccupations and their orientation toward broader literary and stylistic developments, both at home and abroad. In principle, the writers are represented by complete works, poems or short stories, rather than extracts. The presentation is chronological, interrupted by five thematic groups containing individual poems or prose extracts centred around the subjects of the pre-war experience of childhood, nationalism, war and evacuation, human relations, and the role of fantasy in reality. By thus casting different lights on the writers represented, our hope has been to add depth to the portrait of Finnish literature offered by this book.

Drama is excluded, as are literature for children and young people, and essays. Finnish and Finland-Swedish literature appear alongside each other; the original language of each text is given in the notes on writers. The majority of the texts were translated specifically for this volume. A short survey of Finnish history, by Matti Klinge, is to be found at the end of the book.

A way to measure time is published as the result of a commission from the Committee for the 75th Anniversary of Finnish Independence, which is celebrated in 1992.

PENTTI HAANPÄÄ
MIKA WALTARI
AARO HELLAAKOSKI
P. MUSTAPÄÄ
GUNNAR BJÖRLING
RABBE ENCKELL

Pentti Haanpää

AT HIS OWN GRAVESIDE

A passenger, a shortish middle-aged man dressed in a decent but rather baggy-looking suit, got off the bus at a minor side-turning. The bus sped off on its way, lurching and rattling; it looked much the worse for wear after the long years of the war, with the big charcoal-gas cylinder bouncing behind it like a great black goblin. A cloud of dust rose from the dry road into the mild September air, hovered, drifted, and slowly dispersed.

The man stood for quite a while at the roadside and watched as the bus disappeared round the bend and the dust-cloud cleared away. His face was obscured by a thick, darkish, slightly curly beard, in which a close observer might have discerned a few strands of silvery grey. The area covered by this beard was, indeed, exceptionally large: it extended almost to the tired brown eyes with which the man now gazed indifferently about him.

He set off down the by-road at a leisurely pace, like a man in no particular hurry, carrying only a small cardboard attaché case. His eye took in the fields of autumn stubble, with the stooks standing up here and there like grey trolls. It was easy to see that this was not a landscape that had been under the plough since time began: the edge of the forest, black or greenish, was never far away. Somewhere a threshing-barn was belching grey smoke, and the smell of the drying grain reached his nostrils as he walked.

The narrow road was almost deserted. Ahead, for part of the way, a farmer's waggon lumbered along, piled high with its top-heavy load of sheaves. The bearded man met nobody except for a group of young children. Dirt and sunburn had combined to darken their faces, which he scanned with a curious kind of intentness as they passed him.

If this solitary traveller's mind had been as open to view as the landscape, in which wildness and cultivation vied with each other for dominance, one would have seen that this part of the world was not, for him, a dead region, with its inner essence concealed. To him, these surroundings were very, very familiar. It was hereabouts that he too had once been a grubby ragamuffin, gadding around the countryside, like the kids he had just met. Of course, the place had changed since those days: the smooth, green expanses of agricultural land had widened, new dwellings had been built or improvised, and brightened with red paint. Many trivial memories came into his mind as he walked on. Many a time, as a young lad, he had hurtled along this road on his bicycle, on his way to savour the delights, modest in those days but still adequate, of a village dance. Over there were the places where he had worked, or travelled to work. And here, to the music of buzzing mosquitoes, he had sat with a group of workmates and taken his first swig of distilled liquor, out of a blue bottle . . .

The past, so far away and yet within touching distance, seemed composed in equal measure of wistful happiness and bitter disillusion. It was in these surroundings that he had begun by slow degrees to grow older, to wonder uncertainly whether life really had to be so meaningless. It was hard to believe, at least if one was young.

And then, the unexpected: the tempest that had swept him out of this landscape, once and for all, so that his presence on this road at this moment was like a ghostly visitation . . .

The bearded man stopped for a longish while at a spot from which he could just discern the faded red paint of a small cottage. It was the first home that he, or that other man in the past, had ever owned. Dear to him at first, the focus of many dreams for the future, it had gradually become as stifling and oppressive as a prison. His wife Anna-Mari, as he had soon discovered, was not only a slovenly housekeeper but also extremely simple-minded. Life had quickly lost its savour for him, and even fatherhood had failed to re-animate him. Yes, the boy must still be here too, doubtless a hulking great fellow by now. One of those war-orphans. Hm!

The man left the road and began, with some hesitation, to make his way towards the red cottage. A ghost revisiting the earth, he imagined, would have somewhat similar feelings. A return from 'the other side' could bring the survivors nothing but consternation and havoc.

Nevertheless, he surveyed the once familiar surroundings with a certain curiosity. The little red cottage had by no means become a dead relic of the past. Although it showed its age and bore signs of deterioration, it had been patched up here and there. The shed had a brand-new shiny roof, and the fence was new too; behind it a cow mooed insistently, waiting to be milked. In the yard a tethered sheep shook its tail busily, and a small party of hens explored the ground for whatever they could scavenge. Life, it seemed, was still going on.

Since there seemed to be no one about, the bearded man walked boldly up to the door. The feel of the handle, as he turned it, was so familiar that for a moment he almost believed that he was back in the past, and that everything that had happened since had been merely a dream. It was as if he had just been down to the village on some business or other, and was now returning to the comforts – and the vexations – of the domestic hearth. Anna-Mari would be there, the same as ever: in a constant flurry of activity, with little to show for it; and not too tidy either. Nattering on about the same thing for hours on end, like some incompetent song-bird . . .

But the woman sitting at the sewing-machine in the living-room was not Anna-Mari, but a complete stranger to him, as he realised at once.

'Good day to you, ma'am', he said in greeting.

The woman invited him to sit down, explaining that she was not the lady of the house. 'Just sitting in, like.'

The bearded man said he was a displaced person, looking around for somewhere to settle. He asked if he might have a drop of milk to drink with the sandwiches he had with him.

The woman was not sure whether she had the right to dispense milk to strangers, but brought a mugful nevertheless, and put it on the table. The bearded man tucked in to his sandwiches, talking as he munched, and the woman, who was youngish, seemed equally ready for conversation as she set her machine whirring again and guided her material beneath the needle.

The visitor was told that the owner of this little house was a war-widow. To-day she had gone over to the village some distance away, to see the welfare people and all that. So much paperwork these days, always forms to fill in. Yes, there was one child, a boy of about ten; he was out too, gadding around somewhere. The widow, well, she just muddled along somehow in this little cottage, and there was a patch of land too, where she could grow something to help keep body and soul together. And then of course she had this pension from the government, because of her late husband, you know . . .

'Looks as if she could do with a man about the place,' joked the visitor. 'Fair size, is it, this plot of land?'

'Depends what you mean by a fair size: enough work there for a man, certainly, but would it be worth it? I mean, she seems to prefer things the way they are now. She didn't always get on too good with that dead husband of hers, *late* husband I mean, he wasn't dead then, of course . . .,' she prattled on.

The bearded man had finished his frugal meal. He seemed less eager to talk now.

'Oh yes, she could have had a husband by now, that Anna-Mari, it's not as if there weren't none on offer, even now when there's so few men about, since the war. There's one fellow been lodging here from time to time, helping her with odd jobs and suchlike, some of the heavy work. They've thought about getting married, but then they're frightened she might lose her pension.'

The bearded man may not have been altogether cheered by this evidence of how little the living were missing their dead. He relapsed into a moody silence.

Suddenly the door was flung open and a boy burst into the room. He was distinctly dirty, and made a lot of noise. He asked at once where his mother was.

'She's not back yet. Should have been here by now.'

'Had a puncture, I expect, with those rotten tyres.' The boy was already clumping around noisily, foraging for something to eat. He devoured the food greedily, taking great mouthfuls, and glancing from time to time at the bearded man seated on the bench. He, for his part, stared at the boy as if spellbound, unable to take his eyes off him, and unable to speak.

From behind the dense forest of his beard came a faint sound which might have been a sigh. That boy, he was thinking, might be looking at me rather differently, not quite so casually, if I were to open my mouth and tell him certain things. What kind of effect would that have on a young person's life? The boy was four years old when his father went away – never to return. Little does he realise that the arms that carried him that day are so close to him now . . . No, a shock like that could only do him harm. Much better for him to keep his mental picture of a father who died heroically in the war. He had not come back here to do more than have a look. Such a desire as might be felt, on a moonlit autumn night, by a dead man lying in his grave. But in broad daylight, like this? 'Dead men shouldn't peep.' How true!

The bearded man paid for his mugful of milk, took one more long look at the boy, and then got up, said goodbye, and left.

He walked away, quickening his steps. He had the feeling that two pairs of eyes were watching him. He could almost hear the conversation – the boy's childish voice saying, 'That man kept staring at me!' and the woman's deeper tones: 'He certainly did! Reckon he'll know you again next time he sees you.'

Yes, it would be dangerous to hang around. Four years or so isn't a very long time, and behind his whiskery disguise he felt like a hare hiding in a hedge.

Quickly, he walked on. It was getting late, twilight was coming on. He saw a woman coming towards him, wheeling a bicycle, and even though she was some distance away, he realised that it was Anna-Mari. Well, it would be nice to have a close view of her once again. She was not finding the bicycle easy to push: she looked older and more ungainly, and her clothes did not fit her properly, but then they never had. She appeared to take no notice of him as he approached, and he, for his part, seemed about to walk on, merely raising his grey felt hat as he passed.

But the woman stopped, staring at him in wide-eyed astonishment. He realised that Anna-Mari had recognised him. All the strength seemed to have drained out of her. The rusty bicycle, with its deflated tyres wrapped round with string, fell to the ground as she backed away from him uncertainly and flopped down to seat herself on the bank at the roadside.

'Matti!' she exclaimed in a hoarse, horror-stricken voice. 'You've come back!'

The bearded man sat down beside her and said quietly: 'It's all right, I haven't come to stay, and I'm not Matti, really. A ghost, that's what I am.'

'I knew you'd come back one day,' she said in a whisper. 'I was there when they lifted the coffin lid, and the body was all black and horrible, but I knew it wasn't you . . .'

'I *am* all black and horrible, believe me!'

'Oh Matti, what are we going to do now?'

She seemed utterly at a loss and very frightened.

'Nothing', he said. 'I've come and now I shall go. Only, I felt I had a duty to come and see you and make sure you're all right. Well, it seems you are, so . . .'

'I *was* all right, until . . . You see, I had got used to you not existing.'

'Well, I don't exist, don't you see? If I came back now there'd only be fuss and scandal and all kinds of awkwardness. I'm going. I'm better off there – in the other world.'

The woman sat silent, unable to speak.

'You've seen a ghost, that's all', said the man. 'Think of it that way. Good night!'

He got up and began to walk, without looking back, swinging his cardboard case. At a bend in the road, however, he paused and saw the woman still sitting where she had been. A moment later, however, she got limply and wearily to her feet. Looking back along the road, and finding that the bearded man was no longer in sight, she retrieved her bicycle and began laboriously to push it, with its deflated tyres and load of shopping, in the direction of the little cottage with the faded red paint.

All through the mild, cloudy autumn night the bearded man walked, stopping occasionally to sit down by the roadside and smoke a cigarette. By the time he reached the village the sun had risen and it was beginning to get light. Walking unhurriedly, he made his way to the churchyard. He walked along the rows of white crosses, and stopped in front of one of them:

Matti Leväinen
Born 1898
Died East Karelia 1941
Killed in action.

Next to it was the grave of someone called Antti Leväinen: he too had been killed in action on the East Karelian front. The bearded man looked at the rows of low crosses, and then up at the lofty church and bell-tower that rose behind them. Were *they* right? Could it be true that a man does not die when he dies, but lingers on in torment?

The bearded man found the thought of such a fate extremely frightening. Once he had deceived everybody and avoided a hero's death. He did not regret this. The idea of rotting away beneath that cross certainly did not appeal to him. But when the time did come for him to die, he would prefer death to be final. He would like to feel sure that he was not condemned to be an eternal wanderer, that he could never again stand here, revisiting his own grave.

But here he was, doing just that. And he had the feeling that Matti Leväinen was as dead and buried as it was possible to be.

This is what had happened to Matti Leväinen on the East Karelian front, in the year of Our Lord nineteen hundred and forty-one.

The Finns had been mounting attack after attack, inflicting defeats and advancing steadily. And Matti Leväinen had been taking part in all this, though with fear in his heart. For him, this forward surge had something unreal about it, and, anyway, he personally had no quarrel with the Russians. He felt that there was nothing to be gained from all this, except, probably, a soldier's grave. And that was not a thing he particularly yearned for.

It was a continual surprise to him that war, of all things, had given him a taste for life, even a life such as his, which he had thought so stale and savourless. Now it seemed that there was something to be said for it, after all.

After yet another successful attack the fighting had died down, and Matti Leväinen found, to his surprise, that he was still alive and physically intact, though almost dead from fatigue and shocked by the horrors of war. The air had been so full of flying metal that there could scarcely have been room for any more; and Death's scythe had swept the field, killing and maiming indiscriminately. It was just as well that the unit had now been withdrawn from the front line for rest and refitment, a tattered remnant of its former self.

It was here, on the margin of the now silent battlefield, where the dead were being recovered for burial, that Matti Leväinen met his brother Antti, a driver in the Transport Corps. And to Antti he confided the sad fact that he, Matti, did not feel that he was cut out for war. It suited only such people as wanted to die, and even for them it was not really satisfactory, the killing being done in such a haphazard way, and so inartistically.

Life in peacetime, that life of trouble and toil, with everyone beset by his own problems, now took on the aspect of an unimaginable state of bliss. If only one could be back at home in Finland, far from the sound of war, back at one's peacetime tasks . . .

They were walking close to the edge of the battlefield and had spotted the body of an enemy soldier, lying by itself.

Matti's brother was a lively fellow, always apt to come out with any idea that happened to cross his mind.

'So you're not enjoying the war? Why don't you clear out, then?'

'Are you joking?' Matti asked, almost angrily. 'It's all very well for you, you can stay behind the lines most of the time.'

'That's not so. But look, you could get away from here.'

Antti gave him one of his rocking-horse grins. They had just walked past the Russian soldier's corpse.

'There you are, there's a chap with nothing to do, why don't you get him to stand in for you?'

Matti Leväinen began to have a vague idea of what was being suggested.

'But . . . What about me, where could I disappear to?'

'I could take you back to Finland, as far as the railhead. We'll be off in that direction any time now.'

Antti was getting really enthusiastic. He was one of those people whose chief need was always for something to happen, something exciting, adventurous. It so happened that he had filched the papers of a civilian labourer who had been working for the army and been killed: he would be able to provide his brother with these. Moreover, he could give him some useful advice about where to go: he knew of a good place in the south, where he had spent some time as a truck driver.

'There's a splendid widow there, you might even fall for her. It's a good place to live, and no one will suspect a quiet old man like you, working on the land, of being a dead war-hero!'

To Matti Leväinen these fanciful ideas were like bait to a starving fish. He was very tired, very much shaken by the horrors of the war. If only he *could* get away from it all, even for a moment. The thought of civilian life was like the memory of a lost paradise.

They got down to work straight away, without qualms. Antti went off to collect a few bits and pieces of clothing and some food, since Matti could not afford to risk being seen. He himself set about undressing the body they had found in the brushwood. It was a strange and very unpleasant task, for the body already stank horribly. The whole world seemed strange and nightmarish, filled with the fog of war and the smoke from burning forests, through which the sun glimmered palely, like a small red disc.

By the time Antti returned with his bundle, Matti had finished undressing the corpse, and he now took off his own clothes and put on the few bits of clothing his brother had brought him. Somehow, between them, they managed, with much pulling and tugging, to manoeuvre the evil-smelling and now somewhat swollen corpse into Matti's own clothing and accoutrements, not forgetting the identity disc. It was slow, unpleasant work.

'Lucky he was a bit smaller than you', said Antti. 'But he'll soon swell up a bit more in this heat, and they all look the same after a bit. Could be anybody.'

When they had finished, Antti surveyed the result with satisfaction, and said:

'Well, there you lie, Matti, and there you're going to go on lying, till someone finds you. And if no one does, I'll make sure you do get found in the end – but I'll wait till there's no earthly chance of anyone recognising it's not you.'

Matti Leväinen took a last look at the figure that was to deputise for him at a war-hero's funeral. It all seemed like a dream. Larger now, the sun shone wanly through the smoke of war.

They collected the dead man's own equipment and took it to a suitably distant spot, where they buried it carefully. Antti then produced the papers he had spoken of earlier. Matti Leväinen noted that he was now Matti Nieminen, and was two years older than his former self. The photograph, like the rest of the document, was worn and smudged. It would do well enough. They decided on the place to which this new person, this fugitive from the grave, should go to wait for a lift. Antti would write at once to this widow he knew, who owned a small farm, and tell her a friend of his would be arriving, a really good farm worker. Labour was scarce, and he would be welcome. These and other details having been settled, Antti, still grinning toothily, took his departure.

For two days and nights Matti Nieminen was obliged to wait. Summer heat, smoke, the sound of gunfire from the front. How glad he was to be getting away from all that, although in his scanty clothing he found the nights extremely cold, and the food he had did not go very far. At last he saw his brother's truck, showing the signal they had agreed on, a fir-branch protruding from the window of the driver's cabin. It was the last in the column of vehicles, and had stopped at a bend in the road, round which the rest of the column had already disappeared. Matti Nieminen emerged from his hiding-place and quickly scrambled up on to the floor of the truck, ensconcing himself among the empty oil-drums under the tarpaulin, where a few hunks of bread and some canned meat had been left for him.

And so, on a chilly, smoky, foggy summer night, Matti Nieminen began his journey into a new life; munching bread and corned beef, dozing at times, only to be woken again by the rattling of the oil-drums or the jolting of the vehicle as it bumped its way over the pot-holes in the road. With their engines wheezing and grunting, the trucks laboured up the interminable hills, while Matti cowered in his hiding-place, shivering from cold and full of apprehension.

Was it permissible for a mere mortal to flee from the wrath to come? The real Matti Nieminen was lying somewhere beside a military road beneath a wooden cross, and Matti Leväinen's surrogate, a man from another country, lay still unburied in the forest, among trees blown down by the wind. Could these two buy a life, and days of peace, for a nameless stranger?

The column halted. This must be the check-point that Antti had spoken of. Matti Nieminen lay motionless, like a corpse. He heard shouts, voices, heavy footsteps on the gravelly road. He sensed, rather than saw, an unknown face peering over the side of the truck, the sleepy face of a man carrying out his duties. A petrifying moment; but Fate so willed it that the man caught no glimpse, among the empty oil-drums, of anything resembling a fugitive from war and a hero's death.

Then Matti Nieminen saw his brother, who was standing on one of the wheels. Even in the dim evening light, he could make out that wooden-horse grin. Antti whispered:

'God, those bastards are thorough. Had a real good look, didn't he? But it's over now. Enjoying it down there?'

There was no reply.

'Pretty uncomfortable, I dare say. Still, the way most people arrive from where you've come from, their legs are stuck out stiff and they don't feel anything.'

It was a relief when Antti got down and disappeared from view, with his horsy grin and ghoulish, unnecessary whispers.

A further long wait, and then the column began to move forward again. For a long, long time Matti lay there, numbed with the cold and buffeted by the shifting oil-drums. But finally the truck stopped and his brother looked over the side and told him to get up.

The other trucks had disappeared. Antti instructed his brother to go into the woods and hide, till he could bring him a few things and fit him out as a civilian. Then Matti would be able to move among people again, buy a ticket and go by train to his own promised land, the widow's farm, where there would be no war and no fuss. Apart from all this good advice and the inevitable grin, Antti was also able to provide his erstwhile passenger, who was by now so stiff as to be scarcely able to move, with a little food to keep him going.

Accordingly Matti Nieminen hobbled into the wood and began another long wait. In the Karelian forest he had got very dirty, and he was badly in need of a shave. Fortunately he had managed to bring with him a piece of soap and a razor. Having sought out a convenient streamlet, he now set about tidying himself up. He decided to leave his upper lip, with its nascent moustache, unshaven, in the hope that this might make his face look a little different. From this point of view it might have been even better not to shave at all, but he thought this might arouse suspicion. After that, having slaked his hunger with some of the food his brother had given him, he lay and rested, and thought about the Matti Leväinen who was now lying in that other forest, in East Karelia, with the summer heat rendering him fitter every moment for the function he was to perform.

Evening came, and with it, true to his promise, came Antti Leväinen with a passably decent civilian suit in his knapsack. Now, he said, they would have to hurry. He had had the good fortune to meet a fellow-driver who was due to leave, any moment now, for a destination well inside Finland proper; he could give Matti a long lift to somewhere right outside the military zone, where it would be easier for him to board a train without a lot of questions being asked.

Matti dressed hastily and they took a short cut across to the other road, where they were in time to flag down the truck in question. There was no time for long speeches.

'Look after yourself!' Antti shouted, with a wave of the hand, as the truck moved forward again. The scene was to remain vivid in Matti Nieminen's memory: his brother's figure in the summer evening twilight, and the characteristic grin. It was indeed their last meeting. Towards the end of that same summer, Antti was killed at the wheel of his truck by a sniper's bullet, as his brother was to learn much later. And now he lay in a war-hero's grave in the churchyard of his native parish, next to that brother of his whom he had once helped to clothe in a Finnish uniform, somewhere in the backwoods of Eastern Karelia . . .

As for the deserter himself, good luck stayed with him all the way. He got a lift to the nearest town, and then continued his journey on foot: taking the train would mean having to deal with policemen, and that frightened him. But soon the long, deserted road began to frighten him even more. He felt very conspicuous on the long grey-brown ribbon of the highway, a person hopelessly exposed to public view. At any moment someone might come along and ask him 'Aren't you that fellow who did a bunk from East Karelia?'

No, in a crowd one might be able to feel much safer from inquisitive eyes. Accordingly, when he came to a station he boldly bought a ticket and boarded a train. Everything went swimmingly. As things turned out, he was not asked to show his papers even once in the course of the whole long journey. After leaving the train he proceeded on foot, following his brother's instructions as to the route. He had not much further to go now.

There were already tinges of autumn in the landscape, but in the ancient fields the ripening corn still swayed and nodded in all its summer abundance; the cheerful orchards, the neat, well-built houses, all seemed to Matti Nieminen to be smiling a welcome. For the first time he fully understood the distance he had travelled, the magnitude of his own good fortune.

Out there, nothing but the wild forests and the wretched, ill-built road that war had conjured out of the wilderness; war, with its thunderous noises; terror, death, mutilation, the grotesquely swollen corpses; and the smoke – smoke everywhere, so much of it that even the sun was changed into a weird cosmic apparition, an astral portent from the Book of Revelation. Here, a summery countryside, a sky clear and serene, and a deep peace. It was hard to believe that those grim Karelian forests really existed.

Matti Nieminen gave himself up to whole-hearted enjoyment. He felt he had been given something. Even if this could not go on, he had already received something that could never be taken away from him, something worth any amount of trouble – a day of peace.

For a whole blissful day he rested at the edge of a wood, savouring his own contentment. None of the stink of war, no angry voices to fatigue the ear. In the golden light of evening he got up and sauntered on. He thought he recognised the place from his brother's description, and sought information from a young girl he met on the road. Yes, that white house was Vahvaselkä. Matti Nieminen trudged up the path to the quiet building: in the yard he encountered a plumpish, red-haired woman, who gave him a pleasant smile. Doubtless the owner, the widow his brother had told him of.

The wayfarer explained that he was in search of quiet employment on the land. In fact, he said, he had been recommended to try his luck at this particular house. A friend of his had promised to write to the lady about him.

No, she had received no letter, but a worker was certainly needed on the farm. It would soon be harvest time, and even after that – well, someone would still be needed. Come to that, someone would always be needed.

The widow was a talkative soul, the sort of person Matti Nieminen knew he could get on with. He stayed. And after a few days it was clear that the widow would not willingly see him leave. For Matti Nieminen proved to be an excellent worker, with a thorough knowledge of the job. A man like that, at a time like this, was worth his weight in gold.

After a few days a letter arrived from Matti's brother mentioning the possible arrival of this heaven-sent visitor. The widow had tender memories of Antti Leväinen, a light-hearted young fellow who knew how to enjoy life. And now he too, poor man, was caught up in the war. She would have to send him a parcel. Later she received another letter from Antti, telling of his brother's death in action. His body had been found in a badly decomposed state, and some of the men in his unit had expressed surprise, as they thought they remembered having seen Matti Leväinen after the fighting in that area had ended. Anyway, Antti was now being granted compassionate leave, and would perhaps be paying a visit to Vahvaselkä . . .

But he never came, and there were no further letters from him.

Matti Nieminen worked like a Trojan. Perpetually uneasy, and with fear gnawing at his heart, he became a compulsive worker. Especially at the outset, he felt that it must be obvious to anyone that he had come from the Eastern front, that he was in fact one of the heroic dead . . . His beard grew easily, and he let it spread so that it covered the whole of his face. Gradually he began to relax. The war went on. Out there, creeping for cover from the unremitting shellfire, were men to whom it would never occur to send a substitute to lie beneath that wooden cross. And no one would give Matti Nieminen a pat on the head for still being above ground, tilling his native soil.

But one long year of war followed another, and nothing happened. The bearded farm-worker at Vahvaselkä could hardly be described as a stripling, and it never occurred to anybody to wonder why he was not in uniform. The widow herself, who had her own reasons for discretion, had probably helped to still any lingering suspicions. Presumably she had had him registered with the authorities as a permanent employee: Matti Nieminen never asked. He was a very quiet, undemanding person: among his many good qualities was a lack of any particular interest in the subject of wages.

Matti Nieminen found life at Vahvaselkä extremely agreeable. Only the ghosts of the past tormented him: but these perhaps now resided only within himself. His brother was already in a place where the tongue is stilled for ever.

It is possible that the widow, with a woman's intuition, may have divined something of the past that held Matti Nieminen in its fetters. Sometimes he felt alarmingly certain that she had. But such a thing could not be *known*, in the way that the things of this world are known.

At last there came a time when peace reigned again on earth. Outlooks had changed. That a certain Matti Leväinen had remained alive would no longer, perhaps, have been regarded as such a serious crime. Matti Nieminen began to wonder about the family of this deceased person. What kind of life were they living, and how well were they managing?

Matti Nieminen began to feel that it was his bounden duty to find out about these matters. He asked his employer for a short period of leave, which was granted, on condition that he promised faithfully to return.

He travelled by train, and this was the first time he had occasion to show the worn-out identity document made out in the name of Matti Nieminen. The policeman glanced at it casually, remarking that it was time Mr Nieminen got himself a new one. How was he to know that the person in question was sleeping the sleep of the heroic dead, and that the person he was addressing was some kind of ghost?

And now Matti Nieminen had seen the family of a certain war-widow; had seen that the return of a certain Matti Leväinen from the dead was not a thing yearned for by anybody . . .

The village cocks were beginning to crow, the gentle wisps of night-time cloud were disappearing from the sky. The sun leapt into view, the church and bell-tower cast their long shadows over the dewy graveyard and over much of the village itself; here and there a window was thrown open by some brisk early-riser.

Matti Nieminen took a last look at the white crosses on the graves of the Leväinen brothers. He took off his cap, baring a head of hair already streaked with grey, and stood for a while in quiet thought. Rest in peace, you two, to whom rest has been granted. You paid the pricc for another man to buy back a segment of life; and life, when all is said and done, is a very sweet thing to have, despite all hardships.

With his cap still in his hand, the bearded man left the graveyard, and, stepping out on to the road, returned to the land of the living.

1946

Mika Waltari

ATON'S KINGDOM

I

Upon my return to Akhetaton I found Pharaoh exceedingly ill and in need of my help. His face was narrower, his cheekbones protruded, and his neck seemed even longer than before. It was incapable now of supporting the weight of the double crown, which pulled his head backward when he wore it on state occasions. His thighs had swollen, although his legs below the knees were mere sticks; his eyes also were puffy from constant headaches and were ringed with purple shadows. They did not look directly at anyone; his gaze wandered into other realms, and he often forgot the people with whom he spoke. The headaches were made worse by his custom of walking uncovered in the midday sun, to receive its rays of benediction upon his head. But the rays of Aton shed no blessing; they poisoned him so that he raved and saw evil visions. Perhaps his god was like himself, too liberal with his loving kindness, too overwhelming and profuse for his blessing to be other than a blight to all it touched.

In Pharaoh's lucid moments, when I applied wet cloths to his head and administered mild sedatives to soothe the pain, his dark, afflicted gaze would rest upon me in such unspeakable disillusion that my heart was moved for him in his weakness and I loved him; I would have sacrificed much to spare him this anguish.

He said to me, 'Sinuhe, can it be that my visions are lies – the fruit of a sick brain? If so, then life is inconceivably hideous, and the world is ruled not by goodness but by a boundless evil. But this cannot be so, and my visions must be true. Do you hear, Sinuhe, the stiff-necked? My visions must be true although his sun no longer illuminates my heart, and my friends spit on my couch. I am not blind. I see into the hearts of men. I see into your heart also, Sinuhe – your weak and vacillating heart – and I know that you believe me mad. Yet I forgive you because of the light that once shone into that heart.'

When pain assailed him he moaned and cried, 'Men take pity on a sick animal, Sinuhe, and dispatch it with a club, and a spear brings release to the wounded lion – but to a man no one will show mercy! My disillusion is more bitter to me than death because his light streams into my heart. Though my body die, yet shall my spirit live eternally. Of the sun am I born, Sinuhe; to the sun shall I return – and I long for that return because of the bitterness of my desolation.'

With the coming of autumn he began to recover although it might have been better if I had let him go. But a physician may not allow his patient to die if his arts can avail to cure him – and this proves often the doctor's curse. Pharaoh's health improved and with this improvement came reserve; he would converse no further with me or with others. His eyes were hard now, and his solitude profound.

He had spoken no more than the truth when he said that his friends spat on his couch, for having borne him five daughters Queen Nefertiti wearied of him and came to loathe him and sought by every means to cause him pain. When for the sixth time the seed quickened within her, the child in her womb was Pharaoh's in name only. She lost all restraint and took pleasure with anyone, even with my friend Thothmes. Her beauty was regal still although her spring had flowered and passed, and in her eyes and her mocking smile lay something that men found irresistible. She conducted her intrigues among Pharaoh's adherents, to alienate them from him. So the circle of protecting love about him thinned and melted away.

Her will was strong, her understanding disturbingly acute. A woman who combines malice with intelligence and beauty is dangerous indeed – more dangerous still when she can add to this the power of a royal consort. For too many years Nefertiti had been content to smile and to rule by her beauty, to find delight in jewels, wine, verses, and adulation. Now, after the birth of the fifth daughter, something seemed to snap; she believed then that she would never bear a son and laid the blame for this upon Akhnaton. It must be remembered that in her veins ran the black blood of Eie the priest, the blood of injustice, treachery, and ambition.

Let it be said in her defense that never until now could an ill word have been spoken of her; no scandal about her was uttered abroad. She had been faithful; she had surrounded Pharaoh Akhnaton with the tenderness of a loving woman, defending his madness and believing in his visions. Many were amazed at her sudden transformation and saw in it a token of the curse that brooded like a stifling cloud over Akhetaton. So great was her fall that she was reputed to take pleasure with servants and Shardanas and hewers of tombs, though I will not believe this. When once people find something to talk of, they love to exaggerate and make more of it than the facts will warrant.

However this may be, Pharaoh shut himself away in his solitude. His food was the bread and gruel of the poor, and his drink was Nile water, for he desired to regain clarity by the purification of his body, in the belief that meat and wine had darkened his sight.

From the outside world no more joyful tidings came to Akhetaton. Aziru sent many tablets from Syria full of remonstrance and complaint. His men desired to return to their homes, he said, to tend their flocks and herds, to till their fields and enjoy their wives, for they were lovers of peace. But robber bands, armed with Egyptian weapons and led by Egyptian officers, made continual raids into Syria from the Sinai desert and were a permanent danger to the country, so that Aziru could not allow his men to return home. The commandant in Gaza was also behaving in an unbecoming manner and in contravention of the peace treaty, both in the spirit and the letter. He closed the gates of the city to peaceful traders and admitted only those whom he thought fit. Aziru made many other complaints and said that anyone save himself would long ago have lost all patience, but that he was long suffering because of his love of peace. Yet unless an end were put to these incidents, he would not answer for the outcome.

Babylon likewise was incensed at Egypt's competition for the Syrian grain markets; King Burnaburiash was far from content with the presents he had received from Pharaoh and put forward many demands.

The Babylonian ambassador in Akhetaton pulled his beard, shrugged his shoulders, and threw out his hands, saying, 'My master is like a lion that rises uneasily in its lair and sniffs the wind, to learn what the wind will bring. He set his hopes on Egypt, but if Egypt is too poor to send him gold enough to hire strong men and build chariots, I do not know what will come of it. Though my master will ever prove a good friend to a powerful and wealthy Egypt, the friendship of a poor and impotent country is of no value to him, but rather a burden. I may say that my master was severely shocked and surprised when Egypt in its weakness yielded Syria. Everyone is his own nearest neighbor, and Babylon must consider Babylon.'

A Hittite deputation, among which were many distinguished chiefs, now arrived at Akhetaton. These men declared that they had come to confirm the hereditary friendship between Egypt and the land of Hatti and at the same time to acquaint themselves both with the customs of Egypt, of which they had heard much that was good, and with the Egyptian army, from whose arms and discipline they believed they might learn a great deal. Their behavior was cordial and correct, and they brought munificent presents to the officers of the household. Among the gifts they offered to young Tut, Pharaoh's son-in-law, was a knife of blue metal, keener and stronger than all other knives. I was the only other in Akhetaton in possession of such a blade – one that had been given me by a Hittite harbor master, as I have related – and I counseled Tut to have his also set in gold and silver in the Syrian manner. Tut was so greatly delighted with this weapon that he said he would have it with him in his tomb. He was a delicate, sickly boy who thought of death more often than do most children of his age.

These Hittite chiefs were indeed agreeable and cultured men. Their large noses, resolute chins, and their eyes that were like those of wild creatures entranced the women of the court. From morning till night and from night till morning they were brilliantly entertained in the palaces of the great.

They said smiling, 'We know that many dreadful things are told of our land by the invention of envious neighbors. We are therefore delighted to be able to appear before you in person so that you may see for yourselves that we are a cultured nation and that many of us can read and write. We are also peaceful and do not seek war; we seek only such knowledge as may be useful to us in our endeavors to educate and instruct our people. Do not believe the nonsense that is talked about us by the fugitives from Mitanni. They are bitter because in their fear they abandoned their country and all that was theirs. We can assure you that no evil would have befallen them if they had remained. But you must understand that the land of Hatti is cramped and we have many children, for the great Shubbililiuma takes great delight in children. Therefore we need space for our offspring and new grazing grounds for our cattle. And further, we could not endure to see the oppressions and wrongs that prevailed in the Land of Mitanni – indeed, the natives themselves appealed to us for help, and we marched into their country as liberators not conquerors. In Mitanni there is room enough for ourselves and our children and our cattle and we do not meditate further annexations, for we are a peace-loving people.'

They raised their goblets with arms held straight and spoke in praise of Egypt, while the women gazed with desire at their sinewy necks and wild eyes.

And they said, 'Egypt is a glorious land, and we love it. In our country also there may be something for Egyptians to learn – such Egyptians as are friendly toward us and desire to acquaint themselves with our customs.'

They spoke many fair words to the eminent of Akhetaton, who dealt with them frankly, concealing nothing. But to my mind these strangers brought with them the smell of corpses. I remembered their bleak land and the sorcerers spitted on stakes by the roadside, and I did not mourn when they left Akhetaton.

The city had changed. Its inhabitants had been infected by some frenzy, and never before had people eaten and drunk and played so feverishly as at this time. But the gaiety was unwholesome, for they reveled only to forget the future. Often a deadly stillness would fall over Akhetaton so that laughter froze in men's throats and they looked at one another in fear, forgetting what they had been about to say. Artists also were gripped by this singular fever. They drew and painted and carved more diligently than ever as if they felt that time was slipping through their hands. They exaggerated truth to a fantastic degree; distortion grew beneath their chisels and pencils; they vied with one another to produce ever more strange and extravagant forms until they vowed they could represent a feature or a movement by a few lines and patches.

I said to my friend Thothmes: 'Pharaoh Akhnaton raised you from the dust and made you his friend. Why do you carve his likeness as if you bitterly hated him? Why have you spat on his couch and outraged his friendship?'

Thothmes said, 'Do not meddle with things you fail to understand, Sinuhe. Perhaps I hate him, but I hate myself more. The fire of creation burns within me, and my hands have never been so skillful as now. Perhaps it is when the artist is unsatisfied and hates himself that he best creates – better than when he is content and full of love. I create all from within myself, and in every piece of sculpture I hew myself in stone, to survive eternally. There is no one like me: I surpass all others and for me there are no rules to break. In my art I stand above rules and am more god than man. When I create form and color, I vie with Aton and outdo him, for all that Aton creates is perishable but what I create is eternal.'

When he spoke thus, he had been drinking, and I forgave him his words, for torment burned in his face and from his eyes I saw that he was profoundly unhappy.

During this time the harvest was gathered in from the fields, the river rose and fell, and it was winter. With winter famine came to the land of Egypt, and no one could tell what new disaster the morrow might bring. News came that Aziru had opened the greater number of the Syrian cities to the Hittites and that the light chariots of these had driven across the Sinai desert, attacking Tanis and laying waste the surrounding country.

II

This news brought Eie in haste from Thebes and Horemheb from Memphis, to take counsel with Pharaoh Akhnaton and save what might be saved. In my capacity of physician I was present at this meeting, fearing lest Pharaoh become overexcited and fall ill because of the calamities of which he must hear. But Pharaoh was reserved and cold and remained master of himself throughout.

Eie the priest said to him, 'The storehouses of Pharaoh are empty, and the land of Kush has not paid tribute this year although I had set my hopes upon those revenues. Great hunger prevails in the land, and the people are digging up the water plants from the mud and eating the roots; they also eat locusts and beetles and frogs. Many have perished and many more must do so. Even with the strictest distribution Pharaoh's grain is insufficient, while that of the merchants is too dear for the people to buy. The minds of all are possessed of great dread. Countrymen fly to the cities, and town dwellers fly to the land, and all say that this is the curse of Ammon and that it is Pharaoh's new god that has brought them this suffering. Therefore, Pharaoh Akhnaton, be reconciled with the priests and restore to Ammon his power, that the people may worship him and be pacified. Give him back his land that he may sow it, for the people dare not. Your land also lies unsown because the people believe it is accursed. Be reconciled with Ammon while there is yet time, or I wash my hands of the consequences.'

But Horemheb said, 'Burnaburiash has bought peace from the Hittites, and Aziru, yielding to their pressure, has become their ally. The numbers of their troops in Syria are as the sands of the sea and their chariots as the stars in the sky. They spell the doom of Egypt, for in their cunning the Hittites have carried water into the desert in jars. Having no fleet, they have carried thither infinite quantities of water so that when spring comes even a mighty army may cross the desert without succumbing to thirst. They bought in Egypt a large number of the jars, and the merchants who sold them have dug their own graves. The chariots of Aziru and of the Hittites have made reconnaissance raids into Tanis and into Egyptian territory and have thereby broken the peace. The damage they have done is indeed trivial, but I have set tales afoot of terrible devastation, and of the cruelty of the Hittites, so that the people are ripe for battle. There is yet time, Pharaoh Akhnaton! Let the horns sound, let the banners fly – declare war! Gather together all those able to bear arms on the training grounds, call in all the copper in the country for spears and arrowheads, and your sovereignty shall be saved. I myself will save it by an incomparable war; I will defeat the Hittites and reconquer Syria for you. I can do all this if Egypt's resources be placed at the disposal of the army. Hunger makes warriors even of cowards. Ammon and Aton are all one to me; the people will forget Ammon once they are at war. Their unrest will find outlet against the enemy, and a victorious conflict will establish your power more firmly than before. I promise you a war of conquest, Pharaoh Akhnaton, for I am Horemheb, the Son of the Falcon. I was born to great deeds, and this is the hour for which I have been waiting all my life.'

When Eie heard this he said hastily, 'Do not believe Horemheb, Pharaoh Akhnaton, my dear son! Falsehood speaks with his tongue, and he is lusting for your power. Be reconciled with the priests of Ammon and declare war, but do not put Horemheb in command. Give it to some tested veteran who has studied in the old writings the arts of war as practiced in the times of the great Pharaohs, a man in whom you can place full trust.'

Horemheb said, 'Did we not now stand in Pharaoh's presence, Eie the priest, I would punch your dirty nose. You measure me by your own measure and betrayal speaks with your tongue, for you have in secret already negotiated with the priests of Ammon and come to terms with them behind Pharaoh's back. I will not fail the boy whose weakness I once shielded with my shoulder cloth by the hills of Thebes; my goal is the greatness of Egypt, and only I can save it.'

Pharaoh asked, 'Have you spoken?'

They answered with one voice, 'We have spoken.'

Then Pharaoh said, 'I must watch and pray before I make my decision. Tomorrow summon all the people together – all those who love me, both high and low, lords and servants. Call also the quarry-men and stone masons from their town. I will speak through these to all my people and reveal to them my purpose.'

They did as he commanded and bade the people assemble the next day, Eie in the belief that he would be reconciled with Ammon, Horemheb in the hope that he would declare war on Aziru and the Hittites. All that night Pharaoh watched and prayed and paced incessantly through his rooms, taking no food and speaking to none, so that as his physician I was concerned for him. On the following day he was carried before the people. He sat on his throne, and his face was clear and radiant as he raised his hands and spoke.

'By reason of my weakness there is now famine in the land of Egypt; by reason of my weakness the enemy threatens our borders. The Hittites are now preparing to invade Egypt through Syria, and soon their feet will be treading the black soil. All this has come to pass because of my weakness – because I have not clearly heard the voice of my god or performed his will. Now my god has revealed himself to me. Aton has appeared to me, and his truth burns in my heart so that I am no longer either weak or doubting. I overthrew the false god, but in the infirmity of my purpose I allowed other gods to reign by the side of Aton, and the shadow of them has darkened Egypt. On this day all the old gods must fall, that the light of Aton may prevail as the only light throughout the land of Kem. On this day the old gods must vanish and Aton's kingdom on earth begin!'

When the crowds heard this, a ripple of horror ran through them, and many prostrated themselves before Pharaoh.

But Akhnaton raised his voice and continued with firmness, 'Ye who love me, go now and overthrow the old gods in the land of Kem. Break down their altars; smash their images; pour away their holy water, pull down their temples; expunge their names from all inscriptions – enter the very tombs to do so – that Egypt may be saved. Officers, grasp clubs in your hands; sculptors, exchange your chisels for axes; workmen, take your sledge hammers and go forth into every province, every city and village, to overturn the old gods and efface their names. Thus will I liberate Egypt from the thralldom of evil.'

Many fled from him aghast, but Pharaoh drew a deep breath, and his face glowed in exaltation as he cried, 'May Aton's kingdom come on earth! From this day forward let there be neither slave nor lord, neither master nor servant; let all be equal and free in the sight of Aton! No one shall be bound to till the land of another or grind another's mill, but each man shall choose the work he will do and be free to come and go as he pleases. Pharaoh has spoken.'

There was no further stir among the multitude. All stood dumb and motionless, and as they stared at Pharaoh, he grew in their sight, and the shining ecstasy in his countenance so dazzled them that they raised a shout of fervor and said to one another, 'Such a thing was never before seen, yet truly his god speaks through him and we must obey.'

The people dispersed in a ferment with bickering among themselves. Some came to blows in the streets, and the adherents of Pharaoh slew old men who spoke against him.

But when the people had dispersed, Eie said to Pharaoh, 'Akhnaton, throw away your crown and break the crook, for the words you have spoken have already overturned your throne.'

Pharaoh Akhnaton replied. 'My words have brought immortality to my name, and I shall hold sway in the hearts of men from everlasting to everlasting.'

Then Eie rubbed his hands together, spat on the ground before Pharaoh, and rubbed the spittle into the dust with his foot as he said, 'If this is to be the way of it, I wash my hands and act as I think best. I am not answerable to a madman for my actions.'

He would have gone, but Horemheb seized him by the arm and neck and held him easily although Eie was a powerful man.

Horemheb said. 'He is your Pharaoh! You shall do his bidding, Eie, and not betray him. If you betray him, I will run you through the belly though I have to summon a regiment to do it. His madness certainly is deep and dangerous, yet I love him and will stand fast at his side because I have sworn him my oath. There is a spark of reason in his raving. If he had done no more than overthrow the old gods, civil war would have followed. In freeing the slaves from mill and field, he spoils the priests' game and gains the people to his side, even if the result be greater confusion than before. It is all one to me – but, Pharaoh Akhnaton, what shall we do with the Hittites?'

Akhnaton sat with his hands limp upon his knees and said nothing. Horemheb went on, 'Give me gold and grain, arms and chariots, horses, and full authority to hire warriors and summon the guards to the Lower Land, and I think I can withstand the onslaught of the Hittites.'

Then Pharaoh raised his bloodshot eyes to him, and the glow faded from his face as he said, 'I forbid you to declare war, Horemheb. If the people desire to defend the Black Land, I cannot prevent it. Grain and gold – to say nothing of arms – I have none to give you, and if I had, you should not have it, for I will not meet evil with evil. You may make your dispositions for the defense of Tanis, but shed no blood and defend yourselves only if attacked.'

'Be it as you say.' said Horemheb. 'Let lunacy prevail! I will die in Tanis at your command, for without grain and gold the most valiant army cannot long survive. But no doubts or half measures! I will defend myself according to my own good sense. Farewell!'

He went, and Eie also took his leave of Pharaoh, with whom I remained alone. He looked at me with eyes filled with unspeakable weariness and said. 'Virtue has gone out of me with my words, Sinuhe, yet even in my weakness I am happy. What do you mean to do?'

I looked at him in bewilderment, and smiling slightly he asked, 'Do you love me, Sinuhe?'

When I confessed that I loved him, his madness notwithstanding, he said, 'If you love me, you know what you have to do.'

My mind rose up against his will, although inwardly I well knew what he required of me. At length I said in irritation, 'I fancied you had need of me as a physician, but if not, then I will go. It is true I shall make but a poor hand at overturning the images of gods, and my arms are overweak for wielding a sledge hammer, but your will be done. The people will flay me alive and crush my head with stones and hang my body head downward from the walls, but how should that concern you? I will go then to Thebes, where there are many temples and where the people know me.'

He made no answer and I left him in wrath.

1945

Aaro Hellaakoski

THE LAST DINOSAUR

Alone and noble, I remain,
the remnant of my race's reign.
My race's reign? My race's world,
ravaged, filthied and annulled.
Alone, noble, I remain,
alien now, everything gone,
unique in devastation.

We were large and mighty things,
our footsteps made the landscape ring,
our swimming left the ocean shaken,
our flying made the daystar darken.
Large we were and mighty things,
superbly present everywhere,
lords of land and sea and air.

Beauty we had and benediction
and a calling to perfection;
we flashed our scales, we bathed in light,
our curving necks had grace and height.
Beauty we had, and benediction:
that lonely joy and well-bred wisdom
to walk head-high, conscious of freedom.

But slaughter came, creeping and eating,
spurring the vermin we were meeting:
we were few, and they were many,
lurking at each brake and spinney.
Slaughter circled, creeping and eating;
in every bush it crouched and smote,
snapping from shadow its hairy coat.

And who are 'they'? A howling pack
that canter and sniff and bite and track
and pouch their ugly fry, in flight,
tucked in their bellies, out of sight.
They came, they devoured, a howling pack,
louse- and flea-bitten, with burning brains,
ravaging, slobbering our remains.

A race of sucklers, with gnashing jaws,
you finished the tale of the dinosaurs,
but you'll never rise above the earth
as we: you're dust and soil and dearth,
an organised pack with famished maws. –
Maybe you'll rise from your mud one day.
How much, it's up to you to say.

1946

THE NIGHTINGALE

1

EVENING

When the children's games have ended in the farmyard,
and the swallows think it may be time to go,
when the wind is folding wing on yonder hillside,
and nesting in resin, dozing off once more,

the waterlilies, down in the bay below,
sink into thought, bleached by the long day's glow,
and a bell tinkles from the meadowed further shore.

Then it's silence. A single man alone
pads to his paddock gate with tack and harness.
In bayside shadows shores are cooling down,
though rocks across the lake still radiate sun.
A mosquito whines – and the little beast
turns to his bloody work and insatiable lust.
Far-off a reed-bed flickers. A flop of frog
is heard as it panics and leaps from a log.

Head nodding, he plods the lakeside sand,
in tattered shirt and tattered working braces:
toil-torn, a tired-out man with heavy hand
brushes a shade of sweat from his furrowed face –
or something else, some heavier thing, as if he'd
done it in sleep, not knowing what he did.

Lakeside fragrance. He sits on a stone. He takes his pipe,
patiently smoothing thoughts that oft-times gripe.
Evening is cooling, its pulse is slow –
some throbbing heart newly transfused with youth
after decades of trouble and anguish and woe.
Gruff from his throat the syllables slip:
All's well, so good: whatever could I miss? –
except a thankful word, as good as all this.

2

THE SONG OF THE ANTS

Legs strained,
cockeyed for work,
have we ever complained?

No effort we shirk.
The formic race
you'll never efface.

A large boot mows
rows of us dead.
But it only shows
how tough we've been bred:
you'll never annul us:
we sing with cracked skulls.

They've often thought
we're a dying strain.
But the roads we've wrought
will always remain.
Now we snore. Tomorrow we wrest
more straw to our nest.

3

THE NIGHTINGALE AWAKES

Grey maybe, by day, in my feather suit,
chockfull of chores, grabbing my grub,
I scurry around on the rush-hour hub.
Now I shake off dust, I free my flute.
I'm an I again – though what I mean –
flower, cloud, or in between –
I've no idea – leaf of tree or underleaf –
yet this I divine: no grey-plume hick,
grubbing for money, not poor or sick.

When the blazing daystar goes under the hill,
I flower and redden, my hour has come:
my body sings, and if I were dumb
still every fibre would warble and thrill;

feathers are freed from their roots: they trill,
'Could anything fasten us down, and how? –
when everything past and coming still
is always present, is happening now.'

Did that fishsplash drown me in the lake,
as it sparked and flashed an iris flake?
Or am I weightless, a cloud-walk, raking
the wind-ways, laughing and shaking?
That glow on the fellside pines –
I'm it, and a herb-scent where the marsh-pool shines;
I'm bliss of grass, and that butterfly-beat
that broke its wing by its darling mate;
I'm all just now who long to die.
Summer midnight, pierce me and kill!
I wait, and soon the owl will strike his gong.

Whoever's deprived of happiness, I'd move
him here, and get him to feel his love
for this, the loveliest futility that ever was.
Why is it quiet? The evening's alive
and enchanted: shouldn't it burst out and sing,
carolling above the mud? I'm all set to listen.
Nothing is missing, I'm beingless being,
driven from within. I only receive. I sing.

4

MIDGE DANCE

Spawned beneath the water face,
we're grateful for our day of grace;
from larva-touch we redeploy
to take the air and sing for joy.

Over the gleaming bay we go
in our midge-day rodeo,
but, underneath, prosaic maws
spur the perch's bony jaws.

The weather's warm but in it swarm
hungry things on savage wings:

The wagtail and the martin dart
and tear apart our *paso-doble*
and decimate our family
of revelling ephemerae,
who, though flighty, spry and matey,
are not exactly weighty.

That's the end of midge romance.
Yet we choir our song, and dance,
till each airy denizen
for no special reason
is reaped out of season.

5

THE AFFLICTION OF THE NIGHTINGALE

The first bewilderment of night
is a sudden cool.
A gnome drinks from a pool.
And the state of the weather,
summer though it is,
burns like ice.
So much is bursting
in hearts' rock
that night's insomniac,
night's complaining;
every leaf, each fluff and particle

has to be stoical,
feels bitter pain.
The wild wind again,
humming what's been,
lingers on the gravel
and ruffles the bushes.

Maybe bushes complain.
Should that stop my strain?
Would I remain –
would anything be left –
if I cursed and lost my chirrup.

My song is futile –
a superfluous style.
But, open my beak for my self alone,
I'm the most useless drone!
I'm not going to moan.
I'm lent to the world
and put to work
merely to breathe
as a tuneful mite:
above all, always to praise
this night to this night.

6

THE GNOMES

No one is dumb,
no one is blind.
No need to crouch
out of mind in the marsh.
Day's ugly slouch
and harsh glare –
should dive into mist,

surrender to night's white dream.
Everything's open.
Everything's spoken.
Everything's knowledge.
Everything's language.
And behind there's mind.

Our night is a good one.
Packed with magic work,
hums the poetry mine.
Horn, drum and flute
come lilting and praising
from deep, deep somewhere,
rising and raising.

We come picklock on belt
for the soft and hard doors
of the troubled all day.
Blest guests! As you rest,
'Open Sesame!' we say.
We creep in your breasts.
And on the heart in bits
the nightingale sits.

7

THE NIGHTINGALE SINGS
very quietly

Back of all the sounds there came
a presence new, astonishing presence,
and at last there came
a steady silence.
Through it I can only guess
water's stealthiness.
The water's cool, the tree

reflected imagery.
Under leaves, over pebbles,
there's a babble
as happy water weaves a tiny bubble,
and carefully manoeuvres the gleam
down the stream,
under tree, over earth,
kissing moss with moisture
on the way to a berth
in the bell-tinkling cattle-pasture.
I'm happy: a bubble, nothing more.
I'm empty, nothing more.
Only as a reflector,
a listener, am I free:
a bubble I remained, enduring
and praising eternally.

8

DAWNING

Out of shadow – a cloudshed: it gleams
in the first light that tips the horizon, beams
and picks out gables, high, so high; and soon a seam
flames under the summercloud doorframes.
The dewdrop's still asleep. And the harvestman's gauze
that dresses the green arms of the bush in turquoise
is still dreaming too. Yet it wakes skittering,
orchestrating its iridescence and glittering,
as two lovers leave the avenued path
and close the garden gate: still, both,
young enough not to have another thought
but listening to the other's thought
and very seriously affirming: the red clouds are all
wound into a single ball,
and the whisper of a special person
is a nightingale's call.

9

THE NIGHTINGALE IS FINISHING

Taking my way
round the garden of dreams
I'll not go astray.
My bubbleskin gleams.
And my stream of song
bears me along.
I overflow
with astonishment.
My winged moment
is praise of
everything that is.
Always
more and more I prize
the sacred word: is.

The warm waltz
of a poem
races the pulse;
if the dumb days
are tongue-tied,
systole and diastole
goes the songstream I ride,
and I doubt
that its gleam
will ever run out.
Sing, syrinx:
smile your song of thanks.

10

MORNING

The cuckoo takes his cue:
cuckoo, cuckoo!

The nightingale stops cheeping:
he's sleeping.
How long? Maybe for ever,
like the midge who'll never
issue from the perch's belly.
Cuckoo: 'Reveille!'
The mighty race of ants
continue their advance:
off to work in thousands,
they never fear mischance.

Earliest dawnlight shines
in some tiny window among the pines
and wakes a farmwife.
Those glimmering dawnrays knife
her beautiful dream, as Daisy moos.
But cool in the shed,
her youngest doesn't lose
a shred of ecstasy: legs spread,
she sleeps as if it were midnight still.

The nightingale's bill
has twittered within her,
and its song will stay
well into the day.
The cockcrow flies past her
from the neighbour's yard
and across the mooing pasture –
unheard, like the stir of birth,
and the crow of life
in the air, in the earth.

1952

P. Mustapää

THE YELLOW JACKDAW

A jackdaw perched on the churchtop –
a yellow one, not black –
thus a rarity for a jackdaw,
the joker in the pack.

It dawdled about alone there,
mulling over things,
and only rarely fluttered
its pair of pallid wings.

But a black flock of jackdaws,
squawking and 'chaking' around,
were still at it on Sunday
when the holy morning dawned.

When the churchtower bells were welcoming
with their cheerful clangour and thud,
and the parish clerk and the dean
were off to the House of God,

that black flock of jackdaws
with acrobat flip and flop
were rattling like a hailstorm
across the belfry top.

But meanwhile the yellow jackdaw
sat quietly at his station –
which nastily ruffled the feathers
of that jackdaw congregation.

He didn't run with the pack –
or in jackdaw, as they say,
'he didn't "chak" with the jacks' –
and so they pecked him away.

Yes, that black mob of jackdaws
blinded the poor fool:
in the country of the jackdaws
drastic laws are the rule.

A jackdaw perched on the churchtop –
a yellow one, not black –
thus a rarity for a jackdaw,
the joker in the pack.

But the calamity that hit him
has made the jackdaw wise:
'I've still got a backbone,
though left without my eyes.'

And his second aphorism
is definitely on a par:
'It's a decent way to die,
showing what suit you are.'

1945

DROUGHT

The shoreside grass is scorched and recedes,
the water recedes and the rushes bake.
The grebes that nested in the reeds
waddle off to the lees of the lake.

Vapouring away, the fluids abscond:
the lake's becoming a minor pond.

Exposed, a crag is a jagged lump;
instead of water, an infernal rash
of marsh and mud infests the sump
where heavenly water used to wash.
Mist poisons the air, everything's dim
where loon and whooper used to swim.

Stinking knolls infest the mud,
the fishes' fins are turning blue,
yellow lilies rot in the bud,
wort and algae are breaking through
the one-time tremulous waterskein
sprinkled with pearly springtime rain.

Carcases emerge and rot,
centuries of clot on jaws and legs,
mussels open, never to shut,
in a muddy gruel of congealing dregs
where water once showed starry skies
and moon, to please a dreamer's eyes.

Listen to how the carrion-crow
croaks and cronks for a turn to eat
in the wounded water's field of woe.
The Water Sprite admits defeat
and croons a vision of black departure –
a Water Sprite deprived of water!

No hermeneutics wanted here.
Agony. Aridity. Black mud, cracked land.
Burning thirst. Mourning gear.
For the race of swimmers a waterless strand!
A lake once free to wash itself clean
is drowning in a filthy green.

1945

MEMORY

What we got we scarcely got at all,
and what we lost is scarcely lost.
Day caressed your brow
and still caresses it.
And yet, as I look, night has come down,
damp mist is clouding the ness,
and yesterday's shearwater
is quiet or long flown.

1952

THE FOWLER

And up there, over your hair,
where the birds feel no fear,
the dapplewing sang to the transparent wind.
Air, space – what you left –
was a presence to you
and light. Then came the fowler,
crossing the field towards the traps,
and stopped, and everything stopped
and with delicate fingers
felt the twittering in the down.

1952

THRACE

Echo's statue opposite Pan's statue in the temple of Dionysus:

Ruined, the city walls
rose again with rooftops, horns and towers;
casting aside his stick
the old man returned to the lands of infancy,

skipping and playing;
and the seed-pod returned
to the scented flower
and the flower to the bud.
And I, Echo, hurried away
to the forestlands, to Thrace;
and you, Pan;
and stopping under the plane trees
I raised my hand –
towards a rock cloaked in herbs,
towards the coolest of cool brooks –
and heard all the old sounds.
And, accompanying me, Pan –
you blew on your flute.

And Elpis spoke: Hope!
I repeated it: Hope!
And I kept on repeating it.
And the grove resounded with Hope, Hope!
Night's clouds dispersed,
Selene disappeared into the morning,
fleeing with her team of bulls.
Hope, then! The olives flashed
silver leaves,
and flowers filled
the Thracian vines.

Tomorrow, the maiden said.
Tomorrow, I repeated, and kept repeating it.
A dim shadow from her garland
dropped, cloaking
her sweet shoulders.
Never, then – never, young man:
and the reason too I guessed:
never, then – and I knew: today, here, now.
In the mild summer, Pan,
I suffered joy.

Quick, said the bird, a redwing.
Quick, I repeated, ever more quickly.
Quick, said the redwing,
and I: Quick.
O down, O gleaming feather:
it grazed a leafy sprig
and the sprig trembled –
And the valley was a flare of fury, pain, frenzy
and flurried wings –
and I saw it, the hawk – circling – the nest – the birds!
Short, Pan, is happiness.

And a command of the lonely: Go!
That I repeated, still hesitating.
Uproar on the road, a distant rhythm,
that too I repeated, fearing.
Howling of wolves, a cawing flock of ravens, wind in the night
and an avalanche of spears,
uproar on the road, a distant rhythm,
a distant uproar
that I repeated raging
and sorrowing, Pan.

So, Pan, time to go back again.
And how the young trees
sighed as they grew and then returned to the dust
beneath the mosses;
and how, casting his toy aside,
the child got up,
and with sedulous feet
the man toiled off to his field,
and the old man was gathered into the soil!
The city advanced
murmuring with joy, its ardour
was borne from the square and diminished and became one
with the waste and windy sand again.
The fields ignited into flowers,

the fields went out –
repeatedly, Pan, and repeatedly.

Nemesis spoke: Vanity –
O final word
and bitterest.
That I repeated too, Pan.
It tolled three times. And wailingly,
with ash in their hair,
the cortege wound its way
back from the grove,
        remembering Calliope's son:
Beauty he celebrated on his lyre,
to the forestlands, to Thrace.
Now in the temple, here before you, Pan,
from time to time I repeat it –

1952

Gunnar Björling

Tremble, hand, and despair
you have a right, you have a home
in that shimmer, that light
in that blood and the perished
in the thorn-stabbed
in shimmer, and happiness
you dwell, you have a home
in the past's
in blessings'
eternal-loving's
in the never-dying's
in the impenetrable's
twilight and light
it bears your feet
your hand is like creators' pliancy
threads of invisibility pass from all around you
and out of night shine
eyes.

1944

I have no birds' names and text of plants
and out of myself I speak
if I hear that voice
I seek
I find words: and come,
words and more than to understand
words and that no other is.

1945

And when day is not
and morning does not shine
but it is the hour of the great eve.
There will be no more flowering
there will be no more spring
and the flowers will not give fragrance
there will be no brilliance in my eye
and cheeks will have no colour
and movements will not run with the wind.
The struggles will not weave the crown
I will have no fragrant leaves
I will be
gone.

1946

Your hunger your pain
that like the grassblade's scent

like mantles of torment
all things' terror

and cries are for cries
cries are in deeds' hushed halls
in silences' fatal deed

like fox fire all the light
a confetti it is swept away
is a will-o'-the-wisp will-o'-the-wisp

alas despair you
and like starlight!

1948

The leaves did not break
the grasses did not die
the sand did not lose its purple
brilliance comes out of the leaves
shadows play over the road
light beats through the bush
above me stands day
and birds or the sky
all the while burns the sun.

1948

We went not namelessly away
our lives were to give name
and word and form,
give the eye's light
give stone and the sand
to learn that which we did not learn
and under world's name and names
go most deeply
namelessly away

1949

One day the bells will be silent
one day the last footsteps will go
one day those muter sounds
one day the visions will break
memory not speak
torment not reach me
one day the bells will be silent

1949

Now all boats glide away
now all flutters before the windless –
wind away
now it grows still over bay and sea and the inlets
now the summer's sun is dying
and the yachts' white sails
now lights flicker
before the last summer procession of joy
now – as if in the mists
candles of the mists
candles
of grey day-mildness'
dying's not-dying
in the September evening
lights
sounding and heard, and
not quite
– do not listen, you will not hear it
but yet most clearly
sounding and heard

1951

Now is not dead
it is a voice
barely shimmering
in this night of light
and between space and sea

1953

That yet in the night
all to a lightgate
that beside
close to
that in sound and my ear
that to your thought's face
a thought and for you
Thus in dread and seeing

1955

Rabbe Enckell

O BRIDGE OF INTERJECTIONS...

O bridge
of interjections,
you that pass over half of life in silence
and half of death
and yet are filled with life and death,
you that like a river reflect the banks
announcing their depth
without revealing or betraying
what is hidden by merciful trees
at the water's edge,
I will go your way like a Moslem
who approaches the mosque with covered head
led astray neither by what lies to the right or the left of him.

I will adorn my ear with sounds
that are audible only at sunrise
or towards nightfall, when each stars sets out its bowl
to catch a sprinkling of the inaudible.
And I will adorn my eye with light
disclosing things that can be neither hidden nor seen,
such as breathe their scent from a distance
and cannot be lifted up and placed here or there,
since they remain with me always
wherever I am –

Among those lofty things
there is neither you nor I nor anyone else,
neither love, passion, jealousy nor revenge.
There is absolutely nothing to lay us bare
or give us occasion for arrogance or humiliation.
Those lofty things soar towards us
on the wings of interjections, transparent as the dragonfly's:
she glows with all that is behind her or ahead of her;
colourless in herself, each moment paints her anew.
They are like a tranquil air in which scents thrive.
One breathes them in as on a forest path.
But the sea, too, the rock and the storm are lifted
on the wings of interjections.

Whoever is versed in them
is like a skilful spinner: from matted wool comes flowing yarn.
O, is it really necessary to heap up facts?
Then I am lost. In facts I was imprisoned.
What speaks through me now is merely what
is present in any moment,
like rainwater in a crevice: it has gathered there
and dries up again in order to return.

Long we go bowed under the weight of circumstances.
One senses them everywhere – like the members of a jury
they judge us, acquitting or convicting us.
As long as we live we stand like prisoners at the bar.
O who can plead in his own defence other than
in a thoroughly inadequate fashion?
On whose side is the law, on whose true love?
These are questions that cannot be settled at once,
but must constantly be reiterated in the world of the half-hearted.
The defier and the conciliator
dwell in the same breast, in the same heart's chamber,
forever pursuing the same exchange of opinions.
In the long run we all lose out.
For what we win we allow to slip through our fingers

and what we lose comes back to us again.
In the degree to which we give it up for lost, it returns.
It returns by way of the loss that makes us reconciled.
It returns by way of the loss that makes us dream purer dreams.

It returns by way of the loss that makes us think truer thoughts and
will better actions.
Verily: no one can say 'I have won!'
For no one wins in the end, but everyone loses,
loses until they are conscious of it and realise
that only by way of loss can the flood of things that are lost
be stemmed. It is so simple. Tears are the nervous spasm
of our desire to hold onto something, they are the child who refuses
to see
that the sense of loss gives to life its deepest substance.

One can find nothing in life
unless one finds those words
that are transparent with
what the spirit has in common with everything and everyone.
One can find nothing unless one is able to weave oneself
a net that fits every sea and every river.

In interjections I have found a strong thread
that has been dipped in the pitch of eternity – in interjections, which
are born
like the spider's web in the light of morning:
constantly at breaking-point, it often tries the eye of the beholder,
but in holds the spider, its creator,
as the world holds God. What does it matter
that much of it is torn to shreds? It matters nothing!
As long as the thread holds its creator.
I found the pitch-thread of eternity in the spider's web and in those
interjections
which, dipped in my heart, held fast
even when its blood flowed hottest.

When the lover makes those long pauses between the words of love
those pauses that rest in the present like a butterfly on a hot stone,
without desire, need or purpose,
he is outside desire
and is in acceptance, in which his soul rests, open.
As after a violent downpour the sun shines more intensely
than it does on a cloudless day, so our lives are most intense
the moment we set ourselves free and stop thinking about purposes.
There is always something melancholy about one who is setting out on an expedition.

Why does the soul in his eyes seem to renounce
the result in advance? why does the moment of decision
make his stomach turn?
Where does this weakness come from? It creeps out of his soul, whispering: 'renounce'.
Renounce! You must admit that – if, like a parachutist, you took the risk –
only then did you really feel free.

There is within all of us something
that is too fragile not to break,
too fragile or too inexpedient.
Are we therefore to condemn it?
Complete expediency would never
find its way to the life that is more than cause and effect.
Complete expediency is not possessed
by the ox under the yoke, not even by the machine.
The ox contains that which is animal and is not the beast of burden.
The machine contains the incomplete, which is the human being.
Expediency can make no decisive contribution
to the argument about what our lives are worth.
No: sickness, want and hope –
that is life and its redoubts, never surrendered.

Let us therefore not condemn that which has made us vulnerable,
made us fall out with life and brought us face to face with the thieving brats of reality.
The wound proves that there was something
which went beyond the bounds of necessity, something
which demanded more and found less,
was a squandering of energy until reality
converted it into blind weakness.
To me the quarry is free when it is hunted
in mortal terror by a goading pack.

To me the murderer is free when, his soul on tenterhooks,
he awaits the ring at the doorbell,
the quite ordinary ring of an errand boy at the door with a delivery
from the grocer's shop around the corner –
and then another ring, one quite out of the ordinary, one that mercilessly
shoots the bolts of existence, discloses
the next step as a 'come with us' – the soft purring
of the police car from the street sounds like something in a dream –
This is a freedom you cannot escape!
A freedom which leads to something greater, something inconceivable.
One that will perhaps finally release
the most intense delight a human being can attain: the smile that nothing will be able to avert –

In the twilight of the gaol
on the stone floor, pressed
against damp walls and with the cell bars
like a cool and indifferent thought, irrelevant,
I felt for my companion in misfortune the kinship
common shame bestows.
For in a cell there is no concealing
the obvious. In gaol
a man goes free of condemnation and only
the unease of his own conscience examines

what is concealed
behind the ever more tightly knit
meshes of the interrogation. Fear and unease
about the inadequate weapons of cunning and watchfulness
construct a shared world
of hours that melt like hot tin.
Yet, when the fear grows less, even gaol
has its view of eternity
and over its walls, dark with twilight, falls
the shadow of the peace that is granted
to those who rest beneath the open sky.

Never will I forget
how well we got along
over our games of chess: the squares
scratched out on the stone floor with a pin,
the pieces made with cardboard torn
from an empty cigarette carton. Bent
over those scratched squares we found
a peaceful crevice in the now,
a field for the tournament of thought
and at times we would forget
that the morrow had already been lost
before our surroundings let go
their grip on us.
The knowledgeable thief entertained us
with songs from far and near,
always came back
from interrogation having confessed new crimes
always calculating
what they would cost him in months
of life; yes, truly
justice did not scorn
the widow's mite –
Never will I forget
how dear hands sent me
the book about Watteau with its pairs of

silk-robed lovers in parks suffused
with the purple radiance from distant
sunsets.

Thus is our life – Vain
to try to set it on a course
for the better. There is
no 'better' anywhere.
Fear and distress interrupted by
the occasional relief of
sleep and oblivion put man
in his rightful place. Whoever understands this
no longer negotiates with fortune
and the rainbow.

There is something that has gone –
A cloud has gone, a light, a cloud and a star.
I stand staring at that patch of emptiness
where once it was: a cloud has gone.

I do know why this empty patch in the sky
should bring forth such emptiness within me.
I do not know why: since the cloud disappeared
I have felt a thirst that cannot be quenched.

My lips are dry, my soul rocks to and fro
like one whose abdomen hurts.
I know full well that everything is an illusion
and that life builds cycles of illusion.
And that all transformations simply illustrate
that here have we no continuing city.
In spite of every transformation we are kept
on a diet that is far too restricted: it satisfies us before we have stilled our hunger.
Who but a conjuror could love reality for more than ten years at a stretch?

What comes after that is nothing but repetitions, which give us a
certain degree of immunity,
but by no means indemnify us; on the contrary, although the
symptoms grow less noticeable, the disease penetrates deep
down.
Work, leisure, all that is measurable in purely external terms
becomes more significant and the emotions are now the great
stumbling-block we must overcome.
But we overcome them not at all, we merely conceal them,
conceal them from the sight of others and ourselves.
Increasingly we make life into a plan of action, a sphere of activity.
The most precious and sensitive instruments have been lost
in the storm,
But we attempt to manage without them, we trust to our own eyes.

Can we hold the course? Do we care whether we hold it any more?
Chance and our eyes grow more and more closely wedded to
each other.
In this magnetic field everything is simpler.
Even the oarsman, aimlessly rowing, has a regard to the wind
and the waves.

Those who consciously describe themselves as corks before the wind
do not become more so
than those who are, but unaware of it . . .

To be poor is to be on the lookout –
We all stand in the queue ordained by necessity.
We do not know what it is we are queuing for, we join the queue
without knowing what the goods are worth:
desirable or not, it is all the same.
The queue forms like an ice-pattern on a window
and is longest
when one is looking forward to what one cannot get.
Patiently the days of our lives unfold,
frozen and wretched,
soon hopeless – and yet we go on with them

just for the enjoyment of waiting – and when we ourselves are no longer waiting
for the enjoyment of waiting with those who still are.
We warm ourselves at the glow of hopefulness as greedily
as the street-vendor at his brazier.

Toughness our most efficient stimulant,
a decoction of ‘perhaps’, ‘you never know’,
‘as well here as there’, ‘it could well be’.
Joined together by words and thoughts like a wire
the queue winds
binding our hearts somewhere
between belief and scepticism,
‘good luck’ and ‘that’s the end of that’.

Thus we are incapable of dying
and what we live by is what we are unable to cope with.
It is so simple – in this greyness
dwell harmonies, sweet scents that make
our spirits tremble, our hearts hammer
obstinately – in painful contradiction
to all that we know –

To be poor is to be on the lookout,
on the lookout for life and death, to sense
how closely they follow each other
into our hearts, as closely as the windshadows on a flag.
Only the hunter knows the way the quarry moves,
the detours it will make, where he will find it,
only the hunter knows, and the hunter is life.
Our hearts are marshes on which shots ring out,
but we see nothing of the quarry that is felled.
That is the hunter’s secret and a secret too
is the deep silence that is death’s echo –

Like a roe-deer oneness had fled from me –
And where I walk the paths are muddled together

and all the trees look the same.
But however far I may have gone astray in the exitless,
to you, wanderer, it will one day be disclosed,
to you, that wander under happier skies
where confusion's film of blood does not obscure your sight,
that here once the foot of a roe-deer left its imprint,
here in the valley of oneness and longing.

O bright valley, resting always further away
than thought and eye arc so quick to believe!
O bright valley, there you are, glimmering in daylight more clearly
each time the mists of vanity are dispelled.
The wearier grow one's steps the more clearly sounds
the purling of springs, the light across your meadows
and the water of the unattained rock cools
the throats of those who succumb but never
lose sight of their vision –

Long I sat on the bench of life
looking as though I were not looking,
saw the columns, supply vans,
heard the rumble of tanks, the frenetic din of engines.
The man at the wheel: stone gods, totem poles,
isolated, exalted in their din, while the caterpillar tracks
scraped out listlessly burrowing claws in the dust.
How long I sat there looking
looking as though I were not looking
looking as one looks at the crowd on a platform
keeping one's eyes peeled for the one whom one is to meet, only
for the one whom one is to meet,
seeking a voice in the tumult –

Among leaves that have lost their sheen,
among flowers that have lost their colour –
Within the perianth they have their glow
and decay has its incense
of the past – a gentleness without limits –

So listen inwards, to what does not believe,
does not hope and does not remember; a web
of dead things that have lost their forms
and are merely air or nothing!
They have drowsed away from them, they have slept,
slept long, alas, even during their lives they were sleeping
a sleep full of dreams about something
that never was –
Someone is loitering outside,
creeping in at your doors –
in search of warmth and company,
bread for his hunger –
Why does he not just come right in and say what it is he wants?
Why is he creeping about outside?
Drive him away: he has dark designs.
Chase him away! But he is not there. Where is he? Where has he vanished to?
But I know there is someone creeping about outside,
someone to whom I can give neither bread nor warmth –
Is it hope, dark hope?

Strew ashes, abundance of ashes,
ashes on the hard-frozen field,
on the winter snow, so that it melts away
laying bare the brown earth!
For you have an errand to me as you have to others,
sun!
All your mail has the word
Urgent marked on it.
Urgent – such a hopeful word,
so warm, when sent in your letters:
your beams!

How often the gold text in your stamp is borrowed
for things and communications of such little urgency!
Your message passes through so many
bitter intermediary hands that

– when finally it reaches us –
we are unable to decipher the garbled text.
But sometimes it amuses you
to throw you letters down to us
directly from above
and then there is a scent as delicate
as marsh violets –

Spring comes so quietly:
all the herb-gardens already hold
their seeds – all the herb-gardens
the gardener loves before all else.
Filled with the tension of expectancy
the rustle of the seedsticks
in the bag – now they have come to rest
in the soft folds of the soil, sealed in there.
He loves them best:
the sharp and the soft,
the light and the dark.
He loves them for the sake of their bitterness
and for their sweetness –
abundance here is paired
with fine discernment
and an aroma as full as that of the rose
here has its nearness to victuals, the frugal necessities of life.

Interjections,
forgotten by sound
possessed by light!
You are the girl where she sits
in the arbour's shade, bowed over the book that is making
her heart flutter.
Now she averts her gaze, her eyes pause for a moment
seeking coolness on roses and blue lupins
to avoid those pages that come flooding over her
with too great a confusion.
When the voice of her mother calls her to the table that is ready laid

her own voice answers in faltering tones –
She has been far away. Will she finally have the strength
to get up and push away
the soft branches – ?

Or: you are the youth, when during heart-tearing exertion
he shapes words on his lips, words he makes as humdrum as possible
in order to hide his insecurity, his fear, despair –

O interjections
you possess the shortest way to renewal –
you know corruption.
Light as butterflies
you steer from flower to flower.
So much trouble with the manifold
in order to attain the unique!
There is no shorter way
than you:
like the arrow quivering in the target you have already reached your goal
in the honey sac –
the cup of bitterness
O interjections, there you float:
keywords of chance, rinsed clean by the storm,
transparent from the wind,
butterfly-wings capsized on a stone cairn
merely commemorating what remains of
the flight of countless butterflies in the sun –

1946

Childhood

Childhood

The house slowly put out new rooms into the darkness,
new passages and staircases, a courtyard behind the
courtyard,
closed doors there – hush! – someone called, plaintively,
or was it just imagination, shadows, misunderstanding?

At the same time the house slowly shrank, the walls
closed in,
took on the colour of skin, the colour of tired
eyes when they saw
blotches spread over the ceiling, as if someone
was bleeding through the floor, but no sound was heard.

Slowly we grew older and ran up and down stairs
that echoed without response through hot summer days.
Evenings darkened, filled with windows and lamps.

1969 **Bo Carpelan**

THE FAR JOURNEY

Mother was much livelier than Father. She laughed often, and her red lips were nearly always overflowing with humming and song. Her cheeks, too, were red; her hair dark grey, and very thick. She was a little plump; rotund, but at the same time as light as air. She never stayed in one place, not even when she was working, but danced ceaselessly to and fro, hither and thither, without reason.

Father I saw much more seldom than Mother, but he was nevertheless the more exciting. When he came home from work he washed his hands and his face, sat down at the dinner table, quickly swallowed the food Mother gave him, and moved over to the rocking chair. It was his place of rest, and once there it was as if he simply rocked away from ordinary life. Mother never knew or understood anything about it. Father's taciturnity just got on her nerves. But I knew and understood, I, who every evening climbed on to his knee.

Where did we go on those journeys? Somewhere very far away, where Mother's ceaseless chatter could not reach, but where we heard quite different sounds and saw quite different sights. It was very quiet there, and beautiful, just those enchanting sounds and their quiet murmuring.

There, far away, Father talked to me. He told me of his work as a stonecutter and promised that I, too, would be a stonecutter. He told me of his past, of his childhood in the country, of how he came to the town which was now our home, and of the future, when he would be old and I would be grown up. And finally he told me of things which do not belong in this world, but on the other side of the earth and the visible sky, beyond the North Star and the moon and the sun, where God and the angels live. The place where we all go in the end.

I heard of many things that Mother did not even know existed.

Sometimes I woke up to find myself being undressed and put to bed. I could hear Mother's voice clearly again, and saw Father pick up the water and slop buckets and go out. Mother had asked him to bring in fresh water and take the dirty water out. But mostly I fell asleep without this vision, in which Father acted as a servant, and saw him again only on the evening of the next day, when he sat me on his knee again.

Mother I saw all day long, from morning till night, except for the morning moments when she went to the market to buy food. Mother dressed me, fed and washed me and took me out and brought me in. Mother talked to me, kissed me, sang me all sorts of different songs, sat me on her knee a thousand times a day, cried when I escaped from her sight. I loved her very much. But with her we were only on the surface of the bright, sunny globe; everything around us was clear and simple. That was why I left her always when evening came and Father came home. I ran to Father's lap and he took me far away, to mysterious lands and skies.

I still don't know how to explain how Father guided me along the highways and byways of his mind. Only during those short moments when Mother was away did he hum softly to me a song about a star, the North Star. But when Mother came back, he always stopped. And that was, indeed, for me the most important thing: his mysterious silence, the far journey.

*

The house was rented. Outside our room, first came a dusky hall, which we shared with our neighbours, and then some steep stairs. To me, at least, the stairs seemed dangerously high, since they had five or six steps. When I had to go up or down them without Mother's help, I managed only by grasping the banister with both hands.

The yard was flat sand and some kind of trodden earth-like substance. Opposite the house were various low buildings: a pigsty, stable, woodsheds, privies, a cesspit and a well. At either end of the house were high, wide doors giving on to different streets, and I used both equally hopefully, since in front of each was a fine pile of stones to be cut.

I know no more of the yard, for it did not interest me. Neither do I remember anything, at this stage, of the other children. Of people from outside our house I knew at this time only one: the house's owner, the town's mayor.

He did not live with us, but in some better house of his own. But here was his jumble shed, between the privy and the stable, and always when he visited his profitable, poor people's house he deposited something in his shed: a worn horseshoe he had found in the road, a rusty nail, a piece of tin and something metal. Metal he valued so highly that he believed it was nothing short of stupid to leave even a scrap of it in the road or in a dustbin. For him, metal was the foundation of riches. But since his family and friends were not prepared to acknowledge his obsession, an old man's obsession, he deposited his pieces of metal in the shed in our yard.

What, then, was he like? Unfortunately I remember no more of him than that he was a very stern old man and that he had an angry stick in his hand. If I was in the yard when he called, I quickly ran to the nearest hiding place, but at the same time I became mocking and derisive. I remembered what others had said about him: that rich old man is mad. Sane people don't collect rusty, broken horseshoes.

He came to our room from time to time in the evenings, when he was certain Father would be home from work. It was the day the monthly rent fell due, and Father and Mother were waiting for him. I, too, became more nervous by the minute. I was frightened of something, even though Father and Mother assured me that he meant no harm to anyone. Perhaps I was frightened because at home there was nowhere to hide, unlike in the yard where I had laughed at him. As soon as our door opened and our landlord came into view, I slipped from the safety of Father's lap to hide behind him, or threw myself under the bed.

It is strange that I ran away from him here, too, although the owner of our house was particularly polite when he came inside. He shook Mother and Father's hands, asked how we were, praised the good weather, and would have patted my head if I had let him. But I had run away from him, and every time he had to give up his futile attempt and return to Mother and Father. He often rubbed his hands in satisfaction before them, for Father took out his purse, counted out the requisite rent money, and gave it ceremoniously to the landlord. At the same time Mother curtsied respectfully. The landlord grabbed the money happily, counted it quickly and pushed it into his own purse, thanking Mother and Father: 'Thank you, thank you, good people, you are just the kind of people I like. I hope that you will live in our house until the ends of your lives. Thank you, thank you, goodbye, goodbye, au revoir, good people.'

He backed out of the room and disappeared, politely bowing, through the door.

*

What was it like, this room of ours? Although I have long tried to recall its walls and ceiling, its floor and window, what colours there were, the shapes of the furniture, the lamp and the oven, I remember nothing. I cannot imagine what the bed was like in which Father and Mother slept, or the place where I spent my nights. I have some dim picture only of the rocking chair for, rocking there on Father's knee, I experienced all the most wondrous fantasies of life and death.

1953 **Toivo Pekkanen**

HIMMU

Hilma was a young girl; too young, really, for her age – she was 22. She had grown up late. Sent away from home, from her log cabin in the country to the town, when she was ten, at 14 she had already been serving customers in the shop. Her late development, however, had nothing to do with work; it was the result of something quite different.

Papa had given her to his sister, the wealthy Mrs Varonen, to bring up on the understanding that she would be allowed to go to school in the town. Hilma was the cleverest of all Papa's eight children, not counting Tilda, who was dead. Tilda had been a quick-witted girl, so biddable and docile; she had attended the girls' school in Tampere, and Mrs Varonen had loved her as if she had been her own daughter. When Tilda had visited her old home in Saari, in Vähikkälä, she had gone round the farms chatting with the old people, and written down the stories and poems and songs they remembered, and she had sent her notes to the Helsinki gentlemen who were interested in collecting them. So Tilda had really been something special. But she was dead; consumption had suddenly taken her away, like so many others at that time.

Just after Tilda died, Papa sent Hilma to Mrs Varonen, ignoring a letter from her in which she tried to remonstrate with him: 'She will only die here, just like Tilda. I do not have the strength for such a little girl. When I have children of my Own to look after, and Aleksandra agrees that we should not take in strangers Here any more.'

But Papa insisted in sending Hilma, and Mrs Varonen took her in on the understanding that she would be able to go to school once she had gained a little strength.

But Hilma's education had stopped short at reading and writing, which she had been taught by Miss Sahlberg, Mrs Varonen's first assistant in the ladies' clothes department. Miss Sahlberg was a good teacher, and she suggested to Mrs Varonen that Hilma should take the entrance examination for the girls' school. That spring, hoewever, Mrs Varonen, whom Hilma had learned to call Auntie, noticed that Hilma could serve customers better and more nimbly than anyone, and her eagerness to send her to school faded. She liked having a biddable girl to help her, and Hilma was already completely at home in the shop, organising the stockroom and measuring fabrics, not to mention dusting and sweeping the floor. Hilma was not sent to school the first autumn, or the second, and by the third year she had already grown too big for the first form; by the time the fourth came, she could look after the shop as well as someone twice her age.

Hilma was small and thin compared to her sturdy cousins, Mikael and Konstantin. When she arrived from the country, she was wearing a patched frock and Tilda's old shoes and, instead of an overcoat, a grey check shawl wound round and round her body and head, for it was November and terribly cold. She was brought by Papa's closest neighbour, the wife of the tenant farmer and smith; Papa could not bring her, because did not have the clothes or, to tell the truth, the inclination. The smith's wife found the Varonens' house after asking her way a couple of times, wondered for a moment which door to use, went round to the yard and entered through the kitchen door. And there she found a friendly soul, the housekeeper, Greeta. Greeta welcomed the girl and thanked the smith's wife, who quickly went about her business, hoping to catch the evening train home.

Auntie and her daughter Aleksandra proceeded to examine the girl who emerged from the shawl. And exclaimed at her thinness, her chapped, bare legs and her bright, fair hair. 'My goodness gracious me, where are we to find clothes for her,' said Auntie, and Aleksandra complained: 'Why did Mama agree to take her?' But then Aleksandra relented and searched throught her own clothes, and altered one of her old dresses and a pair of knickers, which the poor child shrank from in horror, never before having seen such things.

In front of the living room mirror, Hilma began to cry, refusing to admire her new clothes.

Her fair hair became a particular problem, for on first seeing Hilma the shopkeeper, a grave and sincere man, cried: 'What beautiful hair, just like an angel's.' 'Oh no it isn't', retorted Auntie. 'Fair hair is vulgar.'

After that Auntie tried all the tricks she knew to darken Hilma's hair. Her red, rough feet and hands were rubbed with cream and vaseline, and the ingrained dirt of her nails was removed with the points of scissors, but her hair was accorded a more unusual treatment. First it was cut very short. ('Well, it was full of lice,' said Aleksandra, but this her mother denied.) Auntie mixed oil from the chemist's with a tablespoon of brandy, and this she rubbed, with ungentle hands, into Hilma's scalp. This was repeated every night, with Hilma whimpering and Auntie muttering bad-temperedly. Hilma's hair was now certainly ugly enough, greasy and foul-smelling. And with time it darkened – if not through Auntie's ministrations, then certainly through sorrow.

Greeta said that Auntie meant well. Brandy was an expensive gentlemen's drink, and Auntie was prepared to sacrifice this precious liquid for Hilma's sake. Hilma said that she knew all about brandy, because Papa drank it when Captain Tiileman came visiting on his bay mare. Tiileman brought brandy as a present, and Papa and he would drink it together sitting at the little parlour table, which was brought into the house specially for the captain's visit. The table was in the middle of the living-room floor, the chairs on either side of it. Papa had made them himself. Papa was so clever.

Auntie liked Hilma's hair better dark than fair. But Hilma had other faults that were not so easy to put right. She was shy, and always worried about something. When she first arrived, straight from the forest, it was understandable, but Auntie kept nagging at Hilma when she persisted in thinking that life in the town was the same as in the country. She imagined the kitchen tasks to to be just as simple. At first she was put to serve Greeta, so that she could get used to them. Greeta asked her to wash the everyday town cutlery, the spiky forks and the shiny knives. She was supposed to scrub them under the tap, where water gushed from a hole at the end of a hook and never ran out, Greeta said. This Hilma did not believe. She wanted to turn the tap off after she had scrubbed each knife and fork before handing them to Greeta for washing in soapy water. But Greeta told her to let the water flow, it was much quicker that way. 'But the water will run out,' said Hilma; 'why use more than you need?' 'It won't stop,' said Greeta, and laughed a little. But it did. The stream of water slackened, and then stopped. There was no more water. 'I told you,' said Hilma, muttering between her teeth.

Greeta laughed as she told Auntie what a clever girl Hilma was. Auntie snorted. The water began to flow again that afternoon. Hilma would just have to believe that it had been an accident. Or a mistake. Something. The engineers had turned it off at the mains.

For her first town Christmas, Hilma received from Auntie and the shopkeeper a new dress, a woollen one made specially for her, and three nightdresses, since it was necessary to wear different clothes at night from during the day. Mikael gave her mittens and Aleksandra stockings, Konstantin a scarf and Miss Sahlberg a locket. She liked the locket best, but she thanked Auntie first for the dress, which was red. When she put on the dress and hung the locket around her neck, she was no longer the old Himmu. She would have liked to show the dress to Papa and Mama, but they were far away. At home. She was in the town, in the Varonens' house. Maybe she would never go home again. But when her hair had grown long enough so that it could be trimmed and combed smooth and looked decent, Hilma was taken to the photographer, and she had to stand still for a long time and hold on to a little table and behind her there was a big picture with trees and bushes and she would have liked to look at it. She did not understand that it was part of a picture – of her, and the picture behind her. A picture of a picture and her. It was very funny. But everything else was strange, too. And the trees and bushes in the background picture were really ugly and pathetic looking, not all like real ones. Why did they make pictures that didn't look right?

Hilma's main worry was all the incomprehensible aspects of sheer living, eating, moving about, talking. Aleksandra was a good girl, and although she was only four years older than Hilma, she was already a young lady, and almost grown-up. She took it upon herself to educate Hilma in genteel manners. It was a hopeless task for a young lady, but she did not give up easily. Hilma did not even know the names of the most ordinary objects that adorned the lives of the gentlefolk. Aleksandra decided she should learn them first.

This happened as follows: Hilma was placed in the middle of the parlour while Aleksandra stood behind her, holding her head and directing her gaze towards each object in turn.

'Ceramic stove. That's a ceramic stove. Say it.'

'Ceramic stove,' Hilja whispered.

'More clearly.'

'Ceramic stove!'

'All right, all right. You'll learn it better later. That's an etashere. Say: etashere.'

'Etashere.'

'No, no, say etagère. Etagère.'

'Etagère.'

'That's a pianino. Pianino.'

'Pianino.'

'Those are drapes. Say: drapes.'

'R . . Dra . . .'

'Well, I suppose that's a difficult one. We'll leave it till next time. Say sofa. You must know sofa. Sofa.'

'Sofa.'

Hilma burst into bitter tears.

'What's wrong? Does it hurt? What is it?'

Greeta came to fetch Hilma away. But Aleksandra had to confess to her mother that Hilma was an unexpectedly bright child.

'Just think, she'd never seen an etagere, but she knew how to say etagère.'

Mrs Varonen snorted.

Hilma learned other things, too: how to sit upright at table and how to use a fork, that spiky, horrible object, and how to hold one's elbows and neck and head and fingers. All at once! You weren't even allowed to swing your legs. These lessons took place in Aleksandra's room, where the older girl had consented to eat her meals on account of Hilma. She explained at length to Hilma how kind she was to agree to such a lowering of her status, although she had long been allowed to eat with her parents in the dining room.

The boys ate in the kitchen with Greeta. Now a table was laid separately for the two of them in Aleksandra's room, and Hilma did everything just as Aleksandra told her.

'Look, now you've spilt soup on the tablecloth. Oh dear. Don't hold the spoon like that, look, your elbows are all over the place. Just think if some fine gentleperson was sitting next to you. You'd be nudging them. They'd think you were an idiot. They'd laugh at you.'

Hilma generally broke down before they got to the dessert and let out a great sob. At the same time she tried to run away, and if she managed to escape Aleksandra's grasp she would run either to the cellar or the attic. She was not at all frightened of the dark attic, not compared with Aleksandra.

'What are you doing to that little girl to make her cry like that?' asked the shopkeeper.

'I should never, ever, have taken her,' muttered Mrs Varonen. At the same time she remembered Tilda, and began to search for her handkerchief, but left off. What was gone was gone.

When Hilma had learnt to write, Auntie decided that she should write to her parents, so they could see how well she was progressing. Auntie called Hilma into the dining room, spread a newspaper on the table, brought an inkwell and a pen and some clean paper, and then there was nothing for it but to begin, with Auntie looking over her shoulder on one side, Aleksandra on the other. Hilma's fingers were pressed round the pen, and the dictation began, Auntie's large, sweaty hand guiding hers. Aleksandra said, 'Let me try, Mama'; Aleksandra had a cold, bony hand and it squeezed her twice as hard.

'Shan't!' cried Hilma. 'Let me do it by myself!'

'Tampere,' the letter began, 'the 19 Feb', which was all that would fit on the first line, what with her hand being pushed about and Tampere being written so large.

Auntie dictated what came next:

'Dear loved ones. With these few lines I send you my greetings and assure you I am very and hope you are also.'

'She left out "well"! Mama, Hilma left a word out!'

'Let it stand,' said Auntie. 'As long as she writes something'.

It looked quite good, and it was quite easy to write with guidelines under the paper. But then Aleksandra had to go, because she was expecting a visitor, some young lady from the same class at school, and Auntie had to give instructions in the kitchen, because there was to be a party that evening. There ws nothing for it but for Hilma to go on by herself, just like that, to tell of her life and to ask for news.

Hilma sat all alone in the dining room, and in front of her rose the enormous, empty surface of the table with its two tablecloths, and the newspaper and her writing materials looked tiny and insignificant in comparison. She looked at the pot plant on the column. It looked wintry and undernourished. She remembered her home farm, Saari, just as it was in summer. The large field Papa had ploughed, by the shore, the big fir tree by the roadside, Hilma's stone where she played house with Vennu, the roses by the gate, the aspens that rustled behind the sauna, and the fritillaries under the farmhouse windows. The apple trees and gooseberry bushes. The cows in the pasture and the horse in the meadow And the baa-lambs. And Mama. And the boys and her little sister.

She fingered the tassels of the tablecloth. What if the tablecloth slipped and the inkwell fell on to the carpet?

Her gaze fastened on the elaborately carved arm of the chair opposite. What if a piece fell off it, and the pale wood glared out, an accusing pale spot amid the black stain?

She picked up the pen, reached for the inkwell crouching there a terribly long way away, put the pen down, got down off the chair, clambered up again, and got up on her knees. Now she could reach the inkwell easily. All she had to do was write, to go on from where she left off, just like that.

'Dear Papa, come and fetch me with horse (Polle) and cart, I can't sleep or eat here.

'Dear Papa, I'm homesick, I'm only a little girl and I don't want to be in this strange place.

'Dear Papa, very soon I'll die here, just like Tilda did, and I'm much worse than her.'

And then she went on writing, and what came was what her pen wanted, not her. The pen wanted her to write what she did not want to write. It was Auntie's pen, after all. But although what the pen wrote was all empty talk and lies, it became the truth as soon as it went down on paper.

'It is a long time since I was at home, we were all happy then, but I have been very happy here too because while I have been here all sorts of strange things have hapened Auntie has put me to school (not proper school) and I have learnd to write although it is still not very good but if I practice it will be better and I will be able to write home and that will be nice. Here we had a very happy christmas how was it with you I got lots of presents mittens from Mikael a workbox from Auntie and a red dress made out of wool and 3 nightdresses. A workbox from Rosa a scarf from Konstantin and Miss Saalber gave me a loket. Christmas was alltogether lovly but I know it would have been just as good at home.

'I went to church today the sermon was given by a and reading tests were announced I don't need to worry about them because I'm at school have you had reading tests did Nikolai read well? Have the boys played a lot?'

Up till then it had gone well, but then she began to write about Shrove Tuesday and made an ink-blot and she made it worse by drawing lines and large hoops all over everything. Auntie came in and shouted in a hollow, echoing voice, 'Oh, you naughty girl!' and flicked her fingers at her ear. She would have to send Papa the blotchy letter and Papa would probably lose his temper with her once and for all and he would never write to Hilma again, or ever come to visit such a bad child, said Auntie.

Then there were still greetings to be written from her uncle Kalle, who had come to Tampere from Mänttä for a New Year visit, and from Rosa and Ida, and she had to explain that Rosa and Ida were uncle Kalle's daughters, and that they lived in Tampere, and that Rosa's husband was a shopkeeper, not a very big one, but a shopkeeper nonetheless, and Rosa and Ida served in the shop, and Hilma said that she didn't know how to write such a lot of different things and Auntie said calmly that no, she didn't suppose she did, so why didn't she just send greetings. So that is what she did, and added greetings to her Aunt Miina and her cousin Edla, who were supposed to be at Saari just now, at Papa's house, Papa had said so in a letter to Auntie.

In her early years in the town, Hilma often awoke dreaming of Saari and Papa. In her imagination she was walking along the shore path and looking for Papa, who was supposed to be in the lake field or on the shore. She peered between the birch saplings that grew in the ditch beside the field and was worried. And finally, as she approached the shore, she thought she could see Papa rising from the water and wringing water from his clothes. She was frightened as he began to walk up the path, wondering was it Papa, or the water-sprite who bore away naughty children. But it was Papa, and Himmu ran towards him shouting for joy and buried her head in her father's stomach. And as she did so she started back: Papa was wet through.

She awoke from that dream wet and weeping herself. She was a child, but she had been made to carry a heavy burden: she had to suffer humbly and be grateful to Auntie for everything. Auntie was temperamental, said Greeta, who had known her for many years. She meant well, but lost her patience easily. She gave good advice, but did it angrily, not calmly. She did not suffer fools. She could not tolerate any noise, and if the sound of Hilma and the boys at play reached her in the shop, she arrived red with anger and took the birch to whomever she could lay her hands on. Hilma would have liked to play with Mikael and Konstantin; they were just the same age as Nikolai and Aleksander at home. They were the same in other ways, too. They were always getting up to mischief, playing practical jokes and boasting and pinching her when they thought no one was looking. If they were caught doing anything wrong, it was luckily always Konstantin's fault. Hilma didn't know why, but she was glad that she was not blamed if something got broken or lost.

Aleksandra forbade her to play with the boys. Her voice was severe and full of meaning. And after that, Auntie forbade her too. It was a pity.

But Hilma did have Greeta. Greeta was the best thing in the entire Varonen household, because she was cheerful. She put up with Hilma's prattling, and chattered herself too. She sang long songs, and knew them off by heart. Like the one about the terrible time when the young gentleman Ernst von Nottbeck was cruelly murdered on the Lielahti road. Awful things like that can happen even to rich people, who are friends with God as well as the Tsar. Auntie, too, liked to listen to Greeta's songs, and she was very sorry for the Nottbecks. They were so rich that the Varonens were mere peasants in comparison. But that didn't help their son, and the story went that the lady of the house had died of sorrow on learning of his murder.

They were good and noble folk, those Nottbecks, Auntie said. But when Auntie wasn't there, Greeta said that they were real slave-drivers, foreign braggarts.

Once Hilma told her Auntie that Papa was the best person in the world. She began, excitedly, to explain all the things Papa could do. Plough, sow, look after the garden, grow flowers, berries and apples, drive a horse, look after the horses and the cattle, gather in the harvest, fish and catch crayfish, dig a tar-burning pit and make tar that was sold in Hämeenlinna. He knew how to make malt, too. He could make liquor and beer, too, only that wasn't allowed. In Saari they were rich: they had everything they wanted, and they didn't want anything they didn't have. They were richer than the Nottbecks, because they didn't care if the Tsar had visited them. Carried away with enthusiasm, poor Himmu was foolish enough to chatter on to her aunt about all these things.

Auntie gazed at her with her large, cat-coloured eyes. Himmu fell silent, but it was too late.

'What does your father know? Nothing. It's nothing to know how to farm and tend cattle. Any old fool knows that. Your father is a poor man. His poverty is a punishment from God because he has always been . . . what he is. Always, ever since he was a little boy. Disobedient and loudmouthed. You should be grateful that you have escaped from your parents' wretched house to the town, where people are civilised. Just you remember that!'

Hilma began to cry quietly and wipe away her tears with a new handkerchief that Auntie had just given her. That made Auntie angry, too. Told her to stop crying. Told her a second time, and then fetched the birch from behind the door.

'Will you stop that now?'

Hilma did not stop, and Auntie gave her the birch. It was like a nightmare: her fine knickers were undone at the back and the thin skin of her bottom felt the bite of the birch. Hilma whined. Auntie pressed:

'Will you stop now?'

In the end Hilma came to her senses and screamed 'Yes!' with all her might, and Auntie stopped the birching, pulled up her knickers and buttoned them, and straightened her dress. Hilma had to put the birch back in its place: it was hard, because her eyes were still watering and she could hardly see, and she had to stand on a chair to get the birch back on its hook.

Then Hilma fixed her eyes on Auntie and, still whimpering and sniffing, asked if she could go to the kitchen. Auntie was quite red, and accused Hilma again of ingratitude. She was not allowed to go to the kitchen. Auntie complained and complained that Hilma was obstinate and disobedient. Listening to her words, Hilma calmed down, the intervals between her gulps and whimpers lengthened and her breathing became regular.

'It's like this: God ordains who is poor and who is rich. If you say that poor is rich, you are blaspheming against God.'

'Yes, but Papa . . .' Hilma was still bold enough to hiccup.

'I know your father means well, but he's a poor wretch. Constantly ill, too. And those . . . weaknesses of his. Be happy that you're here. You can even go to school and learn. You can sit down at a groaning table where nothing is lacking. You have clothes and everything. What more do you want?'

'Nothing,' Hilma realised.

'It's not like this at home in Vähikkälä. Is it?'

'No.'

'They're always short of something there. I know that. Aren't they?'

'Yes.'

'God ordained that you should be allowed to leave home.'

'Mm.'

Hilma grew up slowly.

1971 **Eila Pennanen**

A FAREWELL TO THE RÖÖPERI OF MY CHILDHOOD

These streets, buildings, sky above rooflines,
the factory smokestacks, windblown hair,
dinosaur cranes in the harbor, the shipyard,
the sounds of labor, wild banging of rivet-guns,
the greeting calls of ships as they arrive
escorted by seagulls from faraway seas
or take leave from you, hill of Punavuori, old Rööperi,
you, the city, your face reflected in the sea's waters,
a face forever renewing itself.

How many years – more than fifty, now
since I first walked these streets . . .
Was Mother holding my hand then

as mothers hold their children's hands today
on these same streets ?
Did I play on the swings then, like children today
in that pitiful park by the shipyard
in the shade of masonry walls ?
Was there even a park here then – I can't remember,
I only remember you, sky speckled with seagulls,
clouds, and smoke – you, hill of Punavuori, old Rööperi.

Where have they gone, the old wooden buildings, the lilacs
in their yards, the dwellings of skippers and sailors,
fishermen, speaking broken Swedish,
carters and artisans from your streets, the stables in the back yards,
the odor of hay and horses?
Where are the sails in the harbor, sand yawls, schooners,
proudest among them the barque 'Tjerimay'
that carried off many of your sons to distant seas and lands?
Some of them never returned.
Where are the companions of the boy I was,
the Sjöbas, Kudes, Pedes, Haras, Kaltsis, guys from Röba,
inseparable for better or worse, cool dudes –
the street taught them speech, the harbor, tolerance,
and in their struggle against poverty
they learned to be tough and ruthless, cruel and just
in ways unimagined by laws, judges, and teachers.

Where are your daughters, their sisters, sweethearts of sailors and dockers
whom the Salvation Army tried to save, shopgirls
whom gentlemen of the city tried to lead astray –
where, old Rööperi, are their mothers,
fast talkers worn out by pregnancies,
tanned by the lye of their laundry rooms,
hardened by their husbands' fists,
the grandmothers of today's Rööperi, today's Helsinki,
who, fueled by cough mixture and coffee, pushed on like old stubborn tugboats

through wars, revolutions, decades of hunger and deprivation
dragging behind them the barge of daily bread and unpaid rent,
always in danger of sinking, and didn't even know
that the ocean they crossed, the storm they endured
was called world history.

You have disappeared, old Rööperi, disappeared
to live in the images of my memories, the summer of my childhood.
You disappeared like the old maples and lindentrees in your yards
after they grew mossy, decrepit, no longer bloomed.
You disappeared like the scent of lilac in May,
like the musicians in the courtyards, surrounded by children.
Disappeared like the smell of horses and hay in the stable yards,
like the fishermen on your shores, the sunset of my childhood
beyond the straits, the open sea, the forests past Jätkäsaari.
You disappeared like a dream, like a play from its set,
you no longer exist. What remains is stone, iron, steel, old Rööperi,
a new town of brick, glass, and concrete built on your grave.
What remains is the sky, speckled with gulls, clouds, and smoke,
the city, its face reflected in the sea's waters,
a face forever renewing itself.

1962 **Arvo Turtiainen**

Translator's notes:
Rööperi, Punavuori, Röba – names for the same old working-class neighborhood of Helsinki, literally 'Red Hill' or 'Red Mountain.'
Sjöba, Kude, Pede, Hara, Kaltsi – male first names in old Helsinki dialect.
Jätkäsaari – literally 'Docker's Island.'

THE OSTROBOTHNIAN ABOUT THE SEA

Out of the sea all land has risen.
Those who live by the sea have seen for themselves
how land has risen and dried itself with grass
and begun to dress itself in forest.

If one day the sea
should change its mind and start to take back its land
it would mean quite a lot of trouble
for Ostrobothnia's coastal population.

Can one really rely
on the sea that owns three-quarters of the earth
always being so generous to the Ostrobothnians?
Safest not to rely on it too much.

Those who live by the sea
know how it changes, from day to day,
hour to hour, how the water ebbs or flows
but is never still.

And that the inconstancy marks
even that which is thought to be constant.

1984

Lars Huldén

LIGHT'S SOUND

Rainspatter on the water surface
or a cricket here in the grass?
to which hushed song
has my heart awakened?
a swallow whirring past . . .
the sea breathing against the rocks,
or simply the morning light spreading slow
                                                        in the branches,
in the tree's crown overhead

light's sound

1965

5 o'clock and nothing o'clock
        by the sea
the tugboat in space comes thudding
        with silence

no bird no soul frees itself
        from no shadow

everything sinks into the sun

1971

You do not see them
but if you listen
they are already there;

the first grains of snow
among the spruces

space falling
soundlessly apart

1973

From the light of meltwater
echoes
        birdsong

1973

Peter Sandelin

An old cabin in Teisko had
a cataract in its eye
but it could still see
how from somewhere over a meadow of buttercups
the two of them came
a sweaty blond curl on the boy's forehead
in the boy's hand a little ringless hand.

Then the cottage
grey-eyed
and black-browed said
with its toothless mouth:
'Just come home,
come over the meadow of buttercups
here into my arms.'

1954

In grandma's room there's quiet,
the clock with a china face can break it,
I can't.
But in the morning I slip into the quiet
and grandma's not angry.

I show the colours of the flowers on the mat on her bedroom floor
and say:
The flowers are running atbout on grandma's striped mat.
Although the quiet is sacred,
grandma excuses me every morning
I walk along the striped mat to her side
and tell all sorts of stories.

1959

THIS IS HOW IT IS

He has long since
        lost his vigour in these streets,
all he grows now
        is a beard, case histories,
        application forms, protests.

He has built here,
        now they're dismantling infirm buildings
and the street shakes
        from explosions in sewers
        with dim lamps in their stony dust.

He used to suck hard at the air
        of courtyards full of bushes and trees,
now it's leaden clouds
        from beneath car bonnets for an asthmatic to swallow,
        a cough jolts brittle bones.

He's past it, he sits
        on the benches of the public sauna,
bathes his knobbly legs,
        rubs the bumps on his arms,

grumbles
        at the haves and the have-nots,
at how it's always only others
        like socialist ministers
who get privileges of so many kinds.

1972 **Viljo Kajava**

EILA KIVIKKAHO
SOLVEIG VON SCHOULTZ
EEVA-LIISA MANNER
TOVE JANSSON
VEIKKO HUOVINEN

Eila Kivikkaho

SHOUTED INTERJECTION

Do you consume nothing but beauty?
Dig your home in a treasure
like rust
and eat right through?

1951

RAISING THE FLAG

What a wonder – to fly
a great flag in your heart at midnight,
blow a bugle,
blaze abroad:
'Now it's flying.'

Circles of darkness
continually draw in.
No one can see my heart.
What a wonder, the ceremony,
the hoisting of the flag,
the flying of the dishonoured flag
on the pole of honour.

1951

DEFIANCE

When all the trunks and tops are down
the roots remain. The roots remain.
You call it memory? It's more than that:
it's longing and it's pain;
hotter than any tears it is,
more than grief it scorches:
it's your heart, your very heart:
don't mention its torches.

When all the floods are dammed and stopped,
the spring remains. The springs remain.
You call it hope? It's more than that:
it's mutiny here again!
When the mouth chokes back the words,
watch out for the new compliance:
the shout compounds its interest
in the silence of defiance.

1952

VICTORIES AND DEFEATS

The highest treetops
are still visible
on the farthest roads.
Only the path
that broke off there
knows the gorge.

1952

THE GENERATIONS

1
You slap your youth on the table –
a green trump: a living seven-towered
crowning castellation
with not a single grave
in its funeral barrow:
just a road coming and going –
and all the knowledge
inherited: guesswork
culled, inoculated, cross-fertilised.

You slap your
seventimes-crenellated
youth on the table,
not knowing
how empty the pot is –
how out we are
of drugs of endurance.

And yet: could *you*
conquer us?
Our game was up
before you were born.
How can you conquer the defeated?

2
We've camouflaged ourselves like snow,
with the animal kingdom, haven't we? –
clinging to a crevice in the season.

A late flame
spits still in our ash – willowherb.

In the burn-beaten years
reconstruction and a young forest are rising.

Otherwise they'd be greyer,
those city blocks,
the tree more lichened,

and your young forest
would be growing
out of the wind
unscared by our lopped stumps.

3
How empty the pot is,
our only one –
the upside down
steel helmet
bogwater boiled in,
with no condiment
but salt,
no herb but endurance.

Was no sweetsinging tree
left from those forests,
no flower left from the meadows
for the bee?

The herbs were finished, weren't they,
and a battered curse
the only helmet we had?

And if there was a flower
or an unforgotten prayer
still left,
we saved it, didn't we,
for the next grave?

1961

LONG-PLAYING RECORD

Slow circling of the night sky,
a scratched silence,
a grisly largo –
emptiness
inscribing the distances full.

We don't hear
a single scratch, though

a solar system

or the final scraping
of an extinguished instrument.

1961

CHARCOAL SKETCH

Charcoal covers the sheets
with sketches
of its own burnt tree:

leaves in thousands,
shadows of a leaf –

see?
So green it was!

1975

Solveig von Schoultz

DREAM

In the sudden lamplight
skirts became transparent
around the dark core of her body.
Quickly she threw them away.
They lifted like the petals of a poppy flower
flew over the bed, white bells.
The man groped for them
buried his mouth in the cool submissiveness
sank his face into her evanescent scent.
But she stood naked
and forgotten
by the bed.

1952

HEART

We gave her grain, not much,
but so she wouldn't tire,
she got water, a thimbleful
for her to remember the mainspring,
we opened her door slightly
so that the sky hit her eye

and we tied a mirror fragment to her cage
for her to look straight into the cloud.
She sat still, wings jerking.

Thus she sang.

1949

THE BIRDS

At first I heard only the voices
yours and mine
weaving around each other
some words fell behind us.
Later I heard the birds
weaving their nest of rain-threads
in the mist.
Wings shot down
behind us
beaks fought
over diamonds.

1963

SEA IN NOVEMBER

Around the house, quiet under the trees
sit big transparent figures
they don't bar the way
you can walk right through them
only a slight chill
but they're always there
easier to see in wet weather
when the sea is grey
when what has been rises up
towards the window.

1975

GONE AWAY

It's quite possible when you sit in the sun
to sit in the shade, see the rolling waves
merely as glinting lies over the rocks
only see hunger in gulls' yellow eyes
autumn in the sun-dried grass at your feet.
It's quite possible when you sit in the sun
to have gone away, not answer to a call
feel in your innermost room the grey hand
close the windows.

1975

THE BURNING GLASS

As in spring
you catch the sun in a burning glass
watching the heat dwindle
and the paper blacken,
a tiny point in it
begin to glow,
surely that's how despair
should burn a hole in silence.

1980

A WAY TO MEASURE TIME

A wingbeat flashed outside the cave mouth
and the sun's departure was a clear green hillock
as we sank down, swallowed by the darkness.
We crept along damp and narrow passageways
where only chillness breathed, and suddenly
we could stand upright in a lofty chamber
whose ceiling rose up dimly out of sight

and echoes travelled on from wall to wall
confusingly, as if a multitude
of voices from some forgotten time were embalmed
seemingly frozen into the cave's acoustics.
The ceiling's heavy fruit hung in clusters
that through millions of years had been dripping
their liquid lime, a way to measure time.
We shone light on them, dark midnight blue
and red that seemed like flayed bison bodies.
Here sixty thousand years ago lived folk,
our guide said, up there you see a cleft
into the next cave, then people were agile,
could climb, a hundred thousand years ago.
Then as the guide was talking we could see
other people, the most ancient race.
They huddled close together in wet cloaks
and bowed their necks under the low roof
that since the start of time had been dripping
and with each single drop had been growing.
They were a taciturn and hardy folk
who remembered most, cherished their memories
and turned their backs on us with dignity,
intruders and as fleeting as the present.

1989

Eeva-Liisa Manner

COUNTERPOINT

They all fell out of my lap:
the garden, the yard, the house, the voices, the rooms,
the child – a swallow and fish in her hand –
fell to the ground
        which bore the stones.

I'm an empty room,
around me the cardinal points
and snow-folded trees:
cold, cold, empty.

But on my hand
rises everything I loved –
the yard, the roses, the flowerpot house,
perfection:
a house like a capsule: quiet seeds
with death and motion in their tissues,

the little well, the little dog, its invisible collar.
The little room, the little windows,
the little, sprightly lace-up shoes
for the heart' s running.
The shoes run from room to room,

from atrium to ventricle,
and the child-fingers build out into the blood
a stone jetty for the rowers of stone.

Dreams like stones
in the deep,
perused, dedicated to death.

And from the windows
waft in tuned birds –
with chuckles in their beaks:
        drops of Mozart
                zart zart

1956

When shore and reflection are precisely the same,
and flawless and suave is the wedding of sky and water,

when deep and clear is the looking-glass daydream
with animals astray, and clouds, and a forest
soughing darkly in the deep windless glass,

a wingtip dipping in water is apt to crack
the illusion – light and water's infatuated
attestation to the world, silk-slender, but binding.

And the world, as fresh and lovely as after rain
or creation, a change of mind, or a long illness,
is on its own, weighty, alone in all its members.

1960

STRONTIUM

4
No blueskirted rosy-fingered children
run through the cheerful meadows
as confidantes of flowers now
No red hoops bowl the streets
joy brings no news
No trees bend down
their scented burdens
no wind remembers
no well bubbles
no lovers' shadows
unite in the lanes of memory and oblivion
(Die Vögelein schweigen im Walde)

The tank has halted in the ploughland
The trench is sporting a buttercup
The bunker roof has blossomed with a mist of grass
like lace against the emptiness
Peace
And the radioactive families twist in the blast
and dangle in air, stripped bones
down the canal a swollen corpse swims leg-first seaward
the fighting fish has brought his mate into the helmet
and celebrates marriage with shining sides
On the wharf, a newspaper
with open wings
and fading ink:
Holland ist in Not
Holland gibt's nicht mehr
The corpse has come to its port
The world has shed its sickness

And Weltall rises, infinite bat
wings of terror that have no measure,
armies in its wrinkles, a forest of spears,

fame and honour and religious epidemics.
Welt als Wille und Vorstellung
die Welt als Wolle die Welt als Hölle und als Verstelltheit
The squeaking mammal with the wolf muzzle
has sipped all the illnesses gathered all the stinks
is spreading itself
and reaches down to the molten magma.

1960

DEEP AND CLEAR

Sky so clear, it all melts in light.
Day so hot, as if just created.

And still the water has always whispered, the wind
curried the grass, the brook polished its stones.

The marsh horsetail's abstract wheel is old, old. . .
Perception is young, not so old as an hour.

Sky so clear, a bird is seeable through it,
water so deep. . . And all the rest is accidental.

1964

BOABDIL, THE DEFEATED ARAB

on leaving Granada 1492

The sun is dragging its cruel light.
For me it has gone down,
but I hear its sound,
as if skirt-silk or bright straw
were being dragged by a swaying carriage –
uphill? or down? It's the same.

Victory and defeat are the same.
Tomorrow is the same as this day: yesterday,
the sound the same, the carriage's long-drawn-out creaking;
going and coming's themes are the same.
Out of the north came a king in a cloud of dust
and destroyed a peaceful kingdom:
the defeated were dragged in the dust.
Many are the innocents killed for a gloomy faith,
and many are still to be killed. I think of it no more,
the stars go and return, the astrologers are busy enough,
al-Kindi the great reckoned with charcoal and an abacus
that the Arab imperium would last
693 years: he read it in the stars.
Rightest of the right he was, for I feel no astonishment
now, as I myself read my hours in a sundial's shadows.
Sorrow is the sorrow of creation:
it no longer touches me.
Some day, though, I shall have to leave
those tea-coloured rooms and soft arcades.
But I'm reached by the last glow of beauty:
the so-fresh water of the mountain brooks
and its softness, full of roseleaves;
and the wind brushing the Road of Sighs.
Soul of mine, attach yourself to nothing,
and you will never need to be separated.
Avoid attachment.
And I am affronted by the wheeling wheel's useless flight
and eternal recurrence:
as if one were turning a mad millwheel
that is turning by itself.

The sun is a great mill.
Who – whose horses
will help it now to climb the sky?
For me it has gone down.

1968

There are other worlds. Time circles and returns
to its calm heart, the owl-light that is coming
and partly has already come;
we sense it at the moment of night
                                        when unbearable pain stops
and the moment melts like tallow past the plotted limit.
There are other worlds, but they are here:
the candle burns to the candle-end, and there's no candle:
time has waxed back into dawn silence
and a sourceless light is destroying the forest of shadows.

1971

THEOREM

Prose can be hard as you like, let it make you restless.
But poetry is a vibration heard when life is dumb:

shadows move on the hills: pictured wind and clouds,
the going of smoke or life: bright, dim, bright,

a quiet-flowing current, deep clouded forests,
slow-mouldering houses, lanes radiating warmth,

a doorsill worn to a crisp, shadow-silence,
a child's timid step into a room's gloom,

a letter from a far country thrust under the door,
so large, so white it fills all the house,

or a day so steely and bright you can hear
how the sun nails fast the void blue door.

1971

STORY

Childhood: a wildbrook. Often I watched flowing trees.
The river wove them into an ever-running sheer lawn.

I always wanted to be on the other side of the lawn.
Now I know that really there's no right side, or wrong.

Unremembered rivers erupt and escape
from auricle to ventricle, opening, closing the heart.

An underwater tree is stooping over,
and untrodden paths trail into distances.

The peace of death: life is an artful dodge.
The spell of death: the weaving-loom of emptiness.

Weavers weave the wind, songs travel the water:
the story of the weaver finch's domed nest.

Empty chaises drive by, with no one in, and no driver.
Who knows where he's gone, seeking spring in straw boots.

1971

I've walked in distant, deep, subdued worlds
meeting nothing more than a tree
that let go its leaf, the restless red of blood.
Was it a burial? Of my body?
Of hope? Or will? Or just my ears?
The longing to stop hearing the dinning of life,
stop witnessing the grabbing and the scrambling.
And from the last fugue's reverberation
no further sound was heard, no leaf-sound,
water-sound, wind-sound, no bright return of joy
from the brightness, of sorrow from

beyond the looking-glass,
no silver mist-light, no iridescence of water.
Earth was waste, trees bare, water calm,
no need for aspiration further downwards

in the distant, deep, subdued worlds.

1977

The sea-and-skyline died:
it was all a single translucent heat-haze,
white rime, dim pearl.
A boat with glittering sails was swimming the air,
silent as a mirage of snow,
silent as light in a windless landscape:

light's host on the wind's paten.

1977

Tove Jansson

THE STONE

It was lying between the coal dump and the goods wagons under some bits of wood and it was a miracle that no one had found it before me. The whole of one side shone with silver and if you rubbed away the coal dust you could see that the silver was there inside the stone too. It was a huge stone of nothing but silver and no one had found it.

I didn't dare to hide it, somebody might see it and take it while I ran home. It had to be rolled away. If anyone came and tried to stop me I would sit down on the stone and yell my head off. I could bite them as they tried to lift it. I could do just anything.

And so I began to roll it. It was very slow work. The stone just lay on its back quite still and when I got it to turn over it just lay on its tummy and rocked to and fro. The silver came off in thin flakes that stuck to the ground and broke into small pieces when I tried to pick them up.

I got down on my knees to roll it, which was much better. But the stone only moved half a turn at a time and it was terribly slow work. No one took any notice of me as long as I was rolling down in the harbour. Then I managed to get the stone on to a pavement and things became more difficult. People stopped and tapped on the pavement with their umbrellas and said all sorts of things. I said nothing and just looked at their shoes. I pulled my woolly hat down over my eyes and just went on rolling and rolling and rolling and then the stone had to cross the road. By then I had been rolling it for hours and I hadn't looked up once and hadn't listened to anything anyone said to me. I just gazed at the silver underneath all the coal dust and other dirt and made a tiny little room for myself where nothing existed except the stone and me. But now it had to cross the road.

One car after another went past and sometimes a tram and the longer I waited the more difficult it was to roll the stone out into the road.

In the end I began to feel weak at the knees and then I knew that soon it would be too late, in a few seconds it would be too late, so I let it fall into the gutter and began rolling very quickly and without looking up. I kept my nose just above the top of the stone so that the room I had hidden us in would be as tiny as possible and I heard very clearly how all the cars stopped and were angry but I drew a line between them and me and just went on rolling and rolling. You can close your mind to things if something is important enough. It works very well. You make yourself very small, shut your eyes tight and say a big word over and over again until you're safe.

When I got to the tram-lines I felt tired so I lay across the stone and held it tight. But the tram just rang and rang its bell so I had to start rolling again but now I wasn't scared any longer, just angry and that felt much better. Anyway, the stone and I had such a tiny room for ourselves that it didn't matter a bit who shouted at us or what they shouted. We felt terribly strong. We had no trouble in getting on to the pavement again and we continued up the slope to Wharf Road, leaving behind us a narrow trail of silver. From time to time we stopped to rest together and then we went on again.

We came to the entrance of our house and got the door open. But then there were the stairs. You could manage by resting on your knees and taking a firm grip with both hands and waiting till you got your balance. Then you tightened your stomach and held your breath and pressed your wrists against your knees. Then quickly up and over the edge and you let your stomach go again and listened and waited but the staircase was quite empty. And then the same thing all over again.

When the stairs narrowed and turned a corner we had to move over to the wall side. We went on climbing slowly but no one came.

Then I lay on top of the stone again and got my breath and looked at the silver, silver worth millions and only four floors more and we would be there.

It happened when we got to the fourth floor. My hand slipped inside my mittens, I fell flat on my face and lay quite still and listened to the terrible noise of the stone falling. The noise got louder and louder, a noise like Crash, Crunch, Crack all rolled into one, until the stone hit the Nieminens' door with a dull thud like doomsday.

It was the end of the world, and I covered my eyes with my mittens. Nothing happened. The echoes resounded up and down the stairs but nothing happened. No angry people opened their doors. Perhaps they were lying in wait inside.

I crept down on my hands and knees. Every step had a little semicircle bitten out of it. Further down they became big semicircles and the pieces lay everywhere and stared back at me. I rolled the stone away from the Nieminens' door and started all over again. We climbed up steadily and without looking at the chipped steps. We got past the place where things had gone wrong and took a rest in front of the balcony door. It's a dark-brown door and has tiny square panes of glass.

Then I heard the outside door downstairs open and shut and somebody coming up the stairs. He climbed up and up with very slow steps. I crept forward to the banisters and looked down. I could see right to the bottom, a long narrow rectangle closed in by the banisters all the way down and up the banisters came a great big hand, round and round and nearer and nearer. There was a mark in the middle of it so I knew that it was the tattooed hand of the caretaker who was probably on his way up to the attic.

I opened the door to the balcony as quietly as I could and began to roll the stone over the threshold. The threshold was high. I rolled without thinking, I was very scared and couldn't get a good grasp and the stone rolled into the chink of the door and got wedged there. There were double doors with coiled iron springs at the top which the caretaker had put there because women always forgot to shut the doors after them. I heard the springs contract and they sang softly to themselves as they squeezed me and the stone together between the doors and I put my legs together and took tight hold of the stone and tried to roll it but the space got narrower and narrower and I knew that the caretaker's hand was sliding up the banisters all the time.

I saw the silver of the stone quite close to my face and I gripped it and pushed and kicked with my legs and all of a sudden it tipped over and rolled several times and under the iron railing and into the air and disappeared.

Then I could see nothing but bits of fluff, light and airy as down, with small threads of colour here and there. I lay flat on my tummy and the door pinched my neck and everything was quiet until the stone reached the yard below. And there it exploded like a meteor, it covered the dustbins and the washing and all the steps and windows with silver! It made the whole of 4 Wharf Road look as if it was silver-plated and all the women ran to their windows thinking that war had broken out or doomsday had come! Every door opened and everybody ran up and down the stairs with the caretaker leading and saw how a wild animal had bitten bits out of every step and how a meteor had fallen out of a clear blue sky.

But I lay squeezed in between the doors and said nothing. I didn't say anything afterwards either. I never told anyone how close we had come to being rich.

1968

Veikko Huovinen

HIRRI

Autumn was just turning into winter. The birches had dropped their glowing leaves and now were shivering nakedly in the chilly, scourging rain. For a few days more, the autumn storms whipped up whitecaps on the lakes, but then high in the sky one night the stairs came out, and there was frost. The earth turned to iron, the scorched grass was rimed with hoarfrost, and the puddles crusted over with a brittle ice, empty underneath where the water had evaporated. Soon a steel-blue frost stopped the lakes exhaling mist, and then there was a mighty tumult from the heart of the lake: it came yelping, ululating and howling to the shore, as double-quick cracks cut jagged etchings in the greeny-blue ice.

In the lakeless backwoods autumn was working more quietly, creating a somehow more melancholy atmosphere. The bushy foliage of the spruce trees was shaken about by windy blasts soughing in from the pine swamps. In the gloomy dark of a rainy day a hazelhen would send out a discouraged whistling from the young firs, or there'd be a commotion of wings in one of the large spruces: but the nights were haunted by the 'boo-hoos' of a tufted-eared eagle-owl, calling with burning eyes from hollow trees in the primaevally forested hill-slopes. . .

On the southwestern slope of one hill lived the tenant of a grey isolated cottage: Hirri, an old logger. His real name was Heikkinen, but when he signed the pay sheet for his wages, his hand trembled: the letter 'e' became imperceptible, both the 'k' s looked like 'r' s, and the 'nen' at the end often disappeared off the end of the paper onto the pine tabletop. So some assistant ganger christened the old chap 'Hirri' .

He'd been born in these backwoods, in a ramshackle hovel on the edge of a frosty swamp. When he was eight years old he set out into the world, wearing the serious expression of an adult. His first job was as a farm lad, but as his strength grew he took to the timber forests and the withered grass on the banks of the logging rivers. It was a rugged life, he remembered, even though the young red blood was flowing through his veins. Then he was struck down: a severe illness left an aftermath of bad breathing-trouble and the creeping onset of premature age. After his illness, he set up home in a little inland house, in a neighbourhood that always had forest-labour on offer. He'd been occupying this house for going-on forty years, wielding his saw and axe with about a third of a healthy man's power. His life burned with a meagre flame all this time: just a smoky flutter, and the palest of blue lights.

Moments of happiness may have come sometimes his way, but they didn't come thick and fast. There was a permanent expression on his mouth: it was rather like a smile, but it was actually a petrified furrow of pain unintelligible to an outsider. Nevertheless, on clear spring days Hirri's eyes did glow with a warmth as a flock of cranes flew with slow wingstrokes high among the downy clouds over his logging patch, or a high-pitched buzzard-mew pierced across the swamp. Perhaps, too, on a peaceful winter Sunday a merciful languor might steal over him, as he sat with the cat purring in his lap, watching the snowflakes waft against the black wall of the barn, with the wall-clock ticking on in the quiet room.

The autumn sky is bright now as Hirri dodders along, saw on shoulder, to his logging site. Striped restless clouds over a glowing red horizon are definite forecasts of a windy day. The old man takes a duck-boarded forest-track that cuts and meanders, with diversions, to the pine swamps. It's a kilometre's traipse to the islet huddled on the edge of the peatland, Hirri's work-site. Of course, it's less of a haul than for the others: the foreman, an understanding chap, has done his best to fix a slightly closer site for the old man.

So he arrives at the islet where he performs his daily toil. It's no comfort, in fact disconcerting, to see an old man groaning as he bends to the fibrous foot of an ancient, thick, dead fir tree and begins his sawing. He has no son, no family at all, to tell him: 'Go and sit yourself down in the living room, dad: you've done your share, and more, of work already.' Hirri saws away, breathing painfully. Each pull and thrust, each blow of the axe, or haul on a tree, demands an almost superhuman effort from the sick man. The saw gets stuck, jams tight, and nothing will budge it. It makes him swear, but his curses are not the full-blooded expletives of a healthy man: they are irritable, plaintive, bitter whines. Even the autumn seems to respond to the sadness of it all, gathering clay-grey clouds above the lichened firs and sending a dreary swish of wind to accompany the old man's decrepit movements.

Around noon Hirri crunches across a frozen curd of rushes and dips his scoop into a quagmire, collecting water. Back on his islet he uses some resinous wood to start a fire at the foot of a large fir, and he begins cooking his meal. When the water is boiling, he drops pieces of rye crispbread in, and a little dab of butter. That has been his mid-day meal year in and year out, and it hasn't overwarmed his spirit. Parsimony has been forced on him, and in the war years there was little else to eat. Bread-soup like this gives you a real bad breastburn in the afternoon, but what's that, among his other pains, to a skinny old thing like Hirri. Yes, he's got to be careful: 'count the pennies, and the pounds'll look after themselves.'

In the early war-years quite a lot of notes collected in Hirri's purse, unbelievably many considering his modest income. But then, sudden as a hawk from a treetop, the State pounced on Hirri's money, clawed at his wad of notes, and greedily gobbled off exactly half for itself. It was a bitter blow to the old saver: it brought the poor chap almost to the edge of the grave. He'd been advised like everyone else to put his money in the bank and supposedly get some interest. But all his life the old man had found interest and economics foggy and uncongenial notions. The village had a bank, yes, and there they sat, the gentlemen of the bank, and the moneylenders, behind their big window, a cunning smile on their lips. Take your money there, and there it'd remain for ever, you bet: that was Hirri's firm opinion. He'd seen a certain fellow take a large wad of money behind that big window, and all he came out with was a little book with some tiny figures scrawled in it: a poor exchange for a big sum of money like that. Hirri always carried his money about his person, taking care to guard it against loss. His inside coat-pocket was fastened with a big safety pin as well as two buttons.

Now and then, towards the end of a grey working day, Hirri would sometimes start cautiously sneaking around his logging site, like some capercaillie working her way back to her nest. Having established that the coast was clear, the old man would disappear into the trees, pull out his purse and begin thumbing through his notes. He'd put the thousand-mark notes in one pile and the five-hundreds in another. Then he'd count them, often getting them mixed up and having to start all over again. There were twenty-seven of the thousands, and forty of the others. When he'd finished his reckoning-up, a rare smile would linger on his face, and he'd often sing a little snatch of song. These were the peak-moments of Hirri's days, a good antidote to the fear of having to go into an old folks' home.

After eating he starts on work again. So far he has been felling trees and chopping branches off the trunks; the afternoon is spent barking them. He raises a log onto the stripping-block and begins peeling strips of bark off a birchbole with his stripping-knife.

The east wind that rose in the morning has been continually building up, soughing violently across the march. In the big lake of the sky, the shallows have been churned up, and now a mud of dirty-brown cloud is floating over the autumn forest and grazing the tops of the treed slopes. A restless flock of rooks is tossing about in the wind, swirling round and croaking warnings of storm. The flexible birches and the tall firs are swinging long arcs through the air already, but the ancient redboles are still steady, their pine-roots firmly bedded in dry heath. The wind is already wintery, unbearably cold, and it makes Hirri do his best to hurry up with his work, so as to get off back home that bit sooner. The east wind blusters across, building itself up, around three o'clock, into a storm.

Behind Hirri, close to a young pine, ready for felling, stands the high fat hulk of a rotten birch. It's the ruin of a mighty tree, now no more than a decayed corpse. The wind has torn the bark, and it dangles in free strips. Grubs have made a sad mess of its insides, and a tough-necked black woodpecker, going after them, has riddled the hulk with holes. Black fungi are infesting the black and white bark like a cancer, burdening the rotten frame still more and hastening its demise. Now nothing but a few of the tougher fibres and strips of bark are holding it up.

From the far edge of the marsh yet another squall is on its way – this time with a mission: bringing Hirri Death. Drily businesslike and unbribable, Death rides on the wind and gives the old birch-hulk a kick in passing. . . The tree grumbles, crackles, and a huge wodge is dislodged from the top: a hunk of rotten waterlogged wood a couple of metres long thumps down with all its force onto Hirri's back. It is the old logger's departure from this world, sudden as a bird into a snare: he dies without a word. The stripping-knife clatters down between the broken rocks and sticks in the ground, trembling like a tuning-fork making some inexplicable sign.

Shortly after this a gloomy darkness descends on the forest – a darkness such as storm lurks in, a huge soot-black thousand-limbed beast ready to go rampaging, raging, howling and destroying down the forest's tangled tracks. There are savage whisperings, enough to make a lonely traveller glance uneasily over his shoulder, suspecting some insidious tracker. High up on the hill the wind booms hollowly, but lower down, among the red-pine branches, it fusses and whines. Slender pines splinter and break, and many a harassed fir loses the grip of its roots on the earth's crust. Broken branches, needles, withered leaves and other debris scatter along the forest tracks and across the heathland. The tight-packed trees grind against each other, groaning fearfully, while the resinous old pines on the edge of the pine swamp creak with macabre laughter; they have nothing to fear: it's all the same to a bluish-grey dead tree if it has to lie in the tussocky ground. The wind blows eerily, teasing a rough gooseflesh onto the pitch-black surface of the creek that crosses the pine-swamp.

But the dead Hirri hears nothing now: he is frozen to the sphagnum moss, to be found there the next day and carted off to the village. The gravedigger will make a hole in the sandy soil, the parson will say a few warm words, and the cantor will sing, pulling his coat collar to his throat to protect it from the wind scurrying in from the lake. But where will a graveside-speaker be found who might recall the old man's life-work, as happens at the funeral of a person who has served the community usefully? No one will tell the scanty cortège about the frail man's struggles in the harsh forest. There'll be no mention of Hirri's efforts with the log-piles, or his struggles in the icy mist on the logging river at night. His work is in fact so ordinary, so taken-for-granted, it would be unable to move the survivors.

Was it mere accident that Hirri nevertheless received, even before the funeral, a handsome memorial service – a kind influential men never receive? . . . After midnight the humped clouds began to release a shower of snowflakes. The storm took hold of them and sped them along, spreading a white deck over the pine swamp, trailing a ribbon through the thickly clustered young spruce. By morning the wind was dropping, and the snow was beginning to come down peacefully, decorating every stone, stump, juniper-branch or alder-sprout with a white cloak of ermine. When a coppery flame began to rise in the eastern sky, the last storm-cloud disappeared behind the opposite horizon.

Light came filtering into the great forests. The whole immense wilderness sparkled a dazzling white: the first winter snow was here. A blackcock burst out of the top of a felled fir and flashed its silver wing-bars as it flew into the warped crown of a dead tree. The strange whiteness shocked it into opening its beak and cooing out a tinkle of jingle-bells into the sharp morning air. The bells were encased in steely-blue frost, a hint of rimed birch trees, a little autumn mist, but the bell had a little rolling silver bead inside it, crystallized from the freedom of the wild inhabitants of the forest. The frail calling crossed the marsh islet, glided to the far side of the marsh and undulated for kilometres more through the adjacent gorges and along the treed slopes.

When the blackcock stopped its cooing and flitted into a birch to pick at shoots, the white heartland was absolutely hushed.

1950

Home

Home

SUMMER MORNING

I'm still young, and I awake rejoicing,
as amazing morning shines at my window.
My heart is pounding with happy loving –
Oh my land, I love the look of you so.
Silken barley shakes luxuriant tresses
that the July sky is slowly bleaching,
through tufted hair-grass and soft mosses
cloudberry flowers are tenderly reaching
to sweeten the eye. Oh wealth of sky,
squandering light as the sea tosses!
Under that sky, all toil is bliss –
unhappiness takes the face of happiness.

I grew up from the trodden earth,
an aspiring tribe with self-esteem.
For me, humiliation's day of dearth
is a dawn: I see your honour gleam.
As a silver birch glistens after rain –
a golden snood of raindroops in its hair,
let hope shine through your tears again:
rise to the summer gala, and never despair!

1946

Aale Tynni

STONE GOD

God, I hammer and hammer and hammer,
begging, blaspheming, praying I hammer!
Open those gates, open the sky!
Motionless stone, open your eye!
Look: loving mothers are crying:
thousands leap to their children, dying
as walls cave in and ceilings fall.
Our world's sinking under a sprawl
of trash and terror and sorrow.
Tears are scoring bitter furrows
deep in our souls, sour eternal furrows . . .
I crack my fists as I hammer!

Who are you? Shuddering with dread
I see your stone motionless head,
those scornful nostrils, empty of breath,
stone mouth, stone hands of death –
your eyes – oh horror! have mercy! save! –
empty and blind as an empty grave.
Stone God whom nothing can move,
there's no saviour, there's no love!

I grasp your hands, sister and brother.
Dumb from the ruins, we rise with each other
to a waste world, dark as a well.
It's all the same, heaven or hell,
live or die; in spite we rise,
we rise from the ruins, a stony power,
our breast a stone, our face a glower,
with no belief, with no assize,
with no tomorrow, dumb we rise,
hard-faced, with stone faces,
and stone breasts, our Lord's graces!

The feeble dreams we believed are shaken.
Night falls as we awaken,
and eternal dark strafes the day.
The Stone God's face outfaces clay.
We grow as well, we grow with the dark,
ourselves stone, ourselves the dark,
shoulders loaded with granite truth.
Stone God, you wake and persuade us:
in your image you have made us.
Stone you make us, out of your marrow:
cold stone we stand, until tomorrow.

1946

Aila Meriluoto

CONCRETE MIXER

A building site: cranes, lumber, junk,
towers, scaffolding, concrete chunks,
and round it a dead-pan city-block frown:
a large industrial town.

A concrete mixer, I was that,
with lungs of cement and a battered hat,
with crows in my nose,
and sweat in my shirt.

I lolled on a plank.
My morning nosh
quietly sank
in the tummy's squash.
A policeman's shape
statuesque and straight
dimmed by the gate.
A stink of smoking pitch.

The weather's warm: eyes close,
I'm beginning to doze.

Somewhere I'm crawling,
lost and sprawling,
where can I be?
Cemented in, sweating lakes,
in a lizard swamp, swarming with snakes,
sometimes upside down in damp,
sometimes sucking a foot from the swamp,
escaping the Something that pants at my back,
running, tumbling, running, smack!
I swim away, away! –
Ah, and now I'm stuck!
That gap
between the knolls –
bottomless bogholes!
a death trap!

I'm sinking – heaven have mercy
on someone belt-deep and out of breath
in the sucking and swallowing night of death!
The marsh has swallowed my chest, my neck,
my mouth is filled with film and dreck –
I can hardly breathe!
And now, what now! – has the pressure gone?
Like the swirl of a wave that rears –
then breaks – all matter disappears!
Through the dark vacuity
I dive and dive, till thump:
on my plank I wake with a jump.
A little ghost of a cloud had cast
a drop or two on my face as it passed.

It's warm again.
I shift my crotch,
loose my belt a notch –

and my weariness deepening
sink into dreaming
of a long-lost magic ring.

In fact I've arrived at a bony ball:
what we know as the human skull!

Some voice is explaining:
– This is that sick head
in which the lunacy is bred.
Is it a leak in the mould, a blast
in the alloy, or a fault in the cast?
Just for now, it can remain insane,
till it goes to the ladle to be cast again. –
Some caprice, which we can't assess,
seeds the essence of its flesh
with lust and hatred and a morbid mess,
in which the atoms of happiness,
pulsating waves of grief and joy,
are screwed up into hobbledehoy;
dissonance, remorse –
from which the toxins of virtue and vice,
seep to every seedling's base.
Here, mirrored on the dungeon wall,
reason raises a caterwaul,
raving up schemes and sleights,
from which the mildews and the blights,
the arts, the images and the open wound,
the straight, the stooped, the uncribbed, the cocooned,
the molten lava of new-born and dead
are supposed to get their right to spread.
Here the beautiful and bad
monsters of art are nurtured and shed.
But now the show is starting!

The kaleidoscope in the human head
is beginning to turn and change the view;
the voice fades in the hullabaloo:

Images
wake and shake,
from cavities and holes and seams thrust out
the crowding dreams and lusts, and shout,
they steam,
they scream,
they dance, expand and thicken,
they advance, they stand, they flee. . .
angels and devils with wings and horns,
rams and bulls and capricorns;
skeletons, scaffolding – gallows;
wheelbarrows,
concrete mixers. . .!

– Poor us, poor them,
oppressed for nothing, and then some! –

I went unconscious – no joke:
let's say: I woke.

The wincher was poking my leg with a stick:
'Get going, mixer, to your mix!'
The bricklayer fussed, the hodman cussed:

'Thieves and whores! more mortar and bricks!'
Old ladies laboured, toting more
and oozing sweat:
it was life as before:
toil, toil, and toil on yet.

A skilled man, me,
with a trinity
of materials: these three:
with gravel, water, and cement
I conjured concrete, as I was meant –
and some sweat I lent.

I was the Messiah man:
I was the male who poured the pail:
the shadow of The Great Mixer,
The Fixer
who into the deep, deep peace
of The Great Vacuity and Release
pours back the concrete mixer –
a tiny gnat
and a tiny fate
with lungs of cement
and a battered hat.

1947

Lauri Viita

HYMN TO MY HOMELAND

You are crimson as goblets of blood,
and you are black: hopeless century,
marsh stream, with mud in your heart.

Stars die in high skies:
silence's shadow has dimmed them.
The ploughman plods his weary way,
knowing: tomorrow time will be complete.

Houses mushroom in the landscape –
a cry flies from their cellars.
Cemetery-corpses moulder
under their slippery coat of breeding moss.

But ploughman, and sick in cellars – a song now:
wing it like an arrow with defiance
to the land we were born to suffer in
and bear like beasts, unknowing,

blind beggars, eaten by ulcers, going our ways
in ignorance.

Deliver the power of despair to
tomorrow's crushing dawn coming to meet us,
and toast the homeland, toast this land,
sustainer of stunted dreams.

1953

FROM THE INTERIOR

I'm well-acquainted with the dim waters
Päijänne's rainy shores and Näsijärvi's
birds whistling from the dark mountain
to my childhood

Those not freed in June
when the milky sky
wept into the waterways and in the eyes
those not freed are left waiting for
the three hundred days of their winter

I'm well-acquainted with my darling gnomes
I can taste on my lips
the destitute treasures of their dreams
and the bitters of their blood
I think their thoughts and I remember
the unhappening has happened and I hope
the coming will be different
than it will be

1959 **Pentti Holappa**

TRAGEDY, FINNISH STYLE

Had enough, left,
with his sins, with his virtues, long
howled the dog on the grave, then died,
the way dogs die, of hunger.

The house stood empty, the wife
ran away long ago
with Fredriksson, the children
were out in the world, one far away in America.

The family was consumptive, predisposed
to madness, an aunt had seen
Jesus on the roof of the potato cellar,
from then on awaited the coming of the groom.

The uncle, rank-and-file worker in Kazakhstan,
old Communist,
fled from the Whites in '18, took a
German wife, built a sauna, burned it down
while drunk, and died.

The sons went to sea, one
stabbed a first engineer in Stockholm
and is still doing time, the other
went mad in the Azores, started swimming to Finland,
has not arrived.

The daughter, last seen at the Finnish Hall
in Fitchburg, with her seven kids; her husband,
Hunting Wolf, had put on warpaint,
robbed a whisky train and now dwells
with Manitou.

The rowan trees have bloomed. A lot of berries,
the winter will be severe. Wild roses

wave in a circle against the wall
of the house. The door stands open. The curlews cry
in the marsh.

1965 **Matti Rossi**

BEDROCK

I
When I love rock, when I love granite,
let it be permitted me.
It's my childhood's bedrock
that bears people, crystals squeezed
into the holes of crystals, multicoloured and jagged
Out of the jags, the rock, the pine
a language is born and lives
with winter's longest words,
snow's shortest: it is us,
it lives beneath the sky.

II
See the northern sky.
It's not mere black velvet
that deepens the Pole Star's shine.
There the stars of the Plough and the Sword of Kaleva
create high correspondence –
white crystal lights squeezed in the black
where snow follows snow,
frost glares hard,
forest follows forest,
and there's warmth of houses, warmth
of work and love and in the language
sing the loveliest words under its sky.

III
Squeeze a warm hand, crashing down come
trees of the northern forests, there's creaking
of harbour cranes, ships singing:
we're coming back. This is a great beauty.
What is a small one? I asked – and picked
a cloudberry and tasted its juice:
great swamps spread, smell of marsh tea,
and barrenness and dwarf birches.
So tart its taste was.

IV
The holes in the rock are full of birth-spells,
crusty earth and grass,
cultivated clearings and ears of corn.
The spirit of the living finds peace
in the resting places of those
that have done their work. Granite
there too and something living and growing
on the granite's flanks,
and under the northern sky
the mighty song of the wind.

1955 **Helvi Juvonen**

FINNISH WINTER DAWN

We stand on snowy beach
and look across frozen reaches,
and it is still dark
and the cold's pumice scours our cheeks.
We do not know what weather awaits us,
whether sun or mayhap wet snow –
all is so uncertainly possible

upon this beach and we have heard
how vessels foundered
and men on rocks were frozen.

Over there our houses lie
oldsmallgrey,
cowering tight to one another.
And they are not fair to behold
even in summer dress –
now faint the darkling shacks appear
from which not many glints of light
can reach us.
Meagre poverty, mostly, and creeping fear:
our world.

But look, look that way – there, yes there
the sun is seen this morning too ascending.

1948 **Elmer Diktonius**

POEM OF OUR LAND

A matron who reeks of the separator walks across the yard
followed by a flock of chickens. A fly looks into a pitcher of buttermilk.
In the parlor, the master of the house, drunk, sells a lakeshore lot for too low a price.

On the roof of the potato cellar, the cowshed tom plucks a chaffinch.
A halter round its neck, a calf whines, adjacent to a rotting pile of sawdust,
a broken-down shed, a rusty anvil, a sled Grandpa built with his own hands.

The half-grown daughter of the house flicks through old magazines.
The son, younger, loads rat-traps in the cowshed.
The dairy maid steals a glance at a piece or mirror. The hired hand
plants the pitchfork in the dungheap.

At night, mopeds and swearwords crackle in the village.
The boys' necks are as brown as the near-beer sold at the kiosk.
The girls' necks ruddier than the walls of granaries.

And the cuckoo cries hundreds of times before the sun
sinks behind the hay poles, the barns, the lake, the spruce forest
and the fire-blackened crest of the rock.

Clocks tick on the walls of living-rooms, ashes cool in the stoves.
Hands press panting flesh. Four hands. A comfortable number
of loaves with holes in the middle hang on the breadpole under the
ceiling.

The muzzle of the workhorse snatches some clover from under the
barbed wire.
Snails and mist cling to the prongs of the rake.
A boat without oars slides into tangled reeds.

1968 **Juhani Peltonen**

IN A LETTER YOU WRITE TO ME

Sometimes
when one coldly spoke of
slaughtering the pig
drowning all the kittens
and wringing the necks of the hens
the sensitive child would tremble; an
icy wind blew,

felt like frost in the air
like disappointment
and fear
before inconceivably harsh reality
and
a slow-healing estrangement would arise.

The elegant utility of the useless
was
a shy bird for a long time
to come.

1972

Ralf Nordgren

From evening's ragged blue I snatch a piece,
wind it on a reel;
I sketch in my mind a picture of a ringing bellflower.

I'm dumbfounded.
The perfect blue of the bellflower jingles on the hill.
The reel falls from my hand.
My fingers clench in my palm.

1962

In autumn the field grows old,
its stubbly chin rises skyward,
the last insects fly
and one of them stops on the rough field.
The field can't raise its hand,
it thrusts its hand deep into the coming darkness.

The hems of night are stiflingly oppressive in the rain.

1962

THE INVINCIBLE

The cliff alone against the sea,
the sea bites and spits,
but the cliff answers the sea's fury
with glittering teeth of stone.

In the grassy warmth of its armpit it holds
a merry little flower
that laughs its child's laugh, not knowing
how there is a struggle for its life.

1977 **Viljo Kajava**

TREE OF GOD

Raf

Call me Raf Lindermann. Because that's my name. Call me a writer. Because that's what I am. But don't call me anything else, nothing biblical or symbolic, because that would mislead you. And me. Benno, who was speaking in the previous chapters and whose name is Bernhard Lindermann, is my younger brother. I have let him tell you about his childhood, which of course was my childhood too, roughly as I think he would have done if he had been a writing man, which he isn't. I have also let him touch on those things we talked about in reality quite recently, when he was admitted to the hospital and at long last we made some kind of mutual human contact. But it is not he who is writing, but I. Because I am the writer.

I once knew a man who was incapable of any human intimacy or contact and lived his life in an inhospitable world of fabricated necessities and false values of an adamant nature. That was my father. I know a woman who fills every human relationship she is involved in as if with stagnant water of emotions and desire, which pushes it beyond what the meaning of such a relationship is and inflames it, giving it an odor of rottenness and putridness. That is my mother. Benno thought his life lacked meaning, that, like Judas' life, it was predestined for irrevocable sin. So he tried to put an end to it, just as he had previously succeeded in putting an end to that of the person Benno thought he had betrayed and brought to destruction. But I know no man's life is more meaningless than he imagines it to be and that in the end endurance is the only way we can achieve that glimmer of meaning everyone needs to be able to live. Fred, who is a cousin of ours and has been a friend of mine since childhood, doesn't believe this. He doesn't believe in a meaning or even the need for a meaning. He is modern, a modern human being, confused by too much dogma.

During our encounters, my wife often accuses me of actually being incapable of love. I feel I would be capable of murdering her for such a disclosure. And yet, I know she is right. Deep down inside me is a place which is lifeless and empty, dead and calcified, a place which would have been absolutely necessary for love. I cannot love, but I know I must, I know it is the most important thing of all, so I try. Benno can't love, either. And yet there is nothing calcified in his personality. On the contrary, his is a hurricane of love, of desire and willingness to love – leaving utter devastation behind. Fred – he doesn't even want to. He depends on other values.

That year, I was convinced our marriage had failed. I went away with some obscure intention of proving this, and stayed abroad for several months. When Fred's letter reached me, I was in a state of dissolution, apparently sufficient proof of failure in every possible aspect. The letter was typical of Fred. He sees the seriousness of the situation with a greater clarity than most, but it is impossible for him to give expression to the insight which would correspond to the seriousness. Instead he writes so that it could almost be a question of some crude student joke.

'B,

Your brother constitutes an immediate danger to himself and his surroundings. Far from alleviating this, and on the contrary, your mother is increasing this danger with the miscellaneous treacheries of her expansive temperament. Your presence is desired, demanded, and even more desired and demanded if you are able to bring your person back to sobriety and order. Nothing here is more wholly of this world; clouds of insanity pass wherever one moves... (For Christ's sake, Raf, pull yourself together; don't drink yourself to death, for Christ's sake. Be the exception! Be the exception! Honestly requested by your petrified (!) cousin and friend.

Fred'

It's not too much to say that I was pleased to get the letter, but maliciously pleased, insofar as I was pleased to be able to ignore it. I thought Benno's troubles could not under any circumstances be greater than mine. In addition, I had never been able to regard him as anything but a child, hanging onto his mother's skirts, and consequently he would get the best help from her. And yet I returned home from Rome almost immediately. Not, unfortunately, because despite everything I had thought better of it, but just because I had already long ago realised that it was a matter of life and death for me as well, and that here I was suddenly nevertheless being given an excellent opportunity, my disaster prestige still intact, to choose the better alternative. The awful thing, or what was to be expected, was that nothing in my own life or in my relations to my wife had changed from the start. Everything seemed just as hopeless as when I went away. But then gradually something slowly began to function within me, I who had previously been lifeless and incapable of functioning. It was the children. They made me; they almost tortured me into realising what in this whole wide world of thoughts and emotions and imaginings and strivings they represented and needed. And through them, the world.

I found Benno in a state of profound humiliation, more profound and more definite than my own had ever been. I myself have felt insane on a few occasions, but I have never been insane. Benno, on the other hand, *was* insane. Remarkably enough, its was precisely my arrival that brought about his final collapse. I got him admitted to a mental hospital. For Mother this entailed a shock you would have thought would have opened her eyes, but no. She couldn't think, only wish. She never really had any clear idea of what it was all about. If I had despised her before, then I hated her now, for what I considered to be her human baseness and naturally also because of my own incompetence, because I couldn't get her to understand. But later, slowly, even that hatred emerged into something else, something greater, universal, unfathomable, and frightening, but then again more stable, safer, part of me, a knowledge, a condition in which it would perhaps be possible to accept, to love again.

Of course, you all think it is tactless and degrading to turn one's own family's most intimate circumstances and darkest tragedies into public objects, for a book. There are things one simply doesn't write about, just as these are things one doesn't reveal, because they are no concern of any outsider. Perhaps I'd better explain why I am doing what I am doing.

There is a form of consideration which is more destructive and damaging than inconsiderateness. To describe a person in his degradation does not necessarily mean you expose him, that you shatter his human value – it may even mean that you revere him. To describe your hatred is not implicitly the same as describing your impotence when faced with goodness, with life and human beings. There exists a reserve towards evil which in itself is evil because it is passive, because it explains it away instead of getting rid of it, because this means evil ceases to exist as long as it is not talked about, because this entails closed eyes and turned backs while in actuality evil is given the opportunity to grow and grow – quite freely. Making it public does not lessen it. Making it public is a protection against the growth of evil. *Nota bene*: if it is publicity that is respectful. But that isn't why I am writing. I am not so conceited as to believe that I can save someone's soul by writing, however much I would like to. It would be simple to say I write because I have to. Though that is true. Free as I have been to choose whatever profession I care to, I have chosen one within whose activities I have a chance to exist. The same applies to my motives. Every new book is an inevitability, a meeting of free choice with necessity, with its only alternative. One has to see oneself as so exclusive, so delightful, to be able to reach down to the stable basis of one's activity. But that is not a good enough answer. Irrevocability is not like a full stop, or even a dash, but resembles a rhomboid, a polyhedron, a prism.

I write because my knowledge of mankind is greater than mankind's knowledge of itself, especially the knowledge of those people who in half the lifetime of a man have been close to me. I am a clairvoyant. Call me cynical if you like, for I know something about you, something of which you yourselves are profoundly ignorant. That is why I am a writer, because of an excess of human knowledge and awareness of human beings, a natural excess, a rare gift, inevitable and entailing obligation. I do not underestimate myself. Neither should you underestimate me. But I do not overestimate myself, either. I was hideously tormented by this excessive knowledge of human beings, especially in my youth, until I learned to control it, and until I began to understand what it was about. How much easier it would have been to exist as one of those who live and act without knowing what their lives and activities are called in language which is inaudible, which is spoken by the dead, by space and wind and landscape, the time that has not yet been, the silence in the most inaccessible places, or perhaps not even there, perhaps only in the invisible heart to which we never listen. But which I listen to. How much easier and how much more difficult.

It would not be inaccurate to say that I write to bring order into chaos, to share with myself a knowledge that is useful even if it hurts and which would make life more bearable, not only for myself but also for others. That would not be wrong, but neither is it right. What do I know about the ability of my words to reach those they are primarily intended for? Well, I know with certainty that they are to some extent changed on the way, so that when they get there, they are not the same as when they were sent out by me. Why should I then try to teach something, when the only certainty I have is that it will be misunderstood? For words are like the reality they precede, not like a stable body with given curves, angles, soft parts, and a given center, but like a swarm of insects, a swarm of bees of constantly changing shape and form without center but with a vast number of concentrated areas that coalesce and dissolve constantly, anywhere at all in the boundless world created by the swarm. Think about a flock of starlings! No, to set out to be a teacher with such uncertain, unreliable material as words – that is to set off with loneliness and disappointment as your faithful companions. To write so that others are warned! What a blissful temptation and what a difficult trap. But a writer is no priest and what separates me from Benno is probably just that he was to make an attempt to become a priest, while I became a writer. It is not truth I seek. Never believe that. To hell with the truth. The truth is a dream for those with feet of clay, too afraid to allow themselves to be borne by instability, indecisiveness, unreliability – all the *in-* 's and *de-* 's and *un-* 's that together constitute what human beings have to build their houses on, and live by, and from which they derive faith and meaning. No, I do not want to get at the truth, so it should be quite clear to you that whatever I write about, it will always be something other than what it is really about. Life is a series of pictures, innumerable pictures, and to write is to choose a few of them, some of which are appropriate, portraying love and hatred, for instance, and more like them than others. Below the course of events lies a pattern, binding them together, uniting them, a pattern not directly stemming from the course of events and yet meaningful to it, just as the roots of a tree bind together the soil we cultivate in secret ramified symmetry, and the crops are not directly dependent on the roots; on the contrary, we remove them to acquire richer crops and yet – where there are not roots, no binding of the tree, the earth is a desert and cannot be cultivated.

I write to find this pattern, this binding network of roots in the soil that is our reality, of trees which have become invisible, perhaps the tree of God, or the tree of original flesh, or the tree of the spirit, how do I know, which has perhaps died, ceased to exist, dried out and left the earth our reality, this trembling, cracking, wonderful era, a desert, open to disintegration, the end, a tree we ourselves have perhaps ravaged and betrayed. Ask Fred. He believes in the end, but I don't, because I can't, for the pattern has become my passion, and I must go down there to unconver it, if only a fraction of it, for me to learn, to teach us, its ABC, in what way it includes all the particles of the world in its form, this pattern the existence of which I have an inkling, and although I do not know if it exists,

I seek it. Writing is to seek.

If you knew how I have hated life! If you knew how I have hated human beings! Only someone who has hated in this way and yet has grown away from his hatred along the hard, unforgiving roads of helplessness knows what love is worth. And a meaning, a rule, a pattern, however fragile. I must look at the pictures, go through them, look long and carefully at them; and yet I know nothing, nothing at all. That is knowledge. Seeking blindly like a mole in the unfathomable that is the world and life of humankind.

1986 **Christer Kihlman**

THE SPRING

Far across the fields
sounds, faint but clear
the vernal spring.
I listen,
try to get closer.

The water echoes, rippling
through fresh,
sun-scented summer forests.
I go on my way,
searching.

Already plain
among autumn treetops
is the long valley
where a hidden
stream murmurs. I must rest.

As if snow were in the air,
endless as our footsteps.

I listen, it's close.
The voice of the spring, fainter,
still there,
invisible.

1973 **Bo Carpelan**

PAAVO HAAVIKKO
TUOMAS ANHAVA

Paavo Haavikko

No forest or field was out of bounds to our steeds.
        The falcons hunted for me.
Men gathered to fight under my banner.
The women came singly and did not speak my language.

The drawbridge stayed down, the tax collectors did not return.
        I roam through the ravished forests.
I lead the hunters to meet raging death.
I call the elk to face the lancers.
Mine is every woman
        mute, listening to herself
                at the edge of night.

1951

Outside, blind trees have knotted a net,
foxes have called, called for a meeting place,
great is the night, gusty, knocks on palace doors,
nourishes the unborn,
the darkness is a servant, feeds the wicks of lamps,
allow them to leave, allow the wind to whisper
and do not listen, I do not know where to go,
nowhere is there a place for us.

1953

I hear the rain wake up, but what I yearn for is weeping, I would
like to hear weeping burst,
I, too, would weep, would not be alone.
The dream withers, the candles are lit in the five-branched candle-
sticks, I see through the dark,
the cranes are migrating, their cries cut through the night,
they fly, gray birds over nocturnal waters
like a gaze,
o beloved,
you lean on the gunwale and don't see anything,
don't see the birds are gone. Clouds roll out of the dark, rains roll
out of the dark,
those cranes that are watching, they listen through the rain, they fly
East, they hear weeping, the cranes, kingly birds,
they do know sorrow.

1955

Now, when on some night the branches come quite close to
the window
and outside there is wind, a storm,
now, when
I say, searching for words, that
these are things I have not made up,
it's rather that I
am one of them.

1966

I like slow things, and about them how they recur.
How water begins to heat up and bubble.
It took its time.
Great poise is not motionless, it moves.
One has to stumble a bit so it becomes visible
on rising from water, dripping water.

When we make dummies in case of murderers by night
in the middle of the room,
I prop it up with cushions so that it is not comfortable
but would like to change position.
It does not.

1966

IN PRAISE OF THE TYRANT

1.
Twice, three times
may Fate strike. Thereafter
it's the numb beating the numb.

2.
Take heart, Ovid. No sentence
is longer than life.

3.
Look, life has been constructed this way to make sure
you won't ever again yearn for this world.

4.
Hades is an even worse place.
There aren't even any women there.

5.
Don't smile. So you won't become a Buddha
with that lower-jaw smile. Don't laugh,
so you won't be shown, every moment,
a reason for doing so.

6.
When you go to the tyrant. Keep your head on a platter.
Carry the platter in the crook of your arm.
The sharp edge won't hurt.

7.
Before you ask for justice. Make sure
that you won't get it, just by accident.

8.
The tyrant inspires small poems.
He doesn't understand what's so special about him.

9.
Plant trees. Exactly against this tree
may Fascism decisively strike its head.

10.
Precisely the way you divide your small change between two
pockets
the tyrant pours your wages in the form of molten gold
into your ears.

11.
When the tyrant is young. Everyone waits
for him to come to his senses.
Old. For him to die.

12.
It has been proposed that the stars should be removed from sight.
No one has been against that. The proposal has already
been accepted.

13.
I always bow down deep before a small tree and a great tyrant.
Great awareness is greater than a small one.
Be aware.

14.
How decisively
one's brief moments of clear insight
are ameliorated
by a good, plausible ideology.

15.
Don't say this to an old idol that's lost its nose.
It hates everything in existence.

1973

Very carefully, lingering, slowly
for the last time
the old wine tastes the young woman.
What a long journey, its life, it has
made up to this point,
and now it has arrived, truly
arrived,
now it is one with her blue
translucent blood
which is one with her flesh.
It's up to you
to choose the herbs.

1976

CONVERSATIONS WITH DANTE IN THE MARKET SQUARES, ON THE BRIDGES

It is a cruel time when the empire's guts
are all offered up for gustation in the form of tripe stew,
as delicacies, all, and masterpieces, as musical drama,
epic poems from which the story has been peeled,
de-boned, to facilitate the meal.
In the end, when wheat and oil become scarce,
what remains are spices, spices! and carp.
The meal is paradise, the human being its purgatory,
the grave, a hell where the fire has gone out
and which can't be compared with either one of the above.
No food, no carnal pleasures.

Where is the passion into whose fire the carp swim,
        finned, winged, with trembling wings
to get there in time, to be symmetrical, even-finned,
        precise, marvelous, beautiful.

Without hellfire, there is no way to cook the passions of the senses
        of which there are two: metaphysics and spices,
flaming alcohol and hot fire, Indian summer and *mistral.*

In the Florentine marketplace, don't hestitate when they bring you
                                                tripe stew to eat,
                don't ask questions, don't close your eyes:
        soon enough, once again, the executioner
will hold up someone's bloody head.
        And the tripe stew is fuzzy as grass, mighty as the brain,
a thousand eyes.

        And when you meet him on the Ponte Vecchio,
no compliments are exchanged.
        He runs the three-pointed fish spear
called *ottava rima*
        through my throat, it's no contest
in lines, poems, and power. And I say:
        'I have seen your skull
small, bronzed, as if shrunk in smoke.
        You don't look like a winner.
In a moment, they'll bring your tripe stew, and I'll treat you
        to some wine, thin, weak, watery like a stream,
it stays with you no longer than the sound of footsteps.'

        I speak that line only to permit you to sneer at me,
the one still alive, it was really a miserable line.
        Well, so what. We all have our bad days,
the stock market isn't always bullish, or it turns bullish
        just when you've sold your shares, your share, your lot,
your fate, your lines and sayings, your dividend,
        you servant of Two Masters,
Venetian but not a merchant, sell!

How thin is the bread of Georgia, baked
on stones, unleavened, wheaty, crisp, thin
as the moon disc. Out of it, Christ made a sacred meal,
his body which is the moon, his feminine being
which is not a man. His mother was a hermaphrodite
whose son was a daughter, according to the Law of Pisces,
felicium piscium lex.
A confusing family whose exterior man is an elevated being,
whose son is a daughter, and the exterior father murders his
son-daughter
whose garments are then shared out, as no man's would be.
And that evening the bats came, for their free meal,
for truly, it was
in the air. The evening was clear, the forest was growing
gallows-trees, paneling, boards and rot,
and the bats came, softening the air, turning it
into flowers, rose petals
falling, cups, fragrant
to be dried, spices, Bulgarian spices.
Animals are fetuses, fantasies, daydreams,
animals are ideas, incomprehensible.

When I tell you, o three-pointed poet
to be patient, wait, stretch your limbs,
your tripe will be served in a moment, I mean
tripe will be served to you. Not your tripe,
since no one but Christ the Virgin
has a rumen, and it's not on the menu here in the marketplace.
But the tripe will be served. In the cruel empire, this
kingdom of Christ, all interior organs
are served as tripe.

Are you ready to enjoy your virgin meal
consisting of tripe stew and tortured wheat
with bloodless wine, or would you rather
have your wine be red. But even if
you'd chosen or had let yourself

be chosen by the wine, at least soon and here
        the tripe stew walks up to you.
And it isn't simile of anything but it itself.
        It is the sacred eye that never saw the light
that sacrificed itself to darkness.
                                        To darkness.
Thus, not a flounder, walleye, or that
        expensive fish whose name I don't remember,
why couldn't they be kin to the tripe stew,
        gossip and tell you all kinds of things about it.
But that won't work.

But the wine runs out faster than the evening and the night
                                        and the wine!

Then, there's a golden net around the bottle
        as around hair that does not require
a golden net because golden hair does not need it
        any more than a flooding river needs rain,
which was precisely why the hair was not bound
        into a hairdo by anything but the fact
that the hairdo had not been despoiled yet,
        and why do you describe its undoing
by saying it had not been despoiled yet?
        Who is the narrator of this epic of yours,
what is the story, the tale?

That was his question. And the answer is:
An empty house, the man gone, and the women
                                        are away.
An empty house, the man gone, and all the women
                                        are away.

1988

Tuomas Anhava

I've never made a book out of less;
I'll never manage to say more.
No one knows how to hope for his own birth,
and all the rest is speculation.
It's a land of flowing bridges.

1966

I look out: perfect calm:
a leaf falls, and another leaf,
and a third.

1961

House, fir trees,
rainy days all round.
The lake glooms through the forest
like an unassuaged grief.

1961

The soul is in me all over:
thus eternity reforms its form:
when I remember my name, I forget.

1961

It's already dark.
A blind man's eyes are being written on
and he'll know the stars.

1961

The wind is an eye,
darkness all ear
in the nocturnal meadow.

1961

Whoever believes what he sees
                    is a mystic.
In the dark move slowly.

1966

The snow's turned the landscape lucid and quiet.
My mind's uncomplicated and patient.
Down to the last detail I see
the ground unhurriedly growing trees,
and I hold my breath deep, waiting
for it to burst into grass's brief song again, and the flowers'.

1966

War

War

BOXES OF NAILS

To the right was the Gulf of Finland, grey, vast, as smooth as death. Even at midday its horizon was like a dark corner. The waves appeared motionless no matter how long and hard you looked at them. The sandy shoreline went on and on. In front of us spread a small valley three kilometers wide, in which a scraggly forest of leafy trees was growing. On the ridge beyond the valley was a pine forest, just like the one we were standing in. It was raining, but had gone on raining for so long it hardly mattered any more. It was as if the trees were shooting out long streams of spit from time to time.

The front line ran along the ridge beyond the valley. The pioneers were setting up barbed-wire barricades and clearing vistas by chopping down trees. We went over to our own ridge to dig the third line of trenches. They were planning to move the front line here, further back, to a more advantageous position without the enemy realizing it.

The trench site had been marked out for us with chalk lines. In that kind of sandy soil a man's daily stint was five meters of digging. You had to dig the trench one and a half meters deep, one meter wide at ground level, and sixty centimeters wide at the bottom. That's what a trench is like, good and narrow. It was best to do the digging in pairs. I had a strong buddy, stronger than myself.

We finished our stint in a couple of hours and left. We ate at our gun positions and then calmly sat around chatting. In the distance you could hear a rumbling noise like a pot of potatoes boiling; the Germans were shooting, bombarding Leningrad.

'No one's got it very good over there right now,' my buddy said.

'Have we got it good here, then?' I asked.

'Better than there, anyway.'

'Don't forget, that's a city and not just a damp forest.'

'Some people really have it tough. Me, I'm always grateful I wasn't born Russian or a woman.'

'Women sure aren't in any trouble right now. It's us who are here.'

'I still wouldn't switch. What kind of woman would I make, anyway? Just take a look. No beauty, no kind of charm.'

I am a university student. So much for that. I came back from the city of Hamina on the milk train, taking my own good time. Maybe that was better. Then I was late getting back from leave when I got married. In the court martial, they took one stripe off me. 'Since you're taking off that one, you might as well take the other one while you're at it,' I said, and cursed at them, I was so pissed off. After all, I'd already been in quite a few battles. They took it off.

As we were sitting there, along came Major Metsäkuusi, logistics commander of the regiment.

'Where are the food scraps around here?' he asked, even though he was standing in the middle of the scrap heap himself.

'Major, Sir, you're standing right in it,' I said.

He took a long look at me. I guess he could see I was educated and he thought I was sneering at him.

'Stand up straight. Well, what's this? No throwing away scraps on the firing line,' Metsäkuusi said, and started to examine what was in the heap. He dug his hands in among the potato peels and other rubbish, gloves off so as not to get them dirty. I just wondered how shitty they were on the inside. Well, damned if he didn't find a green potato first, then a scabby one, and third, a half-rotten one. That got him all worked up. He studied it up close and scratched at it with his finger nail.

'Just look at what you're doing here. A good potato. If this wasting of food doesn't stop, there'll be no more potatoes. You understand!'

'Yes, we understand,' I said.

I was surprised he didn't eat it up. They said he would eat any garbage he found just to show it was edible. But I guess there weren't enough people looking on, only the two of us.

We had just sat down when the battery commander, Viki Sund, got there. I imagine he was spying on the logistics commander. The world's fattest battery commander, like Göring. He was so fat one of his thighs was as thick as I am around the middle, a real sight. When we were on our way to the front, at the Kouvola railway station people were appalled, saying right out loud, 'Good God, why do they take people like that to the war?' That only made Viki laugh. Viki owns a large manor house. Every couple of weeks half a fatted calf would arrive with a crate full of bread and another one full of potatoes. On it would be written: WINTER CLOTHES.

'What are you boys loafing around for? Go do your stint.'

'We've already done it,' I said.

Viki wouldn't take my word for it, we had to go show him.

'Well, you have, you sure have done your digging,' Viki admitted, offered us cigarettes and left.

I was sitting with my buddy on the edge of the trench on my leather mittens, and smoking. We decided to stay right there for the rest of the day since they seemed to get on your case everywhere else. But then along came a captain from somewhere, not even anyone we knew, a long-nosed, foreign-looking guy.

'Done your stint yet?' he asked, and offered us cigarettes.

'Got a smoke already.'

'Put it behind your ears then, hang on to it. How's things?'

'Could use an end to that rain and this war,' I said.

'You're in the artillery?'

'In the artillery.'

'Nothing to be ashamed of. Artillery is a good thing to have here in this war. Who's the battery commander?'

'Captain Sund.'

'Don't know him.'

'A real big fat guy,' my buddy said.

'I still don't know him. But since you're finished with your stint, you boys could give us a hand. I've got a few odd boxes of nails on the bank over there. They got left there by mistake.'

'We haven't got anything else to do right now,' I said.

The captain started out ahead of us. He wore a large Russian pistol on the back of his belt. We went along the paths leading down into the valley. The barbed-wire obstacle was already finished but there was a hole in it.

'They've laid mines in here, walk right behind me,' the captain said.

'What did he say?' my buddy asked.

'This area's been mined.'

'Hell, no.'

'If you don't believe me, go ahead and walk over there,' the captain said.

'I didn't mean that,' my buddy said.

'That buddy of yours doesn't believe it until he feels it. In this life, that just won't work, believe me,' the captain said.

The opposite slope hadn't been cleared. We walked along it to the left.

'Well, there's a lot of barbed wire, thousands of kilometers,' my buddy said. 'You'd think it would be a hell of a job to make it.'

'Why?' the captain asked.

''Cause it's so full of barbs.'

'They make it by machine,' the captain snorted.

'Of course. I guess you couldn't make such an awful lot by hand.'

'You're a thinking kind of man,' the captain said.

We walked along the slope and the crest of the ridge for at least five kilometers before we stopped for a smoke. It was the captain's treat. We sat back on our heels. There was forest all around us. After a moment we could hear shooting from the direction we had come.

'What's your name?' the captain asked me.

'Hämäläinen.'

'Are you from the Häme district?'

'No, from Helsinki.'

'Of course. There are no Hämäläinens in Häme. Now the shooting's stopped. What's up with you, thinking man?'

'Nothing,' my buddy answered.

'Well, then, let's keep on going. The boxes should be somewhere around here.'

'Listen,' my buddy answered. 'What sort of guy is he?'

'How should I know?'

'So where are we going?'

'They should be somewhere around here,' the captain said, and scratched his neck. 'Where the hell did they get to? I guess somebody else has beat us to them.'

We walked on.

'But he's got a Russky pistol,' my buddy said.

'I can see that for myself.'

'I haven't even got my rifle.'

'Don't talk so loud, he'll hear you.'

Ahead of us, we could hear the sound of trees being chopped down. There were at least twenty men swinging their axes about.

'There goes a tree and then some,' the captain said. 'You getting tired?'

'No,' I said.

'Well, they must be the men from the other bunch. We've gone too far.'

We started backtracking.

'I'll bet he hasn't got any boxes of nails,' my buddy said.

'Shut up,' I said.

'The thinking man's already getting fed up with this. Let's sit down and have a smoke,' the captain said. We sat down on ground wet as a bucket. The boxes of nails were under a bush, three of them, one on top of the other. The captain pulled out the middle one to sit down on.

'How come the thinking man is so serious? Tired? I guess you're just a bit tired. When a strong man gets tired, that's tiredness for sure.'

'I'm not tired,' my buddy said.

My buddy took two of the boxes although the captain would have wanted to carry his own. We started walking. We went down into the valley at the point where there was a thicket of bushes, taller than a man. We waded through it up to our necks for half an hour.

'The opening should be soon,' the captain said in a loud voice.

At that moment, a burst of machine gun fire went off on the other side of the barbed-wire obstacle. It rattled like a toy gun. Did we ever hit the ground!

'What are they shooting at us for?' the captain wondered aloud. 'Don't shoot!'

'Who's that, shouting over there?'

'Jokilehto here!'

Again a burst of gunfire rattled through the bushes.

'It's Jokilehto! Can't you hear me?'

'We heard you all right, but we don't know you!'

'That man's going to pay for this yet. This is Captain Jokilehto!'

'We know some Jokilehtos alright!'

'Well, now we're in the soup,' the captain said. 'Let's try to crawl over to another spot.'

We crawled, and the bushes were swaying; now the others could take aim and shoot us.

'Don't shoot or I'll start shooting too!' the captain shouted.

'Hell, they're still so far down in the hollow that their jaws are still moving,' one man shouted to another.

'I must have left the other box behind,' my buddy said, and started off for it.

'Where did he go?' the captain asked.

'For the other box of nails. He left it behind by mistake.'

'Did that idiot go back for it? I can tell you, they've laid mines around here.'

My buddy returned.

'So there you are, coming back,' the captain said.

'I left the other box of nails by mistake.'

'This Hämäläinen here told me so.'

It was getting dark. We crawled on and on.

'But what if this is mined?' my buddy said.

'Don't talk nonsense. Who would have mined these bushes, and when? Let's listen a bit. Can't hear the sea. What is this? Sand. My God, there's water here alright, plain water if nothing worse.'

The water came up to my elbows. Then a wave slapped my face.

'Can you see any lights?' the captain asked. 'It's so dark you can't even see lights. Where the devil is Leningrad? Should spot some fire over there, for sure.'

'Who goes there?' The shout came from far away, as if from underground.

'Captain Ribbentrop!' the captain shouted back.

'Well, come out if that's who you are!'

'Come on out!' came another shout and a flare flew up into the air. We felt naked and started running towards the forest as fast as we could. There was no barbed wire on the shore. They hadn't put up any obstacles there, guess they'd run out of wire.

'Who the hell are you?'

'I already told you once,' said the captain.

'And the other one, is he Molotov?'

'Is that how you talk to your superior? What's your name?' The captain got furious right then and there.

'Lohenpolvi. Light infantryman.'

'What?'

'Lohenpolvi, Viljo.'

'That's not true. I'll find out whether or not it's your name, and heaven help you if it isn't.'

'Where do these boxes of nails go?' I asked. I had dropped mine on the shore, and I asked only so we could finally shake off the captain.

'You still carrying them? Put them anywhere you like, up your ass, for all I care. This war doesn't seem to be needing three boxes of nails.'

My buddy got mad and flung down his boxes of nails.

'And me, poor devil, dragging these all over the place,' he said tearfully.

'I don't blame you for that. Why are you throwing a fit?'

'This is the last time they'll make a fool of me. Damned boxes of nails, boxes of nails . . .'

'Now the thinking man is getting all wound up. It's time to go to bed. Anyway, thanks a lot for your help.'

'Don't mention it,' I said.

'You joking with me?'

'I'm not joking, Captain, Sir.'

'You're wise not to.'

I got really mad.

'Captain, Sir, I request an explanation. What was really behind this farce? Why were we crawling around there, dragging these boxes of nails?'

'You can keep them.'

'It was the Russians chopping down trees back there,' my buddy said.

'So you finally get it now?' the captain asked. 'What happened was a pullback from the frontline. '

'So that's what it was,' my buddy marvelled and promptly calmed down.

'Now the thinking man has started thinking again. Sounds much better. After this job, I'd offer you cigarettes, but they got all wet in the Gulf of Finland.'

'I've still got mine behind the ear,' my buddy said.

I was crazy enough to feel behind my ear. My cigarette had dropped off.

'Good night,' said the captain. 'When we meet in daylight, we'll all smile.'

We sure haven't met, at least not in daylight.

1960 **Veijo Meri**

SOLDIERS' VOICES

1

Actually, there was no reveille for me at all that morning.

I was on guard-duty from four to six. When my duty started, it was quiet. How, I wondered, could it be so quiet?

We'd a kind of agreement that when dawn came the anti-tank sentry could go off duty. The infantry would take over. It was about five thirty when I came off duty, and I set about making some ersatz coffee.

The troop commander was just off on leave. We drank this ersatz stuff. I was thinking about kipping down. We wished the commander all the best for his leave. He for his part wished us all the best at the front. As he was going, he gave a shout from the dugout door:

'Hey, come and take a look at this: talk about aeroplanes!'

We went out to see. There were a lot all right.

'No question about it, the Bosch is off to drop a few on Leningrad,' someone said.

They were flying low, and just overhead.

As the advance planes zoomed over our stations, flares started coming up from the Red Army lines.

The bomb hatches opened, and the bombs were let go. It was our lines, we noticed, they were falling on.

Not Bosch planes at all, in fact.

2

It was five o'clock.

I was doing my business in the latrine.

I heard noises in the sky. I screwed up my eyes and took a look. I was still in doubt: what were they, coming from over there? – They were still so far off. When they got closer, I'd no doubt about it.

Quite a few of them there were.

3

I was acting quartermaster of the second battalion.

A couple of days earlier I'd been at the front line, hunting up rubber boots: they were supposed to have been handed in, but they hadn't all been located.

At any rate, I finally had no doubts that something was on its way.

Engine-noises were coming from over there. I could see, high in the sky, a Russian observation balloon.

In the morning it was misty, where we were at least, as our billets were on marshy ground. The silence was shattered. A loud drone started, and then the shells were exploding. Smoke began mingling with the ground-mist. The planes were raking along the front line. I couldn't stand the dugout any longer. I crept into an alder bush, lay on my back and looked up at the sky.

4
I was the battalion communications officer.

The HQ was in the cellar of Rajajoki station.

All along we knew that something big was being prepared by our neighbours over there, and day by day we had confirmation of it.

Reveille for me on the ninth day was quite something. The acting adjutant in our battalion at that time was Lieutenant Karanko. He went outside and gave a shout from the door:

'Hey, this is it – what we knew was coming.'

I dashed out in my underclothes to take a peek.

The sky was black with planes.

The artillery was setting up a mighty drumfire. Unimaginable.

5
You'd have said we we were going to have a perfectly ordinary day, the sort we'd been getting used to. It was a really lovely June morning. I was in charge of a base called Notko in the Rajajoki sector. That was it: just before seven – all hell was let loose from the other side, as if the skies had opened.

We dashed out of the dugout to look.

Dozens of bomber squadrons were coming over, with an escort of flighters. They were letting the adjoining battalion have it at the Sormenkärki base on our right, near the Gulf of Finland. After the first squadron had unloaded its bombs, a second came in, and there was a simultaneous outbreak of artillery fire. This bombardment, it was like an electric motor starting up: the shelling and the bombing were a single unbroken racket.

I had two smart orderlies. I was always worried about the base. I and my orderlies darted to a trench. A shell came down between me and an orderly. We were both coated in mud from head to foot. We clawed our way out of it, like out of a tunnel. You could see no sign of life in the terrain ahead: nothing but the remains of a merciless bombardment. You could have shouted as loud as you liked to our comrades, they'd hear nothing.

As there was no letting up, I ordered the men out of this hell into the dugouts, leaving nothing but sentries outside on guard.

Maybe the bombardment slackened off a bit at times, but there was no letting up.

Our eyes were trained on the sky, for there didn't seem anything to worry about in the terrain ahead. As soon as one squadron had laid its eggs, another took its place immediately.

6

On the evening of the eighth, it was all quiet on the Russian side of the front, as if life there had come to an end. We knew different. Every night they'd been gearing themselves up. We'd heard the sound of the trains, the tanks, the vehicles, the troops. We'd seen them training their artillery on the three-inch battery near our HQ. Every man, down to the cook, was aware that something would soon be on its way from over there.

And now, when we'd got to the evening before the ninth and this silence fell, every man-jack guessed that they were all set over there. They were lying low and concentrating, and soon they'd press the button.

So morning came round, and six o'clock.

And six o'clock brought the bomber squadrons.

We stood in front of the HQ and saw the first bombs coming out and going off.

Our commander, Major Tammisto, said:

'Remember this, lads: the Russians' major offensive began on the ninth of June at five fifty-five.'

We looked at our watches. There were three of us officers there. All our watches showed the same time.

Later it was officially confirmed that the offensive began at six, so clearly we were in the wrong.

7

In general I was on the go at my base during the night. I was checking the sentries, because we knew that something was on the way shortly. I was on the job at the base in the early hours that night too. The reinforced guard had been dismissed at dawn: the idea now was to go and get some sleep. My orderly was a lad from Tampere called Aalto. He'd made some ersatz coffee. He said:

'Let's sup it up now.'

We started supping it down.

Then there was a thwack.

The first thump of the shelling blasted the doors and windows of our dugout in. The lads got slightly rattled. I said:

'Nothing that, nothing to worry about. It's come, what we were expecting.'

We had stacked the weapons in the dugout-entrance. I ordered the lads to go and get their weapons and see if they were in working order. Fortunately the weapons had come though the blast undamaged. Battle kit on: we stayed poised. A ring came from battalion HQ: the Russkies were attacking. I replied:

'Actually we had a fair notion of that already.'

I was in the Summa sector during the Winter War, and it was pretty rough there too on its best days; but there was no comparison: this was something indescribable.

8

I was part of the reserve-battalion machine-gun company. We were on the hill called Öljymäki. At nights I reconnoitred the front line and made a situation report in the morning. Every night I saw and heard the same thing: they were getting ready. No doubt about it. I reported everything. I was told to take it easy; there was no reason for worry: there were no end of men and guns at our rear.

When the bombardment started up, I was ordered to reconnoitre. There was this warrant officer called Lukanderi, a weapons officer. He hadn't believed what I'd been telling him earlier. Now he said:

'Listen, Jaska, don't go any more. In your place, hell if I'd go.'

When I did go, the going was difficult. The soil was seething. Boiling under your feet. In many places the trenches had fallen in.

9

I was the battalion commander.

As soon as we turned up at Valkeasaari the previous commander said:

'Quite a lot going on over there: the sort of things they're up to must mean a major offensive. Two week's peace I promise you, but after that I can't guarantee you a thing.'

If fact we had slightly less than three weeks' peace.

We used the time carefully. We set up a dugout-prop factory in the rear. We prepared the props there and then cut places into the dugout for them. We sank new telephone communications two yards deep. We covered the combat trenches with mats of withe, and supported them with props, to keep them in some sort of shape in the soft sand. And we built as many firing-line fortifications as were feasible in less than three weeks.

Who'd have guessed that a single battalion could, in less than three weeks, set up arrangements that hadn't been set up in three years?

There were still a few of the dugouts left over from those constructed right at the beginning of the war, but they were more adapted, I'd say, to keep out the rain than a major enemy assault. The treeless sandy terrain here, and the other conditions, had compounded the difficulties of working at this base. Even the stations were out in the open, not in the forest as in the rest of Finland.

When misfortune hits, of course, no one wants to take the can back. And what's easier than saying, The battalion on the spot couldn't stand up to the enemy: blame the battalion.

We saw that the enemy was digging assault-trenches facing our stations. We let them have it with artillery. The digging continued. Well, we thought: they've been ordered to get the trenches dug, and get them dug by a certain date. We saw black-uniformed men. We knew they were tank officers. They were indicating directions, making plans. Platforms were appearing on the pylons of the Rouhiala-Leningrad high-voltage cables, as well as the trees: artillery observation posts. There was also the continual hum of engines: night and day. And then the artillery. They were often taking a bead on Aleksandrovka church. First they overshot, then they undershot, and so they went on till they got a hit on the church; then this gun's firing subsided, and a new gun took over and began to adjust its sights.

This left no great need for the imagination:

The artillery was getting ready for an assault.

I found the battalion's left flank bothersome. On the other side of this flank was the Twelfth Battalion detached from the second division. The temporary boundary between them and us was the lane cut through the trees for the Rouhiala-Leningrad electricity cable: it was like a broad road and would make a fine tank route. It wasn't a boundary I liked. It bothered me: if tanks suddenly started coming along there, how would we liaise on defence with the Twelfth next door? On the eighth of June I was reconnoitring the boundary with the commander of the Twelfth. I talked it over with him, a Major Ursin. We said: we'll get to see once it starts. He was as certain as I was that something big was on its way. Later the same evening he rang me:

'My next-door neighbour on the left tells me that some Russian tanks have driven up to the rear of my battalion. Have you seen anything there?'

I said:

'There's a droning going on here every night, but there are sand-hills in front of our lines, and canyons between them: makes it quite a problem seeing into their lines there.'

Major Ursin finished our exchange by saying:

'Yes, well, we'll get to see now whether it begins tomorrow.'

I said:

'Right – we'll see.'

At that time we were poorly supplied with means of picturing the enemy's strength: an infantry battalion has no aeroplanes at its disposal, and essentially no other means of getting intelligence about distant movements. I and the commander of the artillery with us, Major Tirronen, sent back to the higher echelons, asking for air intelligence. We sent a letter too, asking officially for aerial photography of our front, as there seemed to be vast amounts of enemy artillery concentrated there, and everything else too. The way I see it, the higher echelons didn't believe an attack was on its way, and that was why they argued a shortage of photographic materials. Our information remained feeble. Not till a couple of days before the attack was any intelligence carried out. Even then no high-echelon personnel rushed to take a look at the results. There were just a few specialists examining them, and they were occupied in cobbling together their specialised concerns. Was there a battery here? And there? How many guns were there at that spot? They were concentrating their attention on the details of the aerial photographs, and the main thing, the evidence that there was an exceptional concentration of artillery, had to wait for the days when the evidence was no use: the artillery was already in action.

It's possible, I think, that some, at least, of the brass were calculating: the nation mustn't be put into a panic. They were intent on calming people down, and perhaps themselves more than anyone else.

I remember saying to the adjutant:

'You know, we've got to give the lads an order of the day about this. Finland's fate is really in the balance now.'

The adjutant said:

'Would it do anything but scare them?'

I pondered and considered: let be then: the men can see how it is for themselves, with their own eyes, day and night. Anyway, no order of the day was promulgated. Instead, there was a tactical order. I have the impression that infantry unit was the only detachment that gave any orders for action when the offensive began. Otherwise, I don't think any leading echelon gave any orders: if they'd given warnings about a coming major offensive, they'd naturally, in my opinion, have had to announce defensive measures: how the assault was going to be resisted; how the casualties were going to be dealt with; procedures for bringing up reinforcements of ammunition; the methods of maintaining communications; and all the other necessary items. And since it's clear that no such orders were circulating in the other units, I came to the conclusion that they hadn't believed any attack was coming.

And then at six o'clock on the morning of the ninth of June:

The previous night I'd gone to sleep as usual in the log house on the back slope of Öljymäki hill. There'd been an HQ there already during the previous battalion's time. There were shellholes in the yard of the house. When I'd turned up there as the fresh base commander three weeks before, I'd said to the previous commander:

'Ah! Shell-holes, I see. This house is kind of exposed.'

'No: they don't seem to drop any,' said the old commander.

And that's how it actually appeared on the morning of the ninth as well. The shells whistled over into the hinterland behind the support hill. After this had been going on for a while, I got up, pulled my trousers and tunic over my pyjamas, and went out. Planes were already showing up forward-left. They were large bombers. I started counting them: nine, nine, nine, nine, wave after wave was coming over, more than you could reckon, escort-fighters buzzing around them and gleaming in the sunshine.

They turned to rake along the front, and obviously, as soon as they were over my battalion's front line, the bomb hatches opened, and the bombs fell.

10

All we could do was lie in the sand at the bottom of a hole and try to keep in one piece.

And the sand flew. It flew, all right.

1966 **Paavo Rintala**

BEFORE BATTLE

Rrrrr. . .rrrr. . .rrrrr. . .

Dive-bombers were sweeping over the front line, off to strafe the command posts and artillery batteries. The sudden row shattered the settled atmosphere; instinctively everyone took a dive into his foxhole.

The unusual respite had lulled them into wishful thinking: they were fancying and hoping that, for some dim reason, a cease-fire might be on the way. A couple of uneventful days had calmed them down; but the tension was so near the surface, they were soon on the point of stampeding – as in the rearguard action. Once the planes had passed over, heads did begin to poke out, but they soon ducked back again as a continuous rumbling came from the enemy lines.

For a second or two the men managed a hope that the barrage might be passing them by, but the first detonations showed how wrong they were. The ground quaked and shook. The shells shrieked and whined through the air, and the lads shrank, their hearts thumping fit to burst in all the hullabaloo. They hugged the soil close, their nails clawing the gravel bottoms of their slit-trenches; and one fellow started childishly picking away with his entrenching tool, a spoonful at a time.

'Battle stations!' – the strangled cry came from somewhere, but it was drowned in the rending explosions. Trees snapped like matchsticks, and flames and smoke went licking up to the tops of others. Splinters, branches and sods came pattering down in a continual hail, and somewhere a whining fragment of hot shrapnel hit someone who began whimpering in terror:

'Orderlies. . . help. . . They've got me.'

Hietanen was face down in his trench, eyes tight shut, mentally registering each blast in his vicinity:

'Whoomph. . . whoomph. . . whoomph. . . whoomph.'

It was a kind of safety-valve – diverted his mind from the terror set off by the hullabaloo. Somewhere nearby, a man was groaning pitifully, whimpering for help, and after a temporary struggle with his fear Hietanen raised his head and looked about. A yard or so off there was one of the recently arrived recruits: he was dragging himself along, painfully crawling, and screaming for help, his face twisted with savage terror and shock.

Hietanen leapt out. He grabbed the man and began to yank him into his trench, shouting and going purple with rage:

'What the hell did I tell you? To bloody well lie doggo! But no. . .'

He'd just given the new lads a serious warning about this, for he knew only too well from his own experience how difficult it was to stay put under bombardment. When fear grabbed you, you were quite likely to fartarse about like this under fire. Could be he'd made it too vivid and actually provoked the bloke's behaviour.

He lugged the recruit almost brutally behind him, fear turning to blind rage against the lad. Shrapnel was whistling round his ears, soil raining down on their heads, and the shell-blasts whamming their clothes against their skin. Hietanen was on his knees, tugging the lad along by hand and belt. The recruit never stopped shouting, more from shock than pain, for the wound was minor.

Suddenly a blast of hot air struck Hietanen's face, and some shrapnel hit his nose, breaking it and ripping both his eyes. He slumped on top of the recruit, who went rigid and silent, seeing the torn eyes bleeding and bulging from their sockets.

He did his best to roll Hietanen off, but he was powerless with terror, as if paralysed. He steered his head round, unable to face the horrible bleeding mug, and when he did finally get a sound out of his throat, it was a long and pitiful wail.

It alerted the others. Koskela and Vanhala were the nearest and rushed to help. They pulled Hietanen off the recruit and dragged them both into the nearest trench. Just then the barrage lifted, and Koskela roared to the recruits:

'You there! The new lot! Get over to those casualties! Dress those wounds! And if we do have to move, be sure you bring them with us.'

The others scrambled to their posts, for a tank was rumbling from the other side of the brook, accompanied by sharp volleys of small-arms fire. Just then, too, they heard the yell of charging infantry; but pretty soon the whole thing turned out to be a bluff. No attack came, the yelling stopped, and the firing too gradually began to peter out.

The men were left mulling over what the bluff meant but couldn't work out much: perhaps the enemy was just trying to get them on edge before a real assault came. They'd come across this sort of ruse before, so it didn't particularly worry them. Koskela ordered Rokka to keep an eye on the platoon and set off to the rear to take a dekko at Hietanen. In the shambles there'd been no time to sort out how it was with Hietanen. Looked to him as if only one of the eyes was a goner.

Hietanen's head was swathed in bandage, and he was just coming back to consciousness when Koskela turned up. His hand went up, fingering the bandage, and he managed to blurt out:

'So how'm I doing?'

Koskela pulled his hand back and said:

'Don't fret yourself, it's nothing. Keep still now.'

'That Koskela, is it?'

'It is. Don't move. You got a bonk on the nose.'

Koskela looked at the bystanders, put his fingers to his eyes, and the men nodded. Then he raised two fingers, and got an assenting nod to that. Blood was flowing from Hietanen's tunic sleeve too, and they located a small wound below the elbow. They bandaged it, trying to blow it up in importance, hoping to divert Hietanen's attention from his eyes. He groaned:

'God, it's a bugger! Hurts like hell. What's up with my head?'

'You got one on the nose. Nothing bad. . .'

'Don't kid me: they've got me in the eyes.'

He was getting more and more conscious, and as he did, the pain got worse. The blow had numbed the wound, but as the numbness faded, Hietanen began to weigh the situation up. He kept clenching his hands, and then stretching the fingers out. For quite a while he held back his groans, but soon he was yelling without break, scaring the recruits off. Delicately, Koskela raised Hietanen's head:

'How about a spot of water? The stretchers'll be here any minute. I'll come with you down to the road.'

'No, don't want any. . . Where are the lads?'

'At their posts.'

'Still there, are we? In the old position?'

'We are.'

Hietanen rolled over to let out a new yell. Then he flopped on his back again. He was gasping and panting.

'Who else is here?'

'The new lot.'

'Hand me a pistol.'

'Don't fret yourself. We'll have you at the station in no time.'

'It's too much. My head! God, it's awful. . . awful. More than I can take . . . Come on . . . I'm on the way out anyway.'

'Take it from me, you're not getting one. No point. You're not going to die. Apart from that bit in the head, you're completely OK. Nasty cuts up there. Nose broken. That's it.'

Hietanen began twisting and turning again. Koskela ordered the recruits to run to the orderlies and get them moving. Already, a couple of other casualties had been taken to the road.

By now, it was all quiet behind the enemy lines, so Koskela told the lads to come over and say their goodbyes to Hietanen. None of them could find a word to say: they'd cottoned on to how badly Hietanen was wounded, and they felt the usual phoney consolations were out of place. Without a word, each in turn squeezed the hand clutching the stretcher-edge. In a pause in his groans, Hietanen tried cracking a joke, realising how awkward everyone felt:

'Got no eyes. So you won't catch me bawling then!'

Not getting any response, he sensed their sympathy, and as if to ward it off, he began his usual line of patter:

'Don't give a bugger, not me! Don't give a fuck. Easygoing type, that's me, you know. Thing like this – not worth a tinker's cuss.'

The orderlies picked up the stretcher and began taking him away.The last sound the lads heard was a long wail of pain. They knew well enough that a sound like that wouldn't come lightly out of Hietanen, and they had a good idea how badly his torn eyes must be hurting.

Koskela walked by the stretcher to the road. The other artillery casualties and already been assembled there, six in all. Kariluoto had intended for an ambulance from the dressing station, and luckily there'd been one available – on hand to deal with casualties from the dive bombers. The doctor had made up his mind to bring in the front-line casualties at the same time, and he'd sent on the ambulance.

It was a converted bus and came swaying along the treacherous road. The casualties watched in alarm as the driver backed it round unconcernedly on a bad bit of rocky terrain. They were dreading that the vehicle'd crack up, and they'd be left there: every one of them was dead set on getting away before the enemy attack came. Their anxiety was pointless, for the driver knew his job. In general, these ambulance drives had spent years negotiating the kind of terrain an ordinary man wouldn't take a horse across. They knew they were driving against death, for a casualty's life often hung on getting to the operating table quickly enough.

The more severely wounded were put at the front. Though the rear end of the bus was the roughest ride. Hietanen stayed there leaving the front to a man with a belly-wound, even though the shaking about was excruciating. The pain stabbed from his forehead to the back of his head, agonising his spine too, and even his arms.

The medical orderly whispered to Koskela: it was on the cards Hietanen might be a goner if the shrapnel had cut deep enough.

Koskela refused to believe that: Hietanen wouldn't be conscious if the wound were that dangerous. He took hold of his arm and said:

'Take it easy, you know. Life goes on, even without eyes. When you pull through, we'll meet again, you bet. See you in the not-too-distant.'

Hietanen was too agonised to fix much attention on Koskela. Groaning and moaning, he turned his head away and managed to blurt out:

'So long, then! Send the lads all the best. And look after yourself.'

The driver told Koskela it was time to get out, and he climbed down. Even after the ambulance had disappeared round a bend, he lingered where he was for a long time, watching silently. Then he lit a cigarette and took his time making his way back to the platoon.

He was even more depressed than usual. His long absence from the platoon had made no difference to his feeling for the lads. Every man-jack that went took something away with him. The old platoon stood for the victorious spirit of the earlier war. Every man lost was a piece gone out of that spirit, leaving a gaping hole stuffed with lowered morale and a feeling of the stupidity and meaninglessness of the whole shoot. And, more than that, Hietanen was also the one closest to Koskela, out of them all. Blindness simply didn't go with Hietanen.

But Koskela knew what had to be done. He'd the knack of thinking what he wanted, and not thinking what he didn't want. Yet again he was shoving out of his mind the torment at this lunatic killing and suffering – just as he'd got over the rage it caused when Lehto shot a prisoner, and the others blabbed about it. There was no place for humanity here, and Koskela began to give his mind to other things: alternative machine-gun emplacements.

1954 **Väinö Linna**

CLOCK TIME

Once off the road, we were confronted by a dense stand of spruces. The trees soon shrunk to saplings, ending in a narrow clearing on the other side of which the forest began again like a wall. At the edge of the clearing were tents; inside one sat Captain Eteläinen and Valli, and by another Manne was digging out a fox-hole. A smart-looking lad was watching him dig.

'Hello!' shouted Manne, and began to introduce us. It appeared that the boy was the group's new man, and not as young as he looked. He offered us real cigarettes. We went inside. The cannon, draught equipment, rucksacks, mess kits, forks and spoons, four radios and tents had been joined by yet more new men.

We had just sat down on the pine branches when Valli came into the tent. He was on official business, you could see that straight away.

'Go to infantry command,' he said. 'You'll find it here.'

His pen showed the place, and marked out the route with a line.

'There's a well-trodden path leading from here, you'll find it easily.'

'What, now?' asked Mikko.

'Now, and take the radio with you.'

'What's up?'

'You'll find out when you get there,' said Valli, and left.

'Typical of him to be so mysterious.'

'Like lambs to the slaughter,' said Mikko.

The path led behind the road along a sandy heath with pines, close to the front, probably following it, and on over a stream and across a small field to a hollow, under a stand of birches and up on to another heath, where the command post was supposed to be. The path seemed to end there. An opening led under gravel and branches to a shoulder-height earth. A flickering carbide flame picked out a few heads against the darkness, without rank or other distinguishing characteristics. This silent brotherhood seemed to have been waiting for us, because they began to file out through the opening. We followed them, one by one, past the gravel ridge and into the dell. Further away, behind a lower ridge, we could see a great cleft in the soil. Grenades came down occasionally and sparsely, as if at random.

No one seemed to know what was going on.

One of my teeth hurt. I didn't know whether what was coming would be bigger than this throbbing pain; if it was, I'd forget all about my tooth. It was as if that which was to come was already present, behind a veil, but you couldn't work out how bad it was going to be. On the other hand, a business becomes really evil only when the evil goes away. The lieutenant, the biggest bloke among us, gave the command to try making contact. There was nothing to say at this stage.

Then a dapper cavalry major leaped into the hollow, and you could see at once that he was expected.

He gave our instructions to the lieutenant, then joked: 'If this is going to be such a dangerous area, I think I'll get out of it now.'

The major disappeared over the ridge as quickly as he had come.

'Our task,' explained the lieutenant. 'After the artillery's opening fire, we're to cross the cleft, proceed to the crag and then carry on through the bog to the road to within about three kilometres of the front line.'

The operation was called on active reconnaissance. 'A feint,' someone growled. It began to become clear what the intention behind our orders was: to distract the enemy's attention from the reflex action behind their back.

That was the manoeuvre that we had been supposed to be part of, we remembered, and now we were caught up in the same plot. It didn't look good. A couple of dozen men, throwing grenades; they flew past the hollow and hit the crag beyond the cleft. They were certain to have heard that we were coming, although neither side had had long to prepare.

We ran, bent double, over the low ridge, across the trench dug in its side, and over the more reliable tree-trunks to the crag, over it, and through some big boulders to the edge of the bog, without encountering a single trace of the enemy. They had left a corridor empty here, beyond the cleft. Plausible: why not attack, if we were to attack from here, but we didn't know that this area was unoccupied; or, if we knew, why waste artillery fire on empty land. Well, there could have been someone there. Now, at any rate, a signal had been given: Watch out! We're coming! Stunted pine trees grew here and there in the bog. We advanced through the scrub behind the lieutenant.

Somewhere it was Wednesday, Thursday, Sunday, a month, a season, a time of year. This was our here and now, and its name was: marsh. It stretched as far as the eye could see, and meaning of life was continuation towards the edge hoping for something on the other side. And that something was not called 'heaven', but 'road'.

About the middle, or so it seemed, we found a ditch. The bottom was almost dry and hard, with only a thin layer of turf.

'Make contact,' ordered the lieutenant. The box into the ditch. The first exploded ten metres away, the rest all around us. The fire continued. From one side, at an angle over the ditch, the machine gun directed its long bursts in a scything action. From above fell the catapults' grenades. All hell had been let loose. Someone panicked, and that quickly had the group running blindly in any direction.

Contact was broken. Mikko and I ran in single file more or less back along our own tracks. Life contracted, all the intelligence in the world appeared at once, bright and clear, and came again in another flash; and noise, the noise said the same. Life flowed fast and vigilant, branches, trees. The gunfire moved ahead of us to the crag, where its power was greatest. Between us and the edge was the sound of victory. This is retreat and they are cutting us off, forcing us on to a stone butcher's block, on to an anvil, and the fiery hammer, many hammers, pounding, thick and hard. A dash between two boulders, bent double along the ground the buttresses, over the anvil, dodging shocks, along the tree-trunks in the cleft at a speed your legs couldn't manage in any other situation even if the prize were honour for a thousand years and eternal joy on top of that. The same speed over the trench, my legs took me over the ridge, then dropped their burden in the hollow.

You're alive, said consciousness, breathe in, breathe in, more air, it's good to gulp it down and to realise, miraculously: two legs, two arms, head still on, to see everything still in one piece. Miraculous to see a few people on the ground.

Someone was standing staring at his hand: why only a thumb. He understood why, and dashed away at a run. Why was someone else screaming like crazy. Maybe he had lost a hand, or a foot, or his innards had been dashed out on a stone. Craziness fell from the air above the hollow. There was a howling. Behind the trench were short bursts of gunfire. Someone was screaming horribly, he was taken away. There he was, and him, and someone with his back turned. Someone was still screaming.

My tooth was aching, pounding.

'Maybe they'll let us go now,' said Mikko.

'Maybe.'

'Your tooth hurting again?'

'Mm. Just now I couldn't feel it, now it's aching again.'

'There'll be aspirin when we get there.'

We waited, all of us who had made it back to the hollow waited. There were a few words, this and that, cigarettes, matches.

Then the lieutenant walked into the hollow and announced that the operation was not over, it was unfinished.

'We'll get reinforcements, and then we'll push the operation through to the end, as ordered.'

'When?' someone asked.

'We don't have exact details yet; maybe in about an hour.'

'Few of us get as much information as that.'

We'd get to run over the low ridge once more, jump over the trench and try not to trip as we ran across the planks of the cleft, would be able to see what the stony field looked like now. Probably it wouldn't happen until we got to the bog. The operations would encounter each other only at the bog, the two antagonists would fall into place, like two logs jointed together, vertical and horizontal. Then it would be time for the orchestra to strike up the dance of death for all it was worth, toes would twitch, feet would fidget: all of us, even the smallest, know this dance, great and wondrous, so they say, this solo number. Everything would go according to plan, everyone would die their own death, meet their own destiny, everyone dies of some disease, but what was the point of growing to be a man to know so imperfectly these three, of which the greatest is lost first, even those who speak with the tongue of angels. Now it felt as if many would die today of other people's diseases, not their own, as if a million men had died of one man's illness, and tomorrow there would be more, and that one man would never die, he was immortal, greater than the gods. Darkness covered the earth.

My tooth ached.

'Soon I'll get some aspirin for my tooth, that'll be good.'

'Yeah,' said Mikko, and fingered his machine.

'How many minutes left?'

'Forty, if we start dead on time.'

Forty minutes had been torn out of eternity and thrown into this hollow. Too much time; forty seconds would have been quite enough, but the group wasn't up to full strength yet, it was still being replenished. Silently men formed a small circle to measure time, clock time, and our own funerals came nearer.

1967 **Samuli Paronen**

THE UNETCHED HEART

'I guess Helvi will be going to visit the grave with me now.'

There was only Helvi, Helvi all day long.

Auntie was clearing breakfast dishes from the table, the empty milk pitcher shaking to the constant tremor of her hand.

'Of course.' Helvi quickly rose from her chair and stacked the plates. But her mother-in-law who had asked her to call her Auntie, took apart the stack, gathered all the spoons and put them on top, and only then carried them to the edge of the kitchen stove.

'I took the wrapped-up flowers down to the basement, so would you be so kind, Helvi, as to go get them and open them here.'

'Of course,' Helvi said again, and felt ashamed at not being able to think of anything else to say, something soft and natural.

'And how about putting shoes on in case someone should happen to see.'

When Helvi ran upstairs, making the worm-eaten steps squeak

under her, for a moment the mother let her hands fall limp in the hot water and listened to words that hadn't been spoken circling in her head like grains in the drum of a mill. For it should have been like this: Please, Auntie, let's go to the cemetery to visit Esko's grave. And let's take along a rake and make it beautiful. And the kind of floral bouquet that will make the whole churchyard festive and show everybody that under this mound rests someone who lives on in our hearts, our Esko . . .

But it wasn't like that. The little grains of words were ground to dust, to ashes, all in vain, and she couldn't even grieve over it, really. That thorn had been in the flesh from the very beginning, the thorn of disappointment from the moment Esko had brought his fiancée home without telling anyone, not even his mother, his confidante. It had always been there, and had sometimes stung, though she hadn't realized it as clearly as she did now.

She began to wash the dishes fiercely, pushing her fingers, swollen at the knuckles, to the bottom of a drinking glass and scraping at it with her brittle nails. My goodness, not everybody could be like Esko, so sensitive that, when he was a grown man he could still fall into her lap and sob like a little child. Yet when all was said and done, Esko had, after all, chosen Helvi . . .

But what, after all, was Esko to Helvi? Only two short months. While for his mother it had been months and years, twenty-six long years. And whooping cough and facial eczema, cold towels every morning during the many long winters of school. And packages and little sums of money, even bigger ones after long night-time talks with the parlor light burning until dawn while Father darkly paced the floor. And what was it Esko had said when he left from his last leave to return to the front, that leave when he and Helvi had been married and he had been home for only one day: Next time I come, I'll spend a long time at home, here with you.

He had kept that promise, too. Esko had come home and been buried in the bosom of the earth, to remain here forever. Even though he didn't belong only to her anymore. Esko had a wife who wore the widow's veil – or at least should be wearing . . .

Mother wrung the wet gray rag in her hands and winced from the pain searing her fingers. A person had to be in a bad way when such a small task took every bit of her strength.

So they started off, Mother and Helvi.

Down the porch steps and along the sandy garden path towards the gate. Atop each concrete gate post sparkled a mirrored glass ball, one leaning slightly towards the board fence. Helvi's tall, slender body was reflected in the slanted ball so that it looked even slimmer than usual. The bouquet of gladioli drooping in her hand was glowing unnaturally large and red, and a green skirt was peeking out from under her dark coat. Her head and legs faded, became smaller and more pointed somewhere on the other side of the ball. But if you looked for them there, you wouldn't find them.

The other ball was shining, almost completely black. Auntie's black coat, black hat and veil, rough black shoes. And a brown paper tote bag, with a garden hoe and a short-handled rake sticking out of it.

'I always keep this bag ready, on a hook in the hallway.'

'Yes. That's – good.'

So they went on, each in her mirrored ball, each in her own steps. Two women whose bodies Esko had hurt and whose souls he had carved into with his boy's knife. Helvi's too, although lightly, sparingly. But Mother's heart was so stabbed and drawn and scraped there was no room for any more lines. Somewhere in the lower corner were the smaller scratches drawn by Father and Taisto, but they were already healing over.

It was a long journey, that two hundred meters from the mirrored balls to the cemetery gate.

If only this could be over and done with!

Luckily she didn't blurt it out, but in Helvi's chest it was pressing and swelling: if only this were over and done with. Because the whole time she knew she was causing disappointment, she didn't, couldn't know how, had no idea how to turn, step, speak. Because not enough lines had been drawn into her; she was too smooth.

But I am the widow. I am the one in mourning.

I am in mourning. She clung to it as to a treasure people were attempting to tear away from her. For although Auntie's every word, every glance testified it was a great thing to be Esko's widow, there was also the doubt: are you worthy enough to bear your burden . . .

Please, don't envy me for it, though my shoulders are young and strong, though I have the strength to bear my grief alone and inside me.

At a fork in the road, a yellow dog came along, giving them a friendly sniff and wagging its bushy tail. Helvi bent down to scratch him behind his ear, and the dog, overflowing with friendliness, rolled in the dust in front of her. Auntie stopped, a look of disapproval on her face.

'Off, Teppo. Off with you, go home,' she said, stamping her heavy foot. 'Dogs are always running around the graveyard and trampling on the graves. That one, too, even though it's the verger's dog.'

That's what seemed the worst thing in the whole matter – a churchman's own dog.

Then they turned in through the small gate and walked along, their shoes grey with dust, towards the new part of the cemetery.

'It looks so barren,' said Helvi.

'And such sandy soil.' Auntie's voice grew tight. 'No grass is ever going to grow here. But what do they care? Even the statue has to curl its hand into a fist. They just don't think of anything.'

Helvi looked at the memorial statue, a fallen warrior who was reaching toward the sun with his last strength. His bony fingers were gleaming green.

'But it's not in a fist,' she said, and glanced over at Auntie. The dense little wrinkles in her upper lip tightened, making her old mouth very small.

'Yes, it is. They don't understand anything, committees, because it's not their own son under the sod.'

It was almost as if Auntie were blaming Helvi too for the fact that the grass was patchy and the memorial statue was repulsive.

Sixty similar white marble slabs, sixty hydrangeas behind the slabs, and sixty green vases in front of them. That hurt a little, too. One small vase, what could you fit into it? Not even a tiny fragment of what one would have wanted to carry here and place on Esko's chest.

Then, the next to last one in the last row: Second Lieutenant Esko Juhani Niskala. And two dates, 8 April 1918 and 14 June 1944.

'We did ask if we could have something engraved in the lower edge, some phrase or verse, but no, couldn't have got it if you'd got down and begged on your knees.'

Auntie was talking softly so that Esko wouldn't hear the worries she still had for her son.

'One time we brought the old mug, the one he always drank from when he was a child, and set it down next to the vase. And lilies of the valley – only flowers, no leaves. But they threw it out, over the fence onto the rubbish heap. One mustn't be any better than another, that's what they said when I asked why. Father had to go dig it up out of the rubbish, couldn't leave it there, that kind of memento.'

There was a lot that hurt here too, where there should have been peace. But tears flowed freely, the bittersweet waters which at home, inside cold walls, among silent, unfriendly people, sometimes went forgotten.

'Esko was always so happy . . .'

She was crying, quietly and high-pitched, as if struggling to get out of some cage. But in vain, for the cage was just swinging and shaking, wouldn't give in. She was inside, she who had ended up there. And Helvi almost envied her, the old woman's clear, ceaseless weeping. If only she had been able to step closer, take hold of those quivering old shoulders and join in the weeping. If only she had a cage around her, or at least some kind of pen. But she hadn't. There had been only a strange awakening after a few short spring nights, the hard asphalt platform of a railway station, and a bundle of letters. Then the casket which couldn't be opened. And nothing else. You couldn't build a cage or pen or even a barbed-wire fence out of those materials; it was not the kind of mourning you could put on display.

At last Auntie had stopped her weeping, settled for the prison of this wealth of memories, and drawn a curtain over her eyes for those who could see her. And Helvi did the same, as well as she could.

'Maybe I'll rake, then,' Auntie said almost irritably, and raked the half-meter stretch of gravel walk smooth and stoneless. Whatever stones she found, she flung off with her rake so that they landed a couple of grave sites away.

'Oh, but the flowers!'

The voice was impatient. Helvi certainly should have understood that you had to put the flowers into the vase first. Now she would trample on the newly smoothed sand.

Helvi hurried off toward the water tank, in the direction Auntie had pointed. She had the vase in one hand and the withered columbines in the other. The green skirt kept peeking out from under her coat, and the mother felt ashamed.

Then the vase was back in place in the meadow with sparse grass, and the flowers were bending humbly toward the ground. Auntie smoothed out the footsteps Helvi had left in the path and put the rake back into her bag. They were ready to leave.

At the end of the gravel path, Auntie turned to look back.

'Anyway, Esko's grave is the most beautiful . . .'

It was a consolation which went a long way toward helping her, one day at a time.

Helvi was walking slowly behind her. It was as if someone had tugged at her heart with a dry palm a couple of times, as though to wipe away dust. It was painfully clear, that heart, bare and deficient in everything. Not a single stroke was etched in it even here, at Esko's grave. The question was whether it could be alive, could belong to a living person. When she tried to find her reflection in it, it showed nothing but her own solemn, searching face, lonely and slightly fearful.

It would be best to come back here alone, when all the others were asleep. At night, under the rain clouds.

1951 **Eeva Joenpelto**

THE FUNERAL

The child turned to look back but could no longer see the place where she had been standing in deep snow by the roadside when the sleigh had come along. Now the man was urging his horse on as the sleigh labored uphill.

'So the dog's dead,' the man said, pulling his fur hat lower over his forehead.

'Yes,' the child answered.

'Died on its own, wasn't killed,' the man said, echoing what the child had just told him.

By now they had made it to the top of the hill. From there you could see all the way across the lake. She had never been there before. She was absorbed in keeping track of the five wavy lines that a few haystalks, spilling over the edge of the sleigh, were tracing in the snow.

'And you're on the way to the funeral.'

'Yes, I am,' the child answered. Then she flicked her hands and glanced to one side.

'That's a fine wreath you've got there,' the man said, and asked whether she'd made it herself.

No, she hadn't. But she had gone and gathered the spruce twigs on her own. And again, as if without meaning to, she brushed against the paper ribbons; they rustled. And she was aware of a strange feeling in her stomach: that she was sitting in a sleigh on her way to a funeral, that this man hadn't driven past her like the others; instead, he had asked her name and age and told her to get into the sleigh. And that, the child thought, came from her carrying the wreath.

'And you're going to be the pastor,' the man said and shook the reins, and the horse trotted on again and the man asked her whether she really knew how to be a pastor.

Yes, she certainly did know. And the child told him that Grandma had died in the summer, and after that, they had found a great woodpecker in the back meadow and had buried it, and she had been the pastor. And they had buried mice and other, smaller birds all through the autumn. And she started talking fast, and while she was talking she tugged at her grey mittens to cover her wrists; of course a dog was more than a great woodpecker but because she had done it before and knew how to go about it, the girls whose family had owned the dog had telephoned her and asked her to be the pastor. And they asked her even though the girl's there were older than she was – one would soon be thirteen and she herself was only seven.

The man stopped the horse at the house where the funeral was to take place, and the child got down from the sleigh with the wreath in her hands.

In the yard there were two boys: the bigger one a ten-year-old from the neighbor's house, and a smaller one from this house, the big girl's brother. 'What's that?'

She turned her back on them. As the boys circled around her, saying they sure did know it was a wreath, she spun around, lifted her chin, and said, 'What's it to you?'

Because she wouldn't argue, wouldn't say anything to the boys. At home, they had told her how one should be at a funeral. And she remained standing at the front door with her back to the boys and waited for the funeral to begin.

They had lifted him from the snow behind the woodshed and laid him out on the sleigh. He was lying there with his legs straight and clumps of snow sticking to his tail. And the children were standing in a circle around the sled. The sun was shining straight down.

'Poor Nalle,' the big girl began, and stroked the dog.

'Poor Nalle,' the others chorused. And the tips of five woollen mittens gingerly touched the black fur. There were yellowish spots under the chin and under the bends of his front legs.

The old grandma of the house came out to join them. Hands clasped over her belly, she looked at the dead dog and nodded several times.

'Let's get going,' the big girl said. 'And you've got a wreath.' She took a good look at it. 'Nalle sure couldn't have guessed. All we've got is these. But these are just as good as real flowers.'

The big girls lifted their hands and showed their Easter decorations, willow branches done up with blue and yellow bows.

They took their places next to each other behind the sled.

'I'll pull,' said the big boy and grabbed hold of the rope.

'No, me.' And the smaller one began to cry.

As the boys were trying to grab the rope out of each other's hands, the sled tipped over and the dead body slid over the icy, slippery edge and onto the ground.

'So that's how you push the poor thing around,' said the big girl.

Since the boys wouldn't listen, the girls called out to Grandma, who was still standing on the steps, that the boys were shoving. 'Pull him nicely, mustn't shove,' came from the steps.

'All right, listen,' the three girls said in one voice.

The big boy was embarrassed and tried to defend himself by saying that the dog wouldn't feel anything because he was all frozen. And he seized the dead one by the legs, lifted him, and dropped him back onto the sled. He fell with a clunk.

'See, he's frozen. All frozen.'

Together, the boys took up the rope and the funeral procession started moving. Wind blew over the procession and the red ribbons of the wreath billowed high up and the one who was carrying the wreath raised it higher and held it in both hands. And the procession went down a hill and past the sauna cabin and the well, where the deep field of untrodden snow began. On the other side of the field stood a tall spruce. That's where they would take Nalle, under the spruce tree, the people in the procession were saying as they waded in the deep snow. You could easily remember the gravesite by the spruce, and when summer came they would take flowers to the grave. For this dog had been a good dog, they repeated in the words they had heard from grown-ups. He had driven off thieves with his barking, had sat quietly in the stern of the boat when they were out fishing, and when he had grown old, he hadn't turned bad-tempered. The sled carved deep grooves in the snow.

They dug a shallow pit under the spruce. When it was done, the boys lifted the sled and when the dead body fell into the pit they took a good long look at it, then lifted their heads and looked at each other.

'Goodbye, Nalle. Now we'll put some snow over you,' said the big girl.

'Goodbye, Nalle,' the others repeated. The little boy looked around in a panic but tried to behave like the others. He seemed ready to burst into tears.

But the big boy kicked at the snow, sending it whirling onto the dead body.

'He can't hear anything cause he's dead.'

The girls said he'd have to go home right away if he couldn't behave properly. 'Yes,' said the one who was acting as pastor, 'you go home and stop that kicking.' She looked at the boy in such a way that he backed off, muttering, 'It isn't your dog.'

'It's not yours either,' the pastor answered.

'And we don't need you here, so stay out of the way,' said the girls.

And they all turned their backs on the boy and covered the grave. When the grave was patted smooth, the one who was pastor said, 'Now you go and stand on the other side of the grave and when I say "Pray!", you pray. And when I say "from dust to dust", you take some snow, it'll be pretend earth, and when I give a sign you toss it onto the grave and look like you're crying.' And she crossed her hands.

'We don't have to say and do all that, do we, 'cause he was only a dog,' the big girl said in a grown-up voice.

They began to confer about whether or not they should say all that.

'Dogs don't have a soul,' someone said.

'No, animals don't,' they insisted to the pastor, who'd threatened to quit and go home if they didn't let her do everything just the way it was supposed to be done.

'But what if it's a sin?' the big girl said in the dark tones of a voice predicting doom.

When the pastor heard those words, she spun around and said, 'I'm the pastor and I've always been a pastor, and I know what's a sin and what isn't. Good dogs will get to heaven more easily than bad people.'

'No, they won't,' said the others.

'That's what they said at home. I asked.'

The congregation fell silent. Then someone said, maybe it's a sin to think Nalle wouldn't get to heaven. They didn't want that.

'Well,' said the pastor.

'Let's go ahead then,' said the big girl. And she pushed away the little boy's hand; he was clinging to the hem of his sister's skirt.

They started a hymn. Their breaths steaming in the frosty February air, the big girls sang in high, clear voices. The pastor sang in a lower register, got out of breath and mixed up the tune, while the little boy was singing loudly whatever words he could make out from the others singing, and he was constantly lagging behind. And the others gave dirty looks to the one who didn't know how to behave and who just kept mimicking them, kicking and shaking snow on the hymn-singers.

The pastor began the prayers. At first she prayed out of sheer devotion, but then she wanted to show them she hadn't been asked to be pastor for no good reason. When the congregation started to fidget, she prayed out of spite, to show that the listeners wouldn't be able to last as long as she did. She prayed all the prayers she could remember.

'Hare tracks!' The big boy spun around and was staring into the forest.

'It's hare tracks, I'm sure.'

'Where? Me, too.' And in a whirl of snow the little one tore after the big one, shouting that he shouldn't leave him behind.

'I'm just not going to do a thing, with the boys acting up like that.' The minister was looking at the two who were still there.

'But you've already done something,' said the big girl. 'My toes are freezing. Let's put the wreaths on the grave and go home.' She stuck the willow branches in the snow and started jumping up and down to warm herself. Then the girls left.

She could hear them calling to her that she should come in for coffee, their voices carrying from across the field.

All the voices had died away a long time ago, but she was still standing in the same position as when the girls had left. She moved her foot, moved her hand, and noticed the wreath she was holding. She looked at the willow branches stuck in the snow and thought: no homily, no final hymn, all unfinished.

Wreath – it was no longer a wreath or anything. She dropped it in the snow. Well, after all it wasn't our dog, she thought.

It was utterly silent and the sun had gone down. She was alone in the forest. And she started off, walking quickly without glancing back. But she didn't dare run.

She stopped in front of the sauna cabin and thought she wouldn't go into the yard, or at least not into the house.

She looked at the icy spout of the well-pump, studied the snow in front of the door to the sauna cabin and saw little black specks, embers that had fizzled out in the snow.

Her fingers were freezing. Her mittens were frozen stiff. She felt her nose; it was cold and wet, and her toes were like ice .

When she opened the door to the house of the funeral family, someone was clearing the coffee table. She sat down on a bench near the door. At the center of the table, on a flowery platter, lay a big raisin bun in the shape of a man, its arms outstretched, its stumpy legs, each one of a different length, spread apart.

She glanced at the kitchen door; she could hear someone washing dishes, and she counted: five buttons. Eyes and a nose. Eight raisins altogether. But instead of a mouth there was a hole. Someone had dug out the raisin with his finger and eaten it although it was meant for her. Or maybe it had fallen off in the oven and burned up. When she would eat the raisin-man – when they would come and offer it to her – she would start with the legs and then eat the arms, and all the time she would look it in the eye. And she would be eating it and it would still feel like it was whole even though only the head would be left. And the door opened. She thought: now.

The door slammed shut, and although she knew what had happened she sat still, staring straight ahead, her heart pounding. And she remembered how hands had picked up the platter and the platter had sailed away over her head. And on the platter lay the raisin man.

She headed home.

And only when she got to her own yard did her legs become her own legs; she started to run, went into the vestibule, yanked open the door. With her hand on the doorknob, she stood on the threshold and looked.

They didn't say a thing. And she stood there bewildered; they didn't notice anything, didn't see what had happened to her, their own child.

She could hear all right that they were talking, saying there comes the funeral guest, and asked her to tell what the funeral had been like. And they came up to her and told her to take off her coat, and when she wouldn't take it off they became angry – at her – and asked again why she wasn't taking off her coat and why she was standing there 'looking like that, with your eyes inside out in your head.' 'They didn't give me any coffee.' The words fell out of her mouth like stones whose weight she could no longer bear alone.

And she lifted her head and looked up. And saw they were laughing.

'What is she saying?' she heard her aunt's voice ask. 'What is she saying?' the aunt repeated and started towards her.

'Did you start fighting with the boys, or what?'

They went away. She was alone.

When the door slammed, someone went to see if a visitor had come in. And from the window they could see the child ski out of the yard bare-headed, and someone wondered where she was heading now, when it was already dusk.

She had already passed the cow barn; she was in the lane behind it, and the snow came up to her waist. She reached the drying barn, skied past it, was up on the high meadow. The wind had blown the snow out of the ruts in the road; the icy edge was slippery and she fell and hurt her hand on the sharp ice. 'They didn't give me any coffee,' she kept repeating, and could see a trickle of blood on the back of her hand: 'They didn't give me coffee – I'll go and take it back,' she kept saying aloud, and her ski pole kept cracking into the crusted snow. She had come up to the grave.

There was a faint rustling sound; the wind had caught the ribbons. The ribbons would stir, then settle. As if poised for attack, she bared her teeth, let go of the skis and grabbed the wreath off the grave, flung it away.

The spruce branch had stopped swaying but she still stared at it.

Then she turned slowly and looked at the grave – took a jump and stood right on it. Jumped, jumped up and down, and her jumps came faster and faster; broken howls and laughter burst from her mouth – 'they'd find out if they came to see their dog's grave' – and her hands were beating the air as in a dance and the snow was swirling, getting into her hair and nostrils – 'they'd find out if they came to see who wasn't given any coffee.'

A foot stopped in mid-air as if it had been seized in a firm grip. And for a moment, that is how she stands there, leaning forward, eyes wide open. She turns her head slowly and looks down out of the corners of her eyes. The raised foot sinks next to the other. She steps back from the grave.

She was staring at a black paw sticking up out of the snow.

She made a slight move, turned, seemed to hesitate. Then she nudged it with the tip of her shoe, nudged again, almost kicking it

– and at once looked behind her. And looked to each side, behind her – bent down and began to dig at the snow with her hands.

Was it? The very same one. And what was it like now? She scraped at the snow. Her bare hand hit something cold and hard.

She had raised her hands to shield her eyes, but it was as if her hands were being twisted away from her eyes and she was forced to look.

A yellow circle. As in a frosted window pane. An eye, the eye of the one who was dead and buried.

But it was no longer his eye, it was made of glass. And through that glass someone was looking at her. And the circle began to widen – and it was spreading out towards her.

She tried to scream but no scream would come out. She doubled over, pain shooting up from her legs to her stomach and chest. And she fled.

At the drying barn she opened her eyes wide for the first time and saw where she was. But she knew the forest outlined against the red sunset was not the black lacy cloth on the parlor table but stakes and swords in the hands of those who, all crouched over, were running towards her. And though the trees before and behind her were still trees, she knew that as soon as she got past them they too would join those who were chasing her.

In the little path between the out-buildings she could see the fence-posts beside the path beginning to tilt and she plunged out from under them; she could see the houses and knew they wouldn't come to her rescue, were just looking on.

But she had made it to the end of the fenced path. And her route had traced a dotted line through the pathway. She had cast off the skis somewhere, and one of the poles too. With the other pole in one hand, she reached her own yard, managed to get the door open and to shut it behind her.

Water was dripping on her hands and face. Through her melting hair she could see the empty house and the circle of light from the lamp. She went into a dark corner.

When someone spoke to her, she answered and sat listening. Who had spoken through her voice? When she was undressing, her hands stopped and she thought: who's undressing, and whom?

She had once fallen from a high place, from a load of hay, and been left lying in the snow bank. Then she had asked quietly: 'Did I die?' And when she had been told she was alive she had sprung up and started running.

She moved her hand and wondered. It moved even though she had no idea whose it was.

The next day they said she had been an especially obedient girl and they offered her some candy. She hid her hand behind her back and looked away. When they asked her why she wouldn't take any, she reluctantly took just one candy. When she was told to take another one, she quickly snatched a whole handful and shoved them into her mouth all at once.

And when she went towards the window, she seemed to be thinking. And there was a sly, surprised look on her face.

1955 **Marja-Liisa Vartio**

A little old lady,
barefoot Karelian,
not knowing where from
where to,
didn't remember her name.

In the midst of war
slept on a train-seat,
on the way to somewhere.

1979 **Helena Anhava**

THE VILLAS OF FORGETFULNESS

Sultry nights, I slept on the glazed verandah in my camp bed,
my reinforcements underneath, their guns trained on my enemies.
I was both in bed and under it, between the sheets
and in the trench,
And the enemy were coming in from the sea and they were
equipped with submarines.
They attempted a landing, the bastards.
During a ceasefire, I looked out of the verandah windows
at my forefathers, the fir trees, and they nodded,
they spread their protective wings and they nodded,
and the sun rose.
I closed my eyes and blasted the last thundering machines
to smithereens,
with a sharp burst of machine-gun fire I shattered
the submarines' periscopes.

When I awoke, there was a flower on the table, some chocolate
and some juice.
I was a dead hero receiving his reward in heaven.
That's what good boys' mothers do.
Everything possible.

1981 **Matti Paavilainen**

WAR'S COMING

'War's coming.'

One afternoon, as we sat around the kitchen table, eating or about to eat, my father pronounced these familiar words in a tone of voice that was quite new. He said them to my mother just as if we children had not been present, as if he did not need to pay any attention to us, or as if the fact that we were only listening meant that we did not understand anything. Or perhaps they simply had no better time to talk to each other, since Father was always off to hunting or to the station, and Mother was always busy in the kitchen.

'Yes, there's definitely going to be war.'

Was it Father who said it, or Mother? Who spoke first, and who answered? That I do not recall; but I do remember the words and the tone of voice and how they struck me, although people had been speaking of the approach of war throughout my short life, and although I did not really know what war meant. Something dreadful, in any case, the most awful and horrible thing there could be. I did not know any way of stopping it, apart from prayer. You had to pray whenever you remembered, pray in your own words under the blankets after evening prayers were over, go on your knees whenever you could on the shores of Raivattalanlampi pond or Linnansuo bog on the way to or from school and pray, without anyone seeing, in the out of doors, sheltered by the woods, so that nothing could prevent your prayers flying straight to the ears of God in his heaven. After that you could forget your fears for a while and go on fishing or playing explorers-in-danger or read or draw or carry on on your journey home even though you had a tummy-ache.

But now, suddenly, I can no longer wait until evening, or for a more suitable moment: I have to go and pray at once. I think no one will notice as I slip out of the kitchen and into the bedroom next door, and pull the door to behind me. In front of the door are my parents' beds, covered with the lacy bedspreads mother crocheted, mother's the nearer. I kneel in front of it, my heart bursting with pain, and clasp my hands in prayer.

Oh Lord, dear Lord, don't let war come.

This has been my prayer for many years. How can I find new words to persuade God; how can I argue my case?

Hear my prayer, merciful Lord.

That is how the grown-ups talk to God: merciful Lord.

Mother opens the bedroom door: she probably thinks I am doing something naughty, pressing a pillow against my stomach, perhaps, like once before. I look at her, on my knees, before I can even pull myself together enough to scramble to my feet. I feel as if I have been discovered, as if I have been sinning, filching apples or reading a grown-ups' book. I am ashamed, even though it is mother who has taught us children, from an early age, to pray.

How I would like to be able to end this recollection with mother taking me into her lap, although I am already a big girl, 11 years old and five and a half years older than my little sister. Or with her saying: Let's pray together.

But mothers mostly make mistakes. And so my mother stands there at the door of the adult world, her hand on the doorknob; she doesn't kneel down with me, but simply says:

'Poor little thing, she came in here to pray.'

And so my prayer somehow becomes a laughing matter: insignificant, unimportant, panicky.

My memory of the incident ends there, but I think my mother urged me to come and eat, to sit at table with the others. And that is, after all, good and kind. Come and eat. Now, long afterwards, one could think that it embraces everything that was important at that time: to eat together, to sit around the same table in our own kitchen for as long as we still can.

*

At about 13.55, there are aeroplanes in our kitchen window, and they stay there for such a long time that I am able to count them. There are nine of them. At the same time the neighbours' son, Lauri Kuivanen, rushes in and shouts breathlessly: 'Come and see the planes, if you haven't seen any before there are plenty for you to look at now!'

Time has begun to pass infinitely slowly. The aeroplanes are stationary in the sky, in the upper squares of the window, and the bombs which have separated from them are hanging there as if suspended between sky and earth. Perhaps they would never have moved if mother had not made the mistake of screaming: 'Oh, look at the bombs falling . . .'

'Into the cellar, and quickly.'

Father takes the lead. We jump to our feet and run outside in chaos, for the cellar door is outside the house. So: first into the narrow hall and then out, down the kitchen steps, a turn to the left and in front of us is the cellar door, behind it the steep concrete steps that lead to the cellar and the sandbag which is supposed to act as a shelter. Now it is just in the way. On down to the left of the pump to the cellar door. And then we are there, the whole lot of us, among the smell of the cellar and the stores of food. Potatoes, carrots, beetroots and swedes calmly welcome these bolting specimens of the human race. On the shelves, oversweet jams containing hoarded sugar. Translucent yellow plums in big jars, they too drowned in syrup. Butter and salted mushrooms. A bucket full of mashed whortleberries. Winter apples wrapped in paper.

In addition to the stationary aeroplanes and the bombs frozen beneath them, another memory; it, too, strangely motionless. Mother is huddled in the corner of the cellar, one arm around my sister, the other around next door's little girl, Lauri's sister. Father stands in the middle of the cellar and tries to see out of the oblong window under the ceiling; I am doing the same, and so is the boy next door, by the grain bin. For some reason I can see myself in this memory, as if from outside. I remember that I was not the tiniest bit afraid. It was as if all the fear in whose grip I lived had been wiped away. I remember even feeling a kind of courage. It was as if all my terrible games had at that moment rushed to my aid. I was filled with a desire to show that I would endure. Above all I wanted to be able to observe what was going on, to see and hear more than was possible from the cellar. When Mother, from her corner, began to moan and pray, it seemed an unbearable distraction. She insisted on hugging me and, pressing me to her for a moment, begged, in an unnaturally high-pitched voice and weeping copiously, for protection and mercy for her family.

*

At some point there is a rumour that an enemy plane has crashed into the forest somwhere nearby; I have some obscure mental picture of this. People fear a reconnaissance parachutist. There is a story of an unknown Finnish-speaking man who fell in with a group of cardplayers, played with them all evening, winning and losing like everyone else, and only after he had gone did the others realised – for some reason or another – that he was a spy. Went on his way. Was never caught. When my young aunt skied or sledged home to Jyvävaara to sleep in her time off, she would have suspected every shadow to be a spy had she not been dropping with tiredness.

There was another story, of granny's second stepson's wife. Or her second husband's daughter-in-law. When this formidable woman had seen a plane making a forced landing on the ice of Ojajärvi lake, she had taken a Browning from the bureau drawer and set off to take the airman prisoner. But the plane had turned out to be Finnish, and instead of an enemy prisoner, she had an airman from our own side, to whom she was able to offer coffee and cakes, which did nothing to lessen her fame. After all, she could have shot him in panic, had her level-headedness not kept her trigger finger steady.

But where could we have found men to search for a reconnaissance parachutist who might conceivably have survived the crash, when there were only women and children in the forest villages, without Brownings or other firearms? I do not know whether my memory is playing tricks when, at this point, it offers me my father's story of the search for the downed Vanyas. I remember how my father liked using the word Vanya, although he sometimes called the enemy Russkies, too. And Ivans. He varied the nickname to avoid repetition.

Perhaps I am making a serious mistake in linking his story with the plane that came down near Jyvävaara, but on the other hand I have often been forced to acknowledge that memories do not follow a chronological pattern. This memory presents itself at this point and becomes an image, as if I had been a witness. Perhaps father was on leave at the time when the plane came down, and was thus able to take part in the search.

I remember the feeling at the time. Somewhere in the forest was the crashed enemy plane. Inside were enemy airmen. Alive, dead, or wounded. Had they used parachutes to jump clear? Were they hanging from the trees? Had they frozen to death in the snow-drifts? Were they frost-bitten? Hungry?

I believe that it was then, thinking about the fate of those enemy airmen shot down over alien territory, which was what Finland was, after all, to them, that I realised for the first time that those whom we called the enemy were human beings. That they could suffer. And that at that moment, shot down and perhaps wounded, they were frightened and in need, just like us. At that moment, probably more than us. That they were at our mercy, just as we, at other times, were at theirs. I remember being afraid for them and thinking, with horror, what our Finnish soldiers would do to them if they found them alive.

Father has told this story many times, and in the end the story has obliterated the original memory; but the image before me is still the same as the one that I saw with my mind's eye as a child, when I heard for the first time what had happened.

After the wrecked plane had been found and the surrounding area searched for long enough, marks of crawling were found in the snow. The bloody tracks led to a hay barn. I suppose the barn was surrounded. I suppose they shouted 'ruki ver' (hands up) and 'iti sutaa' (come here) – words even children knew. I suppose the wall of the barn was sprayed with bullets when the commands were not obeyed.

'Let's set the barn on fire.'

I suppose it was father who made the suggestion. A good one, everyone thought.

That is what they did.

Then human voices, bellowing, were heard from inside the barn. Out of the hay rises first one man, then another. One is dragging a leg, which is bleeding copiously. The other has a chestful of medals, and when father tells the story a respectful note creeps into his voice at this point. It seems that soldiers honour for each others' rank pays no heed to frontiers, whatever the situation; or is it himself that father is congratulating, his part in taking hostage such high-ranking prisoners? The wounded man was not exactly a private, either . . . Hands held high in the air, they came out of the burning barn.

What happened to them? I remember that I would have liked my father to have gone on telling their story, but he always went back to the different stages of the capture of the barn and the high rank of the prisoners. When someone is too close to the situation, he cannot perhaps see it from anything but his own perspective. Perhaps it is necessary to be a bystander, a non-participator, a child for example, before one can sympathise with all sides, even that which is called the enemy. Perhaps that is what is meant by 'unless ye become as little children . . .'?

'Poor things,' I remember my mother saying, at points considered quite unsuitable by others. Often these two simple words were enough to bring a different perspective to some event or opinion. It is possible that it is they that opened up for my inner life the possibility of sympathy and empathy, the unclosed space from which, later, grew my profession, and which may perhaps be one of the few ways to bridge the loneliness of the human condition, the great rifts between individuals. With hindsight, anyway, it is possible to think so, based on that feeling, which I know has remained the same for fifty years. Feelings, too, are memory.

At some point, at the beginning, there was a belief that the Soviet army would surrender in droves on seeing how good life was in Finland, that they would consider it a great piece of good luck to become Finnish prisoners of war. 'Katsho kaupunt' – see the town – the Vanya-soldiers were supposed to have said to each other in their peculiar dialect, to each other on seeing the first villages on our side. These words I remember well, because no one could pronounce them better than Mother's father, our Sortavala grandfather. They had to be pronounced bendily and succulently, palatalising the consonants, as if you had a lot of spit in your mouth. I, too, can still do it.

I began to suspect that there was a lot of nonsense talked about the war. My compassion and anxiety about the shot-down, imprisoned airmen wiped the concept of war hero from my mind, although I did not realise it then. To Father's credit, is must be said that he never boasted of any kind of heroism, if anyone else did. War is war, he used to say. And if mother pronounced her own dissenting words, 'Poor things', I can imagine Father saying, 'War is war.' It probably happened, too. If not then, then sometime earlier or later, and many times; those words are lodged deep in my mind.

*

After the conclusion of peace, the Karelians were given a few days to fetch their belongings – their goods, chattels, things, bundles – from the area to be ceded. They gathered the contents of their homes into heaps by the sides of roads and on station platforms, wrote their name and home parish on chairs, tables and cupboards in the hope that they would follow them, by lorry or train, to the other side of the new border; for life had to go on. For this reason Mother and Grandmother left immediately for Hiitola to save what could be saved. There was, of course, nothing left of the station, for it had been bombed out of existence, but in our house were three suites of furniture bought in Viipuri, the pride and joy of a nouveau riche home (as we heartless daughters called them, years later), and it was worth trying to save them. There was a burr-birch bedroom suite, bought at auction in Viipuri for the newly built house, with a dressing table with movable mirrors; it had been the wonder of all our friends. There was an oak dining-room suite with an oval extendable table and two sideboards decorated with flourishes and engravings; the bottoms of the chairs still bear the legend, 'Hiitola'. There was a gentlemen's drawing-room suite with a tobacco table (although no one smoked), in the functionalist style. All this, and much more besides, was safely loaded on to a train and brought to the Finnish side, and my parents' house has been furnished with these articles ever since. They did not get rid of them at later stages of their lives, as did many others, for example later on when they moved from the country to the town. Indeed, I believe that many a Karelian home was finally broken up only in the 'structural change' of the 1960s.

Mother remembers thinking for a moment whether to leave behind our big dolls, Sinikka and Keiju. My sister and I had been given them for Christmas by our grandmother, and our aunt had crocheted fine woollen dresses for them, red for Keiju, my doll, blue for my sister's. Both of them could open and close their eyes, and both had real hair; Keiju's was dark, Sinikka's fair. Keiju also had china legs with chubby pink knees, just like a real baby. Keiju, who had originally been sent to my aunt by some American relatives, was in mint condition after a visit to the doll doctor, except that she could no longer say 'mama'. The dolls had awaited our return in that cold house and suddenly, amid the bustle of packing, mother had felt it would be terribly wrong to leave them to the 'Russkies'. She had felt that the children's wishes should be taken into account even in this extreme situation. And so she had packed Sinikka and Keiju into a suitcase, and crammed in some of my beloved books, the thick *Girls' Own Book* (from one of the stories of which I had taken Keiju's name), Grimm's stories and the *Thousand and One Nights*. I have all of these still, except that all that is left of Keiju is one eye, which I rescued from Mother's button box. The children of my youngest sister, who was born after the war, played with Keiju until there was nothing left of her. But her eye is still clear blue and vigilant, and looks you straight in the eye.

Many other irreplaceable things, which may have seemed unimportant then, were saved in the same way, among them photographs. It may be that the Karelians' perseverance and willingness to adapt to their new circumstances derives in no small measure from the fact that they brought with them photographs of their old homes. These have maintained contact with the old home and gradually come to replace fading memories; sometimes, perhaps, without anyone noticing, taken the place of memory. Thus their roots have been preserved at least partially intact in people's heart of hearts, even when their original way of speaking has had to make way for the western dialect of profession, education and adaptation.

1989 **Eeva Kilpi**

IN THE SUMMER OF 1941

In the summer of 1941, when Viborg was recaptured and our army advanced to the Karelian Isthmus, my company was marching past Teerilä one morning. We were only a few kilometres away from my childhood home. I swung my bicycle into a bumpy side road leading up to it.

It was good to leave the dusty road full of marching columns, creaking vehicles and swaying gun-carriages. Hitherto, my memories had been of such a distorted nature, I scarcely recognised what I saw. My reason told me it was my childhood landscape I was looking at again, but my emotions refused to accept it. It was like seeing a beloved and familiar face distorted by illness.

Everything had been ravaged by the war, an occasional charred tree-stump rising ghost-like against the sky. The bare slopes were all grubbed up, criss-crossed with trenches and tangles of barbed wire. The familiar villas along the road had disappeared, along it now nothing but blackened fire walls and sooty chimneys. One house had burnt to the ground, and inside the stone base was the blackened skeleton of an iron bedstead, a blue enamel can and a cracked chamber pot staring abandoned up at the sky. A patch of charred grass, a shattered corpse of a horse and the unmoving silhouette of a wrecked tank bore witness to the fighting that had taken place here a few days earlier.

A revoltingly pungent smell reminiscent of funeral wreaths and coffins swept towards me, as if Death himself had breathed on me. The smell lay over the whole landscape and stuck to my clothes, like a perpetual slightly suffocating sense of anguish deep down inside me. It made the whole area seem nightmarish and unreal. The butterflies fluttering among the flowers and birds twittering in the trees seemed to me to be a delusion, intended to lull me into security and persuade me to forget man's ability to destroy and obliterate life. Only the crows seemed real and at home here. They were swarming over us in thick clouds and their shadows swept like gusts of wind over the road and the fields. Croaking hoarsely, they dived down on to the fields and new clouds kept appearing, as if sucked out of the sky by a vast maelstrom. When the last stragglers, flapping heavily and croaking breathlessly, had disappeared out of sight, all was silent and I could once again hear the deep rumble of guns in the east.

As soon as I turned into the side road to Teerilä, the landscape changed character, as if I had left the war behind me as I turned my back on the marching columns and headed straight into the safe and peaceful world of childhood. The sun shone and the birds were chattering away, quite untroubled in the elder bushes. I dived into the flickering shadows of the pine woods where spiders had strung glittering webs of sunlight between the trees. Here I could find no trace of the war. The forest was as silent and desolate as if no human being had set foot in it for years.

When I was a child, this road was the main road above all others. It was the road to Viborg and the longest road in the world, leading to the great unknown. In parts it now looked more like a dried up stream, wheel tracks overgrown with grass, here and there the road completely wiped out or hidden by vegetation so that you thought it had come to an end. But my bicycle flew on, purring quietly and contentedly as if burning with excitement to be reunited with the world of childhood.

Then we were flying out of the forest in an abrupt curve, rushing downhill and following the last stretch of road along the edge of the forest. I felt a stab inside me when the familiar silhouettes of the Kuningasvuori, the Kukkarvuori and St Hubert's Mountain slid out behind each other. There was the lake – now almost filled with reeds. Like a river, it followed the road beyond the meadows and now and again allowed a glimpse of its gleaming surface to appear. A warm smell of resin and pine needles rose from the glade where Grandmother used to rest on her walks. That smell had come to me whenever we returned from our outings, tired and hot, and it still evoked pleasant images of the homeliness soon to envelop me. I caught a glimpse of the stones of my childhood, two gigantic stone faces buried up to their necks in the meadow. There was the pyramid-shaped barn that reminded me of a witch in a grey-patterned moiré head-cloth, now sagging and on the verge of collapse, the face grown small and shrunken, the eyes squinting with horror. I flew into the avenue where I had run a race with the moon, the friendly rustle of the birches guiding me right to the Black Gate, where nothing was left except a fallen gatepost. Uncle Georg's hill. How ridiculously small, suddenly! The bicycle rushed up it without reducing speed. A moment later, I was up on the mound where our house had been. There was nothing left of it but the stone base, a tangle of nettles and willow-herb grown over it. The flowers threw a pale violet light over the whole mound, like the last glow from a fire that can no longer compete with the sunlight. The cotton-waste-like seeds left on the willow-herb stems or sailing slowly through the air stuck to my uniform. Remnants of memories seemed to be still hovering around the non-existent house, bumble-bees buzzing dully in the lush foliage as I cautiously made my way ahead. The nettles had spread enormously and it was difficult to avoid getting my hand stung. Before, they had only covered a small area by the kitchen steps and lined one side of the path to the outhouse and rubbish tip. Now they had crossed the path like a barbaric army, penetrating into my childhood garden and covering the whole of the top of the slope where the stones had once seemed to me to be as high as the Caucasus mountains. They had even conquered the stone base and the squares inside it – the ground plan of the rooms in which I had lived as a child. I found it difficult to orientate and assign my memories to the right places. Their three-cornered pagoda-like tops and saw-edged hairy leaves rose everywhere, their crocodile bite refusing me entry to my memories.

Essentially, I could recognise nothing at all.

The great dark-brown timber house with its dim shadowy rooms, its outbuildings and balconies, which loomed up above me like a ship whenever I returned there in my imagination, no longer existed. When I looked up, my eyes met nothing but a stretch of blue sky. The mound I was standing on looked astonishingly insignificant. The essence of the picture I was seeing again had been cut away and the vacuum filled with blue colour. The house with its timber walls, its doors, windows and knots in the wood I saw in front of me the moment I closed my eyes, now existed only within me. My soul had taken on the form of the house and every room enclosed a particular part of my past life.

1953 **Oscar Parland**

EIGHT STATEMENTS

My dad was a reserve officer, in the anti-tanks.
The summer war broke out I learned to walk.

Packing his bag, my dad remembered a bootbrush and a tin of
polish. 'I'll need these when we get to Viipuri.'

After he'd gone, trains passed our summer cottage with men
singing 'Kaarina'.

Dad wrote: 'Grow root-crops, watch out for air-raids,
it's going well . . . all be over by autumn.'

He fell a day before Viipuri.

We got a parcel: a bootbrush, a pocket watch, a tin of shoe
polish, my mother's letters, a piece of bloodstained wadding.

Winter, we ate root-crops, sat in a bomb shelter and I
learned to speak.

1964

Kari Aronpuro

ANTTI HYRY
MIRKKA REKOLA
PENTTI SAARIKOSKI
VÄINÖ KIRSTINÄ
JARKKO LAINE
JYRKI PELLINEN
MARTTI JOENPOLVI
ALPO RUUTH
LASSI NUMMI
ANTTI TUURI
ERNO PAASILINNA

Antti Hyry

THE DAM

It was late September and had been raining for days. The water-level had risen, flowing deep over the stony bottom of the ditch. The weather had brightened up, and the rain had stopped.

'You could get an electric light going from that ditch,' thought a young lad who had come out now it was morning and was standing at the edge looking at the water. 'The ditch'd turn a waterwheel, and the wheel'd turn a dynamo.'

The boy crossed the yard to the farmhouse and fetched a spade. He began loosening sods. Starting from the lip of the ditch, he cut the surface into squares with the spade-edge and then turned them back with the flat of the blade. He loosened turf here and there, wherever they came easiest, and lifted the sods into a single pile at the edge of the ditch. Of course, he should have been wearing rubber gloves, for the earth was was sticky, and the sods were dripping black water.

The stones at the bottom of the ditch were coated with a brown mould. There was a brisk and dark flow of water over them – not like in the summer sometimes, when the water merely dribbled along, and, if there was a deeper bit anywhere, there were tadpoles in it. Now the willow bush growing in the ditch hadn't a single leaf on it; the current waggled the twigs that touched the water.

There came a shout from the yard: 'Get the fire started under the caldron, and fill it up. The weather's cleared up – she'll be here any minute now to do the washing.'

Easiest way to get them off his back, he thought, was to get the water and light the fire.

He fetched an armful of sprucewood from the shed and some birchbark for kindling. He lit the fire under the caldron and fetched two buckets of water from the ditch. Two and a half gallons each time, he was thinking, as he carried them: the caldron would be full on the fourth trip. The spruce burnt feebly under the cold and sooty base of the caldron.

He got started making a dam. He stripped off his shoes and stockings, rolled up his trousers and sleeves, and got into the water by the pile of sods. He took a sod from the pile, pushed it down to the bottom of the ditch and stood on it to weigh it down. He thrust another sod down and stood on that with his other foot. The water was helping to weigh them down too. He tramped down a whole stack of sods and stood on them for a bit. The dam rose and the water rose above the dam, flowing over the sods, smelling of rain, and cold.

The dam rose high enough to stem the water: now it was blocked and still rising. Quickly, he fashioned a plough-shaped gutter out of boards. With the back of the axe-head he drove two posts into the dam, piercing the sods, then nailed the wooden gutter to them. He sawed the posts off, making them the same height as the gutter; then he stacked sods on each side of the gutter and pulled some stones up from the bottom of the ditch as weights.

The water rose, forming a narrow smooth surface, swollen and dammed: it was now covering dangling willow twigs, stones and the grass sides of the ditch. Then it rose to the level of the gutter, flowed smoothly to the broad end, eddied to the narrow end and tumbled down to the bottom.

The washerwoman came over from the yard. She was carrying a bucket in one hand and a packet of washing powder in the other. She took note of the dam and the boy and said:

'My word, you've got a dandy place for getting water there, haven't you? Goodness me.'

And she climbed down into the ditch, her red checked scarf and apron swinging, and put her bucket under the spout. She peeped into the bucket and the gutter. The water splashed onto her apron, while she kept a tight grip on the bucket-handle. The bucket was full up in no time, and she set off back with it brimming.

The boy laughed to himself.

'Oh that old biddy!'

And he remembered how she looked drinking her coffee, relishing it, nattering and sitting a bit askew in her chair.

The boy set to, making a watermill. With an axe and a saw, some boards under his arm, and his pocket stuffed with two- and three-inch nails, he went behind the shed to the cowbyre. He remembered there was a pitchfork handle tucked away in there – just right for an axle. There it was, and he reached down a bicycle wheel from a nail on the wall as well, and carried his stuff over to a door lying by a log behind the shed.

The grey door had a stain of dark damp on the corner under the log, due to the rain. High clouds were showing on the horizon. Overhead, there were white clouds, but they didn't cut off the sunlight. The sun was shining brightly. The dogs were loose: they could scamper about pretty well everywhere they liked; sometimes they'd go barking round a tree-root in the forest, and in the evenings they'd be off sniffing out wild duck in the dark fields. When it rained they liked to lie in the cowbyre, and in bright weather they'd pick a sheltered side of a wall for a nip at their fleas or to laze about.

He sawed off six pieces of five-inch board, each a foot long, to make blades. He nailed first one, then another piece fast to the centre of the axle, pointing in opposite directions. Then he did the same with the other pieces of wood, in between the first pair, so that they formed a series round the axle. There was now a propeller of three pairs of blades extending outwards from the centre of the axle.

The boy got up and stood on the door, revolving the device in front of him. It didn't feel as sturdy and firm as it should: infuriating, that, like someone poking you in the back, the shoulders and the hands. He'd been forced to drive a lot of nails through the axle, three two-and-a-half inch nails for each piece of board. All going through the hub, they'd weakened it.

He fetched a brace and bit from the cowbyre. He sawed two square pieces of board and drilled holes as broad as the axle in the centre of them. He put the axle through the holes, pressed the boards up against the blades on both sides and nailed them to the edges of the blades. This strengthened the whole millwheel.

He made two-inch high sides for the ends of the blades, and each blade became a small box.

The bicycle wheel was a back wheel with no hub. With a bit of whittling, the watermill's axle fitted into the hub-hole. He slammed the wheel onto the end of the axle, where it gripped firm. As for the other end of the axle, he wound some wire round it and tightened the wire into a neat row. Putting a thin bit into the brace, he drilled holes in the centres of the axle-ends: then he stuck long sleigh-screws into the holes. The millwheel had to revolve on those. The axle-ends couldn't split, because one end was gripped by the bicycle-wheel hub and the other by the wire.

Holding the axle between the blades and the bicycle wheel, he carried the mill down to the dam. He fetched a crowbar, and then set off to look for suitable posts.

'Take that tub over to the clotheslines,' came the shout.

'Right,' he replied.

The washerwoman and the boy carted a full tub of newly-washed clothes to the lines stretched between all the suitable trees.

'Weather just right now. . . and jolly good water,' said the washerwoman.

'Pegs are over here,' came the shout: 'Come and get them.'

The washerwoman hung out the clothes. She hung shirts by their laps, and towels by their ends in a row, each peg nipping two towel-corners. Heavy underpants were hung from the reinforced waist, and sheets were folded over the line, to hang by their middle. The clothes hung heavily, dripping water onto the ground. The lines sagged, the bottom edges of the clothes almost touching the ground as they dripped into the grass.

Using the crowbar, the boy poked two holes in the bottom of the ditch just beneath the dam, near the mouth of the gutter, and an axle-width apart. Then he took the posts and beat them upright into the holes with the crowbar and sawed them off just beneath the mouth of the gutter.

He blocked up the gutter with a turf, stopping the water flowing through. Then he took the watermill and set it on the top-ends of the posts, arranging the sleigh-screws so the blades of the waterwheel fitted over the mouth of the gutter. He drove nails into the top-ends of the posts to keep the sleigh-screws firmly in place. He turned the wheel with his hand; the mill revolved, and every moment a box-shaped blade was over the mouth of the gutter.

He removed the turf from the gutter, letting the water flow, and it ran into the narrow mouth of the gutter, fell into a box-shaped blade and filled it. It forced the box down, filled the other box, forced that down and filled the third. And the mill started revolving. The bicycle-wheel on the axle revolved with it.

He dug a hole with the crowbar in the ditch-bottom near the wheel and hammered a post in there to fix the dynamo on. He went indoors, unhooked a bicycle-dynamo from the wall and took an empty bobbin from the sewing-machine drawer, a needle, a bobbin of reinforced yarn, and a bundle of narrow lampwick.

He unscrewed the dynamo knob that rubs against the bicycle wheel and replaced it with the empty bobbin, fitting the axle-end of the dynamo's revolving rotor into the bobbin hole.

He turfed up the gutter; the water stopped flowing, and the mill stopped turning. He nailed the dynamo fast to the top of the post, so the bobbin was close to the revolving wheel. He wound the lampwick round the groove in the rim of the bicycle wheel, and then round the empty bobbin on the dynamo; he drew it tight, cut it with a sheath knife and sewed the ends together with the reinforced yarn. The lampwick now formed a belt. When he turned the wheel, the belt spun the bobbin, the bobbin revolved the dynamo rotor, and electricity was generated in the dynamo.

When he released the turf from the gutter-mouth again, the water started to flow. Powerfully it revolved the watermill and the bicycle wheel. The wheel and the belt revolved the bobbin. The dynamo hummed. But the bobbin didn't hold: it twisted to one side and fell off; the belt dropped onto the axle and began turning on that.

He pushed a sod back into the gutter and stopped the mill. He wound some reinforced yarn round the end of the dynamo pivot, making an even and tight row, and pressed the bobbin back into place, where it now held firm. He straightened the belt and replaced it. And he took the turf out of the gutter.

The water started the mill revolving. There was a continual swishing and splashing as the radial boxes filled, swung downwards, emptied and returned upwards. The dynamo hummed on the end of the post.

It was already evening, and it was dusk, since this was autumn. The sky was completely overcast, but it had not rained.

'Tea's ready. Come and get it,' came the shout, as he lingered by the ditch.

He went to have his lamb soup with pearl-barley; there was bread and butter, milk and beetroot.

'Where've you been – for no one's had a sight of you all day,' he was asked.

'Out.'

There was a funny atmosphere, for the washerwoman was eating with them too. No one was being normal. The washerwoman seemed to be gobbling down her bread especially fast, he thought: suddenly it struck him how pathetic she was, and he felt so sorry for her, he found it hard to go on sitting at the table.

In the wall near the telephone there was a hole for the telephone wire to go out. He pushed two leads through the hole, fetched the lamp from the dynamo, twisted one of the bare lead-ends round the lamp, used an awl to make a hole in the metal at the back of the lamp and stuffed the other lead through that. And he hung the lamp on the wall near the telephone, so that it dangled in a suitable position on the leads. The other ends of the leads hung free on the wall outside.

He went out. He stripped the ends of the leads coming from the wall, fetched a bundle of telephone wire from the cowbyre, and attached that to the leads. Then he ran the telephone wires to the ditch, two lengths running along the ground up to the watermill.

The washerwoman came out and caught her foot on the wires.

'What's these wires here? How can I get past?'

She was on her way home. She lifted the hem of her skirt, bag in her other hand, and managed to scramble past.

The wires, he realised, would have to be raised up in the air later.

He wound the other ends of the telephone wires round the nails fixing the dynamo to its post by the watermill. He drove in still another nail, to make sure one wire touched the body of the dynamo. The other wire-end he twisted into a small ring, using pincers, and put it under the coupling screw on the dynamo; he used the pincers to tighten it firmly on the coupling screw.

He went indoors. The lamp was glowing. The coil of wire under the glass cover was glowing red, lighting a small area of the wooden wall behind and around the lamp. The light dimmed and brightened rhythmically as the watermill boxes filled and emptied. It was not bright, but when he looked at the hot wire from very close up, an inconstant reddish light spread; as when your eye is fixed on the luminous numeral of a clock, and you see a pale light, like daylight dimly reflected from the ceiling.

'Can't see a thing with it,' he thought.

He went out. He bundled up the telephone wires and took them to the byre.

He removed the mill and the dynamo from the posts, hung the dynamo on a nail on the byre wall, and propped the mill and its wheels against the back wall of the byre. He went indoors, took the lamp off the wall, pulled the wires out of the hole, rolled up the leads and put the bundle and the lamp in the drainage-board drawer.

Outside the washing was hanging in the dark. The fir trees and birches stood supporting the lines. The air round the lines smelled of washed clothes. The water flowed into the gutter, fell to the bottom of the ditch and passed between the stones into the current.

It was morning.

'Get the fire started under the caldron, and fill it up,' he was told. 'She'll be along to do the washing first thing.'

He went out. The sun was dazzling in the autumn sky, its rays enough to warm your hair and the back of your shirt, and the air smelt of sunlight. The clothes had dried and got lighter, and the lines had risen up higher, the white cloths and sheets dangling freely. The water-level had gone down in the night. It was flowing cold and clear through the gutter. He lifted out two bucketfuls from above the dam and carried them to the caldron.

1958

Mirkka Rekola

What is this intractable water
with the ship veering laboriously round in it
what that island crush of pines
and in the distance that mobile song
which is mine
                                        ours.
Don't name as you hear
don't like the crowd get accustomed to
things' soubriquets, saying Baltic
don't say
                                        when you say
the swallow slips off from the tongue immediately
you don't hear a thing you don't reach back.

1961

You remember the elks
setting off sunward
and it still darkened,
you remember death in the yellow tree,
the lampwick,
and this is no more than a yawn and a rock
projecting towards the great region.

1961

One wouldn't want to see that in anyone at all
                              head hanging
familiar spoon in the hand suddenly thin and light

1965

It's here
like a knot in white scarf,
                              winter,
and it's flowering in my summer,
the bird cherry, the mountain ash.

1968

I laid my pack lunch on the park bench.
I sat down, I looked at the sea.
It was as if someone was beside me who waits at home.

1968

Today they're so ideal for me
                              the city's faces
are living their own times

and, there, a brown whitewingtipped bird
flies slantwise over the water
as if choosing a long wave for company.

1972

How could I walk so long
over so small a lawn?

1977

A peoplecloud burst out black as thunder.

1981

Before water I touched this bed,
before water it was
so open to looking
                                        and quiet
I certainly heard
I heard with my eyes
how quietly sand flows through sand.

1983

Pentti Saarikoski

We were a people,
a people of peoples,
even though our horses did swim across
                                        and founded Europe.

1959

The sea and forest were ours, the fish in the sea, the birds in the trees,
the birds sang to the women, the fish went in the men's traps,
until the time had come, the trees withdrew, back into the earth,
sea swilled between bones; the fish in the sea, the birds in the trees.

1959

The men rowed over the sea and through the sky.
One got a flounder, flung it in a tree and revelled: The moon!
The women's bellies glowed,
we declared the flounder sacred, ate it with a flourish.

1959

Life is given to man
to make him consider carefully
the position he'd like to be dead in,

grey skies pass over,
the sky's a hanging garden
and earth comes into the mouth like bread.

1959

HORSE

I'm a spider-rider, inkfishes
in the sea like night's free-floating skies.
On my way to the vice-consul's birthday,
sea in my boots, the vice-consul asleep.

Oh to be a goose, I'd be a verb: I'd gabble,
Ancilla the wise shooed the geese home.

No going where someone's sleeping,
time goes by, I die, but someday again
I'd like to hear the vice-consul saying:
When he was in the womb, the whole woman glowed.

One day a dog'll be hooved, a wolf feathered,
a horse'll bark, a hawk'll howl, and then
there'll be all kinds of creatures and hunters
hidden under trees in the royal forest;
words, ferns catch on your ankles, I
was alive, but a mythologist knew how to kill:
bit my prick off and grafted it under my armpit.

My mother was egg-white, my father black,
I appeared and they thanked heaven for me;
I glued wings to my shoulderblades to fly
over the house from the yard like a horse;
so old egg-white said a person shouldn't

sauce sacred wingers, and old black laughed like
a horse, and I opened out into flight and

flew like a cloud: I was snow and water,
and by spring I'd reached Springswine City,
where the leatherbellies set up statues
giving the lower pig the higher place;
I hung the statuarists from their statues,
and when I left, I sang 'Throw your pearls
before swine or don't throw pearls'.

I hounded that big woman, and her belly
filled with a bad smell from cheek to cheek;
an eternal love is an eternal lamb, I sang,
and took her to a meadow to graze, big she was all right,
and she ate the meadows, ate the clouds, and from her mouth
dangled trails of the sun's petrified slobber;
I grabbed her by her belly-wool, and she ran.

I got so old I became a grasshopper,
and the morning of the grass got a mouthful
of my narrow hips, the flutes, and a flawless spear
pierced the sky like a shield of fur;
the earth was rising to meet me all the time, I sang,
I lived I died mouth open eyes closed,
and larvae tattooed my skin with flowers, suns.

1959

THE OBSCURE DANCES

a girl
dandy as a dandelion
took me by the hand and said
I'm the light that leads you into darkness
No crop to brag about when I dig the potatoes

summer was dry, I was lazy
dandy as a dandelion
We have to sleep half on top of each other
legs curled up
these beds aren't meant for people our size
I natter with the magpies about how all
the world's people
are my children and you're the light
dandy as a dandelion that's leading
me into darkness
I've eaten of the knowledge of good and evil
the heavens are cloudy
the philosophies and policies crack like dry twigs

when I was a delegation and a theory
I rake leaves, count
my eighth autumn here
the sea's black, I meditate
a letter to the emperor, I despise him
Nothing's as green
as the mountain slopes in the morning with the sun rising
I was a mycologist, self-taught
went to the forest, picked a mushroom
studied its tint, bit a piece off
tried it on my tongue
spat it out
Now I'm here

black bread and cheese
on the table, and a winebottle, cigarettes apples
on the floor in a blue coffeepot russet dahlias
I eat black bread and cheese
drink wine smoke a cigarette
Now I'm washing apples
pop reeds in among the dahlias

A car drives along the road, turns into the forecourt
I'm trying to speak simply enough for an adult to understand
a car drives along the road, turns into the forecourt
the house is painted white

I'm the Way
I walk along
a delegation, a theory, painfully
since I'm old and an acclaimed man
chosen for this task
to plod up the mountain, to a pedestal
to see the world from
the cornfields, the ocean,
people at their labours, a working man
turns a concrete mixer, a farmer
studies
his ploughlands, and in the post office
the post is being sorted and in the cemetery
the crosses are rotting
I've come up to the top to say my goodbyes
to poetry, here they are, the carved statues
I don't need to mention them by name any more
they wrote books, founded religions, ordered
themselves to be embalmed and they were embalmed
No blackberries at first this year
then a few came
tiny ones that finally when it rained got waterlogged
I sat on a stone, the stone I'm sitting on
I reflected
This world's a universal cemetery,
a goodbye and finally
I'm going that no one's saying goodbye to
propping a cross on my grave to rot
it's getting dark and the days
are uncoupling like foul-smelling railway carriages
Freed from the sun's protection

they're creating an art
that all the churches
curse, I've seen
that gesture and can never forget it

You're not invited here, and you're not here
the cities, those evenings
I'm lonely, longing for loneliness, the only experience
that city, for instance, where the telephone catalogue
is a bibliophile's collectors' piece
there I sat on the riverbank not thinking a thing
then there's another city but spring
or was it summer then
I read a great poet's verses on the housewalls
The lonelinesses, cities
where the traffic snarls up
even though the streets are wide and the cars few, I don't
now I've understood why it's unavoidable
want to go into it
I'm lonely, the day's on my hands like a rotten spud
I sat in a boat
the others
are long since dead or living in some other city

Night gets no shorter with shoving
smoke dips to the earth
now I begin to remember
I'd found an old boot on a tip
hung it from the ceiling
put a right-sized tin inside
tied a string to the string the boot dangled from
tied the loose end to my braces
and now I'd got an ashtray
Night gets no shorter with shoving
nor a spade sizier with singing

Now I remember, smoke dips to the earth
There was a branch of alder in my hand
I'd been absorbed into the labour market

The Obscure is dancing
alone, the trees don't talk to him
the bird
doesn't look
the bear's gone to his lair
to sleep, no thought of waking now
The Obscure is dancing
he's forgotten
not only what happened but his memories too
study spiders, the cobweb
is the spider's face and fingerprint
The trees have other things to do, shake off their leaves

– –

Build your room, build your room, but leave me in peace
So people
kill each other
I went off to think about this
walked across the field and pondered
As long as wars are portrayed as catastrophic events
they'll never stop
must I
go through all the periods of history
to get some peace
I climbed onto the university roof and shouted
logical thought leads to war and oppression
not a soul is listening
I'm just
tossing down tiles
from the university roof to the street
when I grip the eaves with my toes
It occurs to me

my toenails
need cutting
This society isn't quite advanced enough yet, he says
our leader
that gets buttermilk up his nose every time he
drinks buttermilk for breakfast
Unemployment, environmental problems
a balance-of-trade deficit, inflation
a shortage of kindergartens
flagrant alcohol-abuse
tax-fraud almost a necessary condition of life
et cetera
that leader of ours burbles on
What he intends to do
when this society is sufficiently advanced
he's now been put over great possessions
doesn't he see
he's a cultured man
that an advanced society is a *contradictio in adjecto*
I'm not up to arguing any more
yellow wagtails have flocked in the yard
motacilla flava
they've got into a brawl with the magpies
Labia swell when I lick them, clouds thoughts
like everything living
flinches, doesn't want, but does want

When I'd sailed my third stint round the world
I'd scraped together enough
to buy my dad a cottage
then got a job on a building site, the ladder
it was somehow skew-whiff
that did my back in
now every morning at
nine o' clock
I've got to be there

reporting
for sick pay, 'cos they think
otherwise I'd drink all the money
I said if my leg was broken
would I have to turn up here every day
and report like this
your leg's not broken, Sir, they said through their teeth,
it's your back, Sir
and that being the case
you've got to report
obviously
they were Siring me like that because I'm so
unSirlike
He tells me his life, this ship's cook
but I'm already off in the middle of the spruce forest,
I think about him
his hair
sticking up on end and his nose like a rotten spud

on the longest night of the year
it's a starlight night
the girl sits on the draining board and sings
the mice are constructing their corridors
He decides to kill the girl, for he's scared of death
he helps her on with her coat
puts a sheath knife in his pocket
they set off for the mountain
the blackberries are hoary and the girl says
you didn't pick them
they go up the mountain, the Minotaur's asleep, the girl says
he takes her hand
they walk down Theory Road
get to the dustbin
and see the stars again, heavenly bodies

1983

Väinö Kirstinä

If you come to the land of winds, to the bottom of the sea,
there are few trees, plenty of icy wind
from shore to shore.
You can see far
and see nothing.

1961

Around you screech the newborn plains
still wet from fog
but clear as a dream

at the edge, the sea

beneath, the deep earth
above, the wide expanse
shouts to you and to the plains

about being
it looks at you and asks

1961

One roof intersects another,
from below, a humming rises from the plains,
the bank slopes downward.
From the rain, a sea gull on sheet metal,
the image glides in metal,
shrieks.
Your roofs are ringing,
fragments,
sooty ones, alive.

1961

Horse, hoofs, stones, sparks, plains
and the picture is full.
But the landscape sways, ditches fly back,
the horizon flees.
Distant forests and houses
are dark against the sky.
Hoofs strike sparks.
Horse flies swarm against my face.

1961

Above the blackening ground
of a September night
the scent of turnip on the breeze
and frost high in the treetops.
The cheekbone is delighted.
How simple and cool
the scent of death.

1961

Through my face drifts a spruce forest,
branches, snow, clearings.
I see through my face
when I press my forehead to the glass,
and observe, in the middle of the forehead, an eye.
In the eye I drift
home and away from home.

1961

The bird lived on air
and of the bird's weight, the tree,
and of its shadow, the earth.

Wings are raining under trees,
an expanse is born, a vastness of trees,

when silver coins
wend their way
to earth.

1961

THE FIRST OF MAY

I
It was the first of May.
We went to drink a bit and dance.

She asked me to take off my wrist-watch,
she asked me not to hurt her with a ring.
She offered, in turn, an ice-cold apple, and then
one that was too hot.
Green plains booming with a naked horse.
Out in space there were a thousand bulls, a thousand bulls!
All that we touched burst forth in roses!

Houses staggered past and past.
Lines bent. Walls caved inside each other.
Past us went an unknown man who had legs.

II
I have read a thousand books,
and a clean page is as beautiful,
more beautiful than one filled with writing.
I am tired of studying what you look like, death.

I already know

that the time will come when you'll draw back the moving parts of a submachine gun,
that the time will come when you'll blast off,
that you'll burn the cabinet minister's corpse, too, to ashes,
that you'll finally lay a mine also in the path of a tyrant,
when he expands the empire
and wants to get rid of his shadow.
That you are written under the young ebony faces
when they shout and dance;
that you'll try your pistol on them just for fun,
that they'll fall headlong into the clay of night,
headfirst against a rock; a curtain.

The clean page is now beautiful.
Hell is a sure thing.

Let's go drink a bit, and dance.

IV
An immense taxi:
ten storeys high, and speeding,
and we in its pigeonholes.
Everything's at stake at every moment.

The green light goes on – and it is red,
and iron bends,
and cloth tears, and flesh.
Drink, brothers, it's already evening.
And night is coming, night without end.
Helplessness knows no bounds.

1965

Jarkko Laine

THE HOTEL OBLIVION

The women are driving to town in their Buick
Clouds wrap themselves round its exhaust.
They stop to ask Homer, is this the way to the World Exhibition?
No, ladies, it isn't, he replies.
This is the street of the Hotel Oblivion.

By the parking space, in a wicker chair,
sits Billy the Kid, shoots arrows at the sun.
The women get out of the car:
Are we still headed in the right direction?
No, he replies, and spits out his chewing gum.
That's the Hotel Oblivion there, across the way.

In the hotel lobby, chariots circle the arena,
a gilded Boeing rises off the runway.
Ben Hur sits in a tub with earphones on,
the radio plays Bill Haley and the Opera Choir.
The Delphic Oracle at the switchboard
whispers into the phone:
Hello? Yes, this is the Hotel Oblivion.

Nietzsche, in a busboy's uniform,
runs to hide behind a rubber plant

as the whole Court appears on the terrace.
Sleeping Beauty takes off her Bonnie Parker mask
and shouts to the soldiers: 'Behind that rubber plant!'
A volley of rifle shots rings out in the Hotel Oblivion.

Catherine the Great and Rudolph Valentino
ask the orchestra to play an Argentinian tango.
The women walk up a staircase covered with grass.
The elevator door stands open, Nietzsche is weeping quietly.
Candles burn in the chandeliers,
and on the silver screen Marilyn Monroe smiles:
'Yes, you can always have room here, come to the Hotel Oblivion.'

The women open the door to the room.
Attila sits on the bed reading 'Paradise Lost' out loud.
The women withdraw. Now Attila notices them:
Don't worry, he says, all rooms are the wrong ones
in the Hotel Oblivion.

The circus has pitched a tent in the sixth floor lobby.
Cyrano Bergerac climbs a ladder,
invites the women to the performance.
The trapezes have stopped swinging,
it's almost time for the fireworks in the Hotel Oblivion.

Now it's the morning after the beauty contest,
the Queen has been left alone with her mantle.
In the lobby, policemen are filling a grave,
the jukebox is vomiting coins.
Valentino has fallen asleep on the orchestra dais,
the TV sets have closed their eyes.
In the street, the Buick has been turned on its side,
and the wind is driving the reflection of flames
toward the Hotel Oblivion.

1970

OH MR. Q., DEATH WITH A THOUSAND FACES!

Take off your mask
and the sun like ice
burns our city.

We are all of us angels,
we are blind and see Birth.

Pigs have risen to power
and we are the children of the black snow.

Pigs have risen to power
and we are the wasteland and the throng.

The blazing Alphabet!
Out of the middle of the street
rises a café
and in a corner of it
groans a pinball machine
carved out of flesh.
How the fingers dance!
How the eyeballs flash!
The jukebox cries out like a song
and the floor is autumn, a dark cloud.

Pigs have risen to power
and we are a door without hinges.

Pigs have risen to power and we are
the abundance of flowers in hospitals.

We are a chasm above a chasm,
accelerating all the way down, a roar.

1970

Life, when you taste it,
        is handsome and fateful,
a tall dark stranger who at a corner table
                sips whisky, perhaps a woman
        in gossamer finery, nipples like living ice.
Life, romantic even as a word,
        when you taste it, Robin Hood, oak tree,
        somber unfettered like a great river,
glass flames before death.

Life, whiter than linen. But also dark, and dangerous.
When you taste it.
        A chunk of granite with veins,
                dark meat and herbs.
Life, when you are alive. Cautiously, sharing it out.
When you taste it. It is a brimming water.

1973

PICTURE POSTCARD

It was Titian who painted the woman
who reclines on the divan, her hand
over her privates. That hand is bluish
as if the woman were cold,
and that picture is a postcard.
Every autumn I remember that woman
when the wind drags leaves down the street,
the trees stripped, the palms of the leaves
soon earth. That woman, certainly
earth for centuries, trees grow out of her
or if she became a battleground
saw barren mankind, lovers
of art, artists, skewering each other.
Like a pig at a feast, mother earth
devoured its children. And that woman

was a model. And earth. Twice
silent, and cold. The rain fell to earth
the way it does today. Who can tell
if the rain consoles
or wipes things out. Or if those actions
are one and the same. Oblivion.

1973

I know the scent of cold stones,
the soil is frozen, the sun has no color.

On the whole journey I haven't met anyone,
dried leaves rustle underfoot,
that is the only sound, an incessant rustle.
At such a moment no one should be allowed to die,
the meaninglessness of everything is so clear,
there is nothing to build one's life on,
nothing but existence.

The dark sheen of water, the windowpane
on which a moth stops for a moment,

yearning has entered the blood, won't disappear,
even the room is tired of waking.

1984

Jyrki Pellinen

I think I'm mature in my mind. So
calm, so quiet, and I don't let the din into my ears.
I'm on both sides of all this, I mean
one thing alone and my mind is of the same mind.

1962

Close to myself I know once more I'm a pine growing
for ever. Close to myself I know once more I'm a sky growing
for ever. I hear music, playing
from simple instruments not difficult to understand.
Yesterday I celebrated my birthday, yesterday I thought
how long and difficult the road is backwards.
Let flowers flower, let days come, let lights go out.

1962

The depiction of life is not sweet
only blue rooms with one mistress in the cupboard
a blue shining room with secreted memories in
and then at the very last one must go back again to daylight: it means those songs must be sung again
and there's nothing else

but I that now am this and that
can speak a sheer lie, it is

nine months south, it's a place
like a blue cinnabar: and the sea's yachts-
men are worthy of praise, let times fly up
let songs be raised up, I mean
but then remember how this
would be mirrored by the woman in the cupboard
my cyclorama is not my conception
wise eyelashes from the sky: they flutter down
from above everything and such shadows
always come to the earth
as are seen against the cyclorama everywhere
in all the literature of the world

Light is a light substance you can't gather it
into one basket and, if you could, the
rooms would have to be blue, the lovers would have to be
sorrowful, some like best to walk by river
banks and others play with French
pistols, but the archives have to be able to be everywhere
in castle-dust (the children sit aside, perhaps in trees,
but if needed there are no children, there's a sublime sorrow,
the reason we beat time) and Musset, Musset the king
of poets, whom we serve, this is no world
here no goodbyes are said even in a blue room
when friends arrive and the loved one is in the cupboard
alone the winds alone the remains of them I
claim the world is actually a wrong one
this time the king of poets is Corneille!
fires eyes I love the poets of all
times, so that they'd have their names taken away so that
there'd be a castle like a full stop: there's a big house
that looks into the water that lurches inside a book
a book read, this is a May through all the aeons
and not a single detail has been told
of the most challenging deed of valour

1964

TREE

A tree grew in a bar. It was an oak from altogether elsewhere. The people gathered casually round to look at it: no one laughed at it. They were all creatures of habit and wouldn't have been surprised even if the tree hadn't grown there. It pushed all the dishes as it moved, the animals didn't understand their joy. The joyful animals. And the tree turned into a road, so that all this had to be wiped out. The dishes survived all right. The people survived all right. A man walked across the yard. The man looked doggish, but there was nothing doggy at the other end. What next: the parlour ceiling collapsed into the field and the children died. The event was an event and aroused great sadness, but not sorrow. Since this tree could apparently do anything whatever, it settled down there and died. That's the way everything at the roadside and in the bar dies. Since the boy had heard this – that his father had indeed preceded him – or so they pretended. Thus boredom led to everything accidentally coming to a halt in order of seniority. The fact is, the boy didn't get his wish. The tree alone grew, and grew wrong, as it grew from the roof down to the earth. He left the road – thought the ones who all think alike – they too saw the tree behind the road. Now it so happened that once there was a tree that didn't sidestep anything. It grew all over the place under the bridges, became a beam, then a railing everywhere. This tree was a proper tree, it kept order of seniority, but didn't care where it went, it was everywhere, so contrary to what anyone thought it also grew into God, and then it turned green and flowered when it grew old, it was the same tree, it had seen life as it had desired, but now it had failed and it didn't forget that, later it came out of the north country where it settled in the middle of the road, because there wasn't a single bird there.

1965

spring days in the harbour or somewhere else
spring days I think of the brooks
fabulous sunshine that falls on empty

buses that go like great mobile parlours
to deserted suburbs when clouds
shift dimly somewhere in the sky

It's as if the nights were quarrelling with each other
                                        about the point
where the forest heaves more darkly.

1970

I was a quiet child
in the way a cherry
has a stone inside

1983

I almost wrote close up to myself away from here
I flew as far as Italy to rage new words
into phrases that did not exist and I fell
into a room that wasn't there but deeper
underneath these others; loneliness was like a carving

I saw myself happening wrongly and the paper
straightened out like a bullet I breathed edges and I began
to make portraits from memory I lived a question that
others ruminated about on the phone I was later and later
until the century separated me from those present

and they no longer trusted my luck, and anger
and friendship joined hands here like a galvanised expectation
who presses a button that makes the market square ring
why do you become victims and a bathtub is thrown
into the street I breathed my great matters in a small voice
I skated inwards and thus I grew in the North Country
in a land free of slavery in the cradle of ghosts

this place remained it was hot when I walked
round it thoughts grew plants my diaphragm ran out of
oxygen and the voices and the men stood behind the door and
a child wept to continue its own war a child's mindless weeping
as if it'd lead the Bourbons I was in the Finland of the North
and humour is far from those lands always when I came to this
place the words rose into the air and my arrows broke
I was thrown in a cellar as a dwarf Oh Kasper the great
voice like an animal's

1987

Martti Joenpolvi

THE GUEST OF HONOUR

'All the historically influential ideological trends of our time may be characterised as egalitarian in tendency,' said the Principal, now a quarter of an hour into his speech.

A little earlier, at this gathering to celebrate half a century of the college's activity, he had given a short résumé of earlier phases in its institutional life.

'The ancient world lived in what may be called an officially inegalitarian climate, nor did the medieval world envisage a larger share of equality than that before a theoretically egalitarian God. But we' – the Principal's hand sought the edge of the lectern, purposefully squeezing the hardwood – 'we, the people of the modern age, think otherwise. We hold in principle that human beings are equals.'

The platform curtain rippled as if someone were moving behind it. The Finnish flag hung limply and somehow wearily on its worn wooden pole, the brass socket casting a radiant nosegay of sunrays onto the wall. The red tulips on the lectern had opened: one of the petals fell, and the Principal picked it aside from his text.

'The so-called bourgeois social philosophy already takes, as its starting point, the notion of equality. But to a still greater degree the socialist world-view is an egalitarian doctrine, for the labour movement desires to remove the inequitable factors deriving from private ownership.'

Klaus Hermelä, one of the labour movement's very own men, an alumnus of the college and today's guest of honour, a well-known party politician and municipal chief executive, felt a slight nausea as he looked askance out of the Main Hall's window. The pines were so sharply defined against the clear Easter-Day sky that he could almost make out the individual needles.

'Many imagine,' the Principal went on, 'that the egalitarian factor is sufficient, and that the labour movement is sufficiently idealistic if it takes its stand simply on the principles of personal and social equality and their political requirements. This however cannot be the case.'

Klaus Hermelä could see his chauffeur, who was smoking beside the official black car. The driver amassed a pile of slush with his foot and shaped it with his boot-toe. Finally he scattered the pile with a sudden kick, spattering the side of the car with wet snow. Nieminen's getting restless and impatient, Hermelä reflected. Talks with annoying familiarity on official trips.

'Behind the political and social demands lie deeper principles acknowledged in western culture,' the Principal continued. 'In the last analysis it is precisely these that create the spirit of the labour movement. Without the *notion of humanity*' – the Principal emphasised these words – 'the labour movement is little more than social aspiration relying on civic privilege.'

True enough, thought Hermelä. He noticed a response in himself, for the first time, to the Principal's speech. Of course, Rantamaa's still quite idealistic considering his age.

Hermelä heard a movement behind him in the student-packed hall, a dry creaking of the varnished wooden chairs. Why don't we tell them straight out, these socialist youths, that in our market-economy days the labour movement gets very little support from the notion of humanity?

Rantamaa continued his speech. 'Today, we have reason to ask: have the men and women of the labour movement succeeded in turning the principles of humanity into a practical reality? Have we always respected humanity both in ourselves and in others? Have notions of human love been realised in practice?'

Klaus Hermelä looked along the front row: men and women of the labour movement, distinguished members of the college's Patrons Association, the teaching staff, long-serving lecturers.

Crossed legs, splayed knees, hands crossed in laps, arms folded, fingers fidgeting. All this was so familiar to Hermelä that recently it had begun to seem somehow unreal, unnatural. If for instance someone smiled or laughed without Hermelä seeing why, it might start him pondering on the vast amount of needless laughter in the world, or the tears – all the various reflex actions of the human face. Somewhat uneasily, he noticed how the phenomena of human life seemed to be drifting loose from their moorings, turning at the same time into incomprehensible, irrational occurrences.

The Principal had switched to the labour movement's internal disharmony; he was studying the question from the humanitarian viewpoint. With a practised ear, Hermelä noticed a growing tension in the Hall. He knew that here and there among the invited guests facial expressions were tightening. The Principal too was aware he'd taken his speech into a more sensitive but, in his view, unavoidable area. For his part, Klaus Hermelä was not worried. The Principal was confining himself sufficiently to generalities: Rantamaa wouldn't specify Hermelä's line, any more than other internal party trends. No one would walk out of the hall. Hermelä was not bothered. He even hoped he'd be observed: so relaxed, so politically trained he knew his expression to be. It hadn't shown a quiver even when the major issues were at stake. Nevertheless, he fingered the outside of his coat pocket. Yes, the box of heart pills was there. His fingertips felt the pillbox's shape: it was the shape of life. He heard a whisper behind him from the socialist youth: 'Christ, tough words.' Hermelä was amused; he relaxed.

A demanding spring, this. These days, amusement amounted to renewed awareness of his fundamental weariness. During the winter he'd begun to be ashamed of his deteriorating physique and his altered features, which were giving the officials cause for talk: 'You'd hardly credit a man could go downhill so fast.' Hermelä knew what it meant to call a person a psychophysical entity. He knew the feeling, when you no longer enjoy the self-confidence emanating from a strong body and a large frame. And sometimes he was bothered by the absurd thought that during the past decades it was the weight of his frame that had broken the ranks of the opposition. It struck him, too, that the chairman's gavel carried a bit of weight as well.

Klaus Hermelä, the guest of honour, saw his driver standing at the foot of a pine, straddled, looking up at the top. Nieminen, ordinary name, ordinary man. Seen a squirrel, perhaps: there are some here – were in the twenties too. Hermelä noticed he was longing for the soft back seat of his large official car and the journey home. It'd still be light: he'd watch the snow of the fields diminishing, see the human dwellings where his name was known. They'd traverse the neighbourhoods where he'd spoken about the possibilities of a better life, the division of the national income, a juster society. Gradually the landscapes would become more familiar: he'd see the outer reaches of his life's work for the city – those remotest from the city centre: once they were in the outskirts of the town, these concrete achievements would increase in scale, visible for miles. He'd recall the past struggles, bits of city-council meetings: Hermelä giving speeches, a large, strong man. Lights would go on in the windows of the working-class quarters on the outskirts of the town.

The guest of honour listened to the end of the Principal's speech while staring at the bronze bust of the college's founder. Hermelä remembered sitting for his portrait himself: the conversations with the artist, and, later, saunas at the artist's summer villa. But *did* something of him finally remain fixed in bronze, to be placed in the college hall?

2

The still-hard rough frozen snow of the morning had softened into a watery slush as the celebrants took their way to the college founder's grave.

The long file of the student body advanced with devout slowness in the rear of the vanguard formed by the guest of honour, the other invited guests, and the regular teaching staff. One of the youngest part-time teachers was carrying a wreath over the crook of his arm. It had red carnations in it, and two ribbons, a red one and a white one. The leading group stopped in front of the perpendicular flank of a large rock, from which the snow had been carefully spaded to one side. In a chamber cut into the stone, behind a relief riveted to the rock, rested the ashes of the college's founder.

The guard of honour took up its station. The student body gathered behind the leading group. Hermelä heard a wet scraping in the mess of slush: looking over, he saw a group that was having difficulty squeezing into the somewhat cramped space. All had come straight from the Main Hall, wearing overcoats, and hatless. Their faces looked pale and shivery in the wintery light. From where he was standing Hermelä saw the college's old wing. It looked long and complicated like the labour movement's struggle.

The Chancellor of the college, a veteran manager of a co-operative retail society, stepped forward, walked to the front of the burial chamber, took up a position among the guard of honour and began his speech. 'Humanity and society,' he pronounced. It seemed to Hermelä like two similar-sized and shaped objects being placed side by side on a table. 'These words are immortalised on the memorial plaque of the man whose resting place we stand by in gratitude.' Dampness was oozing through Hermelä's shoesoles – his galoshes had been forgotten in the car.

Some snow fell from the rock, flopping behind the speaker. It caused a stir in the crowd, as they looked to see if any more snow was coming. But when no more did fall, the heads sank back again into their respectfully bowed posture. That allowed them to see that the speaker's feet were buried in snow. However, he did not move from his position. Back in the car I'll be able to take my shoes off, Hermelä reflected.

The speaker reminded them of the college's thousands of alumni, many of whom had borne the heat of the day in the service of the party and society. Hermelä was aware of respectful glances being cast his way. 'Equality doesn't exist,' he reflected: 'the inequality's not in me, it's in the looks of these socialist youths, whose very youth allows them to display their naked sincerity.' He was also in no doubt about how these respectful looks of today could conceivably change in a few years. Hermelä knew the process. On committees, in delegations, in various governing bodies, as well as in the government of the country during his ministerial years, he had seen people's natural expressions distorted by envy, hatred, grudge, prejudice and ungoverned careerism. Hermelä knew the look of a pressure group's feelings and claims finding expression on one human face. At the graveside there was room for humility, a relaxed face, good words. Objects of homage are out of the game.

The Chancellor finished his speech. He was already an old man, somewhat moved as he left the burial chamber. Many of the youngest were moved by the old man's emotion, and they gulped seeing his trouser-legs wet with the snow from the rock. A delegation of several went to pose the wreath. The bronze-relief profile looked sternly to one side.

Hermelä had a dizzy spell; it was over as soon as it came, but he nevertheless began to plant his feet as firmly as he could, and he took a look at the person nearest to him. Then they sang 'Struggling On'.

It brought back the past New Year's Eve to Hermelä. After the final stroke of twelve, he had stepped out onto the brightly floodlit balcony of the Town Hall, standing blinded in front of the microphones. Gradually he began to make out the mass of people gathered below in the square, expectant in the winter night. Something irrelevant, going back to his childhood, thrust its way into Hermelä's mind: sticks of red, blue, green and yellow. The image was so powerful that it summoned a sensation of smell: the smell of plasticine, for him, had always signified the smell of innumerable possibilities. On that New Year's Eve, quite likely, a lot of people were getting round to asking, Isn't Klaus Hermelä going to begin his speech? For a while he hadn't been up to it. A certain thought had to be thought through first. In those moments he got an insight into what it was like to be Hitler, Mussolini, Stalin, all the major shapers of history. The awareness faded, but later Hermelä realised that, during those wintery New Year's Eve moments, after midnight had struck, something in him had finally broken. He'd resisted it so long, he'd resisted it so many times, as he stood before the masses; but now, floodlit on the Town Hall balcony, he felt as if the mob spirit had got loose from the crowd and was standing next to him, looking scornfully at the text of the speech he was holding in his trembling hand. Indoors, he could collect his thoughts by concentrating on some detail of the back wall, say. That New Year's Eve offered him nothing for the purpose but the stars, burning with their cold fire in the black nightsky.

'. . . A new world we are building,
So lift up high your heads!. . .'

The occasion was over. The students began to disperse. The celebrants left the grave in reverse order.

3

Lunch was served in the college dining room, its shape and furnishings familiar to Hermelä from forty years back. Life seemed a short thing measured against some panelled supporting pillar, preserved almost intact for forty years, apart from a slight darkening of the varnish.

At the staff table situated in front of the great bright window, the conversation was centred on the country's economic problems. Hermelä was eating pickled herring salad and potatoes; he drank a lot of the excellent buttermilk, but he didn't participate in the talk about economics. From his post at the head of the table the Principal looked at Hermelä while he spoke, as if dedicating his opinion to him or encouraging him to join in. Only when the talk turned to the left's aspirations for coalition – this was during the plum pudding and cream – did Hermelä say a word. People stopped to listen; quite clearly the guest of honour was expected to say more, but Hermelä finished off the last of his plum pudding in silence. The conversation at the table didn't get going again, and pretty soon they rose from the table. The students, who were providing the table-service, towel on arm, began collecting up the dishes. At one of the tables, an earnest bunch of the rank-and-file were still going on with their discussion after the others had left. A politically motivated youth moved over to their table to listen in on the talk of the campaigners.

The smoking room filled up with students. Hermelä withdrew into the coatracks lining the smoking-room wall: he'd said his goodbyes to the Principal, and he was ready for off. He could see the new library building through the window, and a recently extended hall of residence. Hermelä estimated the costs, and the Patrons' Association's resources.

The overloaded coat-racks gave a feeling of human closeness. Hermelä gave the overcoats a close look: they seemed unanimous, but not particularly socialist. Fine that way, he thought. These racks have seen other kinds of coats as well – and times when there weren't anywhere near enough coats to fill the hooks. Hermelä went over the Thirties in his mind, the goings-on of the Forties, the years of danger, and the political events of the Fifties. Capitalism has changed since those days: it's by no means a straightforward affair any more, a physical obstacle. From the angle of the labour movement, the opposition has dispersed into the terrain, into the Finnish community; and clothes are no longer a give-away, a clear-cut red or white.

Hermelä's ears picked up from the smoking room a ringing, almost blustering voice: 'That's how he is, by nature. Never has much to say. His policy is: even the medium projects have been so carefully researched that all the council can do is rubber-stamp them. That's tactics. The old fox. If he's not confident some job'll go through, he drops it just like that. Takes it up again when the power-relations are right.'

Before he left, Hermelä dropped into the empty Main Hall and closed the door behind him. The chairs ticked among themselves with little outbursts of tension after their recent burdens. Hermelä stood in the middle of the simple hall, and he felt as if he were bidding goodbye to a quiet, modest man of the people.

The chauffeur, who had been stuffing himself in the kitchen, was asleep at the wheel when Hermelä came out. Drowsily, the driver tried to get out of the car and open the door for his passenger, but he was only in time to close it.

'Take a look at that bit of woodwork,' Hermelä said.

The driver turned the way Hermelä was pointing. He saw two naked human figures, the larger resting his hand on the smaller's shoulder.

'Mmmm,' said the driver: 'Sort of like father and son.'

'It is father and son,' said Hermelä.

'What, no Holy Ghost?'

'No, no Holy Ghost,' Hermelä said. 'Wasn't very fashionable in those days.'

Hermelä took off his shoes as planned at the grave. 'One morning, as we turned up for a lecture, we noticed someone had slung an old tyre round the father-figure's neck during the night,' Hermelä said.

'This was, oh, in the early Twenties.'

The story tickled the chauffeur.

'They'd tied a red ribbon on the tyre,' Hermelä went on. 'It was the local middle-class kids' way of demonstrating their respect for the working-class students.'

The driver started the car. 'Concrete politics, it was,' Hermelä said. The car moved off, drove through the gate. Incredible, Hermelä thought – the rage the motor-tyre wreath and its red ribbon had stirred up, even in himself: today that old prank struck him as the best trick the bourgeoisie had played on him in all his long political career.

The chauffeur snorted with laughter. 'Well, blow that for a lark. A motor tyre, eh. Did you feel a bit punctured?'

Hermelä purred; at his best Nieminen was quite perceptive, though a bit slow, yes. And slowness is not a virtue in a driver.

As the distance from the college grew, Hermelä felt himself being spiritually distanced from it too: by the time they got to Hyvinkää, current everyday affairs were seeping into the car. Hermelä began to concentrate on the details of his plot to get an observatory built. The communists'll have to be won over. Why will the thing be necessary? Well, it'll create employment. And how many will it employ? That'll have to be investigated. And besides: the observatory idea has been the sort of natural province of the bourgeoisie for long enough. The proper communists'll swallow it. It's time to get the proletariat mixed up in the marvels of astronomy. He can point to the Soviet Union's great achievements in space research.

This observatory project'll go through, he decided, if it's the last thing I, as municipal chief executive, push through by sheer willpower.

This, regardless of his immediate responsibilities, would make them recognise his farsightedness. From the projected observatory they – the future councillors, secretaries, high-level civil servants, bourgeoisie and labour-movement characters – would observe Klaus Hermelä, by that time delayed for ever on the longest official journey of his life.

1969

Alpo Ruuth

FURY

Koskinen felt good. He undid his tie and breathed in the air of a summer evening. The evening tasted of lindens.

Koskinen walked into the park, past the red flowerbeds, to the sports field where girls in yellow sweatshirts were finishing their *pesäpallo* game. The ball rolled under his feet. He threw it to a girl who thanked him with a smile and started running to the field house. Koskinen stopped to light a cigarette. Above the linden trees, a steady line of smoke moved along, a train on its way somewhere. A black cloud hovered for a moment above the trees, thinned out, finally dispersed in the air.

A man came staggering across the field. The hems of his tattered suit jacket flapped in the wind as he stood watching the girls emerging from the field house. The man walked behing the group of girls, then stopped as he saw Koskinen. They were roughly the same age and size. In the dark, Koskinen's wife could have mistaken the man for her husband.

'Good evening!'

'Evening,' replied Koskinen.

'You got a cig to spare?'

'No, I don't,' Koskinen said calmly.

'Why not?'

'I don't smoke.'

The man glanced at the cigarette dangling from Koskinen's lips. Then he swung. Koskinen didn't have time to duck properly, and the blow landed on his right cheek. Koskinen punched back. The man got a grip on Koskinen's arm and they fell down on the sand, holding on to each other. Koskinen managed to get on top and was able to hold the man still for a moment in order to pound him. The blow made a crunching sound on the man's face. The man kicked Koskinen off. They rolled around for a while. The man managed to punch Koskinen's forehead, twice. Then he tried to crawl off on his hands and knees. Koskinen got entangled in his own feet. The man turned onto his back and kicked, the heel of his shoe struck Koskinen in the chin. Koskinen spat his front teeth into the sand. Once again, the man tried to get away.

Koskinen got hold of the man's foot, and he crashed on his face. For a moment, they stopped to stare at each other. Koskinen spat out a bloody gobbet and attacked, pinning the man down. Koskinen pushed his knee into the man's groin and stabbed him in the eyes with his fingers. The man cried out in pain and raked the sand with his hands. Koskinen felt something smash into his head, lost his grip. Koskinen's head felt hot. On his knees, Koskinen staggered about looking for the man. Another blow struck the back of his head. Koskinen fell forward and saw the man. The man was on his knees, waving a broken brick. Koskinen tried to crawl away, the man followed and stopped him just as he was about to reach the lawn.

The new blow glanced off his neck. Koskinen turned onto his side and wiped his eyes in order to see the man through the blood. Koskinen started crawling about aimlessly on the sand, then saw, two meters in front of him, the other half of the brick. The man saw it, too, and reached Koskinen just as the latter was about to get hold of the brick that might be his salvation. The man jumped Koskinen, smashed the brick down on Koskinen's forehead. Things went dark and Koskinen struck out blindly. The man's blood poured down on Koskinen. Koskinen struck again and felt the man's weight rise off him. The man rolled onto his side. Koskinen no longer had the strength to pursue him, he flopped onto his back and saw the distant fountain. Through the veil of blood it looked red.

Painfully, Koskinen rolled over onto his stomach and started to crawl towards the man, dragging his brick along. The man revived and crawled to meet Koskinen. Both of them on their knees, they met. Both had trouble raising their hands to strike. Koskinen's brick ripped the man's forehead. After concentrating for a moment, the man managed to strike Koskinen on his right ear. They retired a short distance for a break, then approached each other again.

A police car appeared on their field of combat. Two policemen got out and separated them, dragging first the man and then Koskinen into the car. Koskinen resigned, let himself be carried to the car, but when he saw the man, he reached out for the man's bloody neck. The man had enough time to punch Koskinen in the left eye. One of the policemen sat down between Koskinen's knees.

The car swung to a stop in front of a hospital. As soon as the man was taken out of the car, Koskinen attacked him. Then Koskinen's legs gave way, he fell to his knees, shook his head, fell on his face. The man, held by the policemen, tried to kick Koskinen. A doctor and a nurse appeared and helped carry them inside.

They were put in the same room. Koskinen tried to attack the man, who was lying on a bed, struggling with the policemen. Koskinen was thrown on another bed and strapped down. The man laughed at Koskinen until he, too, was strapped down. One of the policemen sat down on the edge of Koskinen's bed. The doctor started to clean Koskinen's head wounds.

'Looks pretty bad.'

'Your name?' the policeman asked.

'Koskinen, Albin. Thirty-five.'

'Married?'

'Yes. Two children, a girl and a boy.'

'Occupation?'

'Engineer.'

'Now tell me what happened.'

'There's nothing to tell. This ain't over yet.'

'Damn straight, it isn't,' shouted the man on the other bed.

'Shut up, both of you,' said the policeman. 'How can we notify your family?'

'You can't. You see, I'm a grass widower. There's no phone at my in-laws' place.'

'One of these days, I'll kill you,' the man shouted.

'Fine by me! Never mind when or where, we'll finish this off!'

Koskinen yelled, struggling with his restraining straps.

'Take that man to another room,' the policeman said.

The nurse pushed the man and his bed into the hall. The man raised his bloodied head from the pillow and shouted:

'Wherever! Whenever!'

Koskinen nodded and closed his eyes, the room was turning, it seemed that he and his bed had started floating upward, and the policeman didn't stay put either but split into two policemen, losing his outline in the process, so that all that remained was the row of buttons on his uniform jacket.

'He's out cold,' the policeman said to the nurse, and put the notebook back in his pocket.

1968

Lassi Nummi

RECITATIVE

So rise: pen, word, voice
        with studied steps
        in noon glare,
inscribe a sign on air: celebration.
Inscribe spring-streams, sun, clouds, seagull cries,
        a rising wing,
inscribe a white hall and white columns, a cembalo's chords
        between the columns,
inscribe our listening selves, celebrating: forty years.
    'In the desert?' Perhaps. Or in fertile gardens.
Desert and garden, they're in ourselves,
and the cloud-statues and the revelations, in ourselves.
    'A somewhat commonplace truth – out of fashion.'
        I only wanted to say,
we're celebrating –

No, that's not what had to be said.

Forty years: a bridge, with supporting vaults.
But a day is more than forty years, a moment is,
and a bridge wakens to life
as someone steps across it.
        We say so many

pointless things. Pointless words, with no lightness in them –
 no weight.

A footstep weighs – in the desert –
 a footstep is a light dance-break
and music, cembalo chords dart through empty halls –

But that's not what had to be said.

The word must be light, the word must weigh –
 an elated lightness and weight!
No, all I wanted to say was how
 there's a child somewhere:
someone desired to fly, to rise sunward – once,
 a thousand times.
Someone built a house, planted a tree, built a bridge and a wall.
And earth was an element, untouched.

 Now tunnels of shining beetles pierce the earth,
cities spread their steel wings wider and wider,
 mirrored in the fast stream.
Flown up on their wings
they hit strange whirlwinds, higher and higher,
everything hastening faster and faster,
anxiously seeking life's images in water
but the stream is too fast

 What I wanted to say was: this brilliant century –
 cursed and bloody like all the centuries,
with young forces against giving-in
 and the thought of destruction. . .
All I wanted to say was: this moment of celebration is valid,
 the marble and the laurels, valid.
 But space has exploded:
we're off with immeasurable speed every moment away.
All I wanted to say was, the world is enjoyed elsewhere,
 is paid for elsewhere.
All I wanted to say –

  – and lightning flashes, columns rise,
    music returns shockingly altered
booming like silence
bursting its sides
with silent cries
of joy and rage and pain.
Maybe we're merely the Deity's finger-exercises,
a magician's diagram inscribed on air,
a clay maquette to be cast away.
Merely a discord, fumbling fingers.
    Maybe we are –

  – a dust rising in wind, the world's dim eye,
we, the insignificant that everything happens in.
We, winged caterpillars, a tribe
mined into life's sweetness
or hurled into open wind –
we know: in vain,
we know: in spite, and just because.
Air-currents waft us.
High in the strange currents
we're a violently working wing
towards the sun or the night.
And we know: the birds are greater than the wind.
We know: each moment is a solution, and a choice,
a detonation exploding us close to space or deep in ourselves

darkness, a cloud-statue, a flaming face

  and yet again either/or,
  a whirlwind, a wing: we
shall not stay where we are, either we rise or sink

we rise

1980

AS A SHIP GLIDING

As a ship gliding over open water in the archipelago
approaches a forested shore – and sinks into it –
into a narrow channel that opens astonishingly
between the trees, curves past the headland tip
and continually opens a new view that captivates the eyes
or astonishes, leaving you meditating or scared –
        and in the broadening after the channel
careens, firm-keeled, to more open waters,
to the mounting blasts and the flashing storm
which, as its last rage subsides, leaves behind
        a strange sweet light –
and in the continual brawl of the heavy swells
the ship skirts its curving sides along the shore again,
        steep rock through which, again unexpectedly,
            a gleaming way opens –
and it slants through gorges, past foaming rocks,
        through lock gates, under sinewy steel bridges
in the day-brightness and the night-dark,
        on the serene mirroring-surface,
            in the rain-grey, the translucent mist,
in the scent of resin and bark, in the far-carrying
        smell of forest-fire,
keel and waves whispering soporifically, monotonously,
        one to the other from hour to hour,
the bright waters and the black waters night after night,
            day after day,
persistently looking their companion straight in the eye,
        the passive traveller leant on the rail

– just so those years of life have passed, so
        crowded with happenings, meetings, and doings
that nothing now can come to mind but
    a haze of pictures, faces, shadows, and low lights
intermelting, faster and faster, or merging with background

– the ripples, the shivers
on the water's settling surface.

1980

BALLAD OF A HEAT-WAVE MORNING

The room is charged with light. I know without opening my eyes.
That's the way now as long as I remember, forwards or backwards.

Suddenly my eyes are open. I don't remember opening them,
I haven't, as usual,
fumbled the visual field for the face of the clock:
seven? nine? time to get up? time to go back to sleep?

A tone on the skin, the feeling of sunny light, a light stab
in the lungs, and in the conscience,
and luxurious languor of limbs after long sleep –
proving: it's going on,
still here, this endless abnormal summer heatwave.

I turn with care. On the ceiling
light-graphs of childhood.
In fact, childhood, with its torments, pains, terrors,
it too is a luxury. Though one didn't know it then.
Like the heat, the light, the languor. Like love.
Like all life, just visible
in dreams of stone.

I take a further turn, till
I'm completely resting on my left side.
It's good for breathing. The right lung can now have its go
with the oxygen, though a light pressure weighs on the heart.

Breathing like a child, and back towards me,
in her robe that goes regally with the lighting,

lies the endless origin and end of all my tenderness,
who has been and is, I can't help it,
however the years go by.

Never have I said she was my only love. But in this love
there's something stubborn. As a heatwave can,
it continues and continues, overpassing
all meteorological norms and all predictions.

She's real as a cloud. She's an image.
A cloud is unseeable when it surrounds you. You can breathe it.
Far off it can be seen: an image
and through the image a series of images,
insignificant rainshowers, an endless summer.

And behind the image, further back, in the double glazing –
a reflection, a second image: world confronts
world, unrealised counterpoint, a moon. Punctus
contra punctum,
endless fugue, endless legato! And long ago
I overshot the limits of good taste,
used up the colours and attributes, the honey and the gold.

So doesn't she change? Naturally. Everything changes, streams
from the eyes and the hands
at a dizzying speed. But some dimensions, some tones
persist insistently. Through all the changes some
basic colour, touch, basic disturbance remains the same.

And the heat continues. So it's heat we're speaking of:
we focus on an interesting meteorological phenomenon
with possible occult social dimensions:
fields may parch, the harvest spoil, perhaps
a travel bureau will go bankrupt, the sick-list may take a leap:
the heart's a delicate instrument,

delicate. . . And heat is hard on it. But warmth.

And if the warmth lasts weeks, or years. . .

She rests and breathes, so innocently. The day before yesterday
was childhood, and yesterday youth;
and now we know so well that life, our real life,
is short

but a heatwave – when once it comes – is not,
is not real or short, it continues and continues
beyond the limits of all life, infinite as an eyeblink
or the thirst for nearness, or the moment of violence
when metal goes through the person, thrust by no one, or
the world's blind will.

1989

a shallow ditch, bedded with
dark-grey aspen leaves

and through the surface-shimmer
a whole great birch tree, all its twigs branches
is pursuing
from deep down
a flying cloud

1989

Antti Tuuri

MELANCHOLY TALE

Miettinen came as soon as he could get away from the fair. It gave me time enough to wonder how long it'd take for him to get from there to here: would he hire a taxi and now be stuck in the snarl-ups, or take the underground, and get stuck there, but then get through after all?

He rang my hotel-room doorbell in a way that said don't keep me hanging about outside the door. When I opened, Miettinen stalked in, circled the room, looked under the bed, and examined the table's lower newspaper-shelf. After a turn round the room poking into everywhere, he whipped his jacket off, threw it across the bed and took a stance right under my nose; he was small enough to have to rise on his toes to make his face level with mine.

'Decided, have you, to take to the bottle regardless?' he said.

'Haven't touched a drop,' I said.

He didn't believe me, and tried to sniff my breath. I moved aside and passed the door to the other side of the room, taking a seat in an armchair by the window. Miettinen didn't sit down even though I invited him.

'So, what the hell's up with you?' he asked.

'Beats me,' I said.

Customers, Miettinen said, had been round asking for me: ones I'd fixed meetings with myself – consultations, lunches and evening get-togethers. They'd been wondering why I hadn't turned up at the stand at the agreed time. He'd told everybody I'd been held up for a day in Finland due to urgent business, but I'd be in on the evening plane. He'd already set up an evening meal with the Italians who'd been taking our stuff for ten years. I said I'd not be coming. Miettinen couldn't credit it.

'Believe me, I'm not coming,' I said.

'Listen: you've got to,' Miettinen said.

I asked him to let me be, and he left, assuring me he'd be round at seven to pick me up; he told me the sales secretary had booked us a table in a restaurant on the left bank. When he'd gone, I sat in the armchair and looked at the pictures hanging on the wall: printed reproductions. The originals were, I knew, in the museum at the end of the Tuileries Gardens, the Jeu de Paume. I used to go there and look at them sometimes, when I was young. I used to dawdle round both levels, spending quite a bit of time there, and as I looked at the reproductions I remembered them all: Monet's flowery meadows, those robust nude girls of Renoir, Dégas's horse races and ballet girls.

I rose and took a look out. From my window I looked down into an inner courtyard with a few horse-chestnuts growing; in the middle there was an illuminated telephone kiosk, with someone in it from the kitchen, wearing a white apron: a dark curly-haired man.

Miettinen turned up at seven. He was wearing a dark suit, with a grey tie and a white shirt. He gave his shoes a polish on the hotel towel in my bathroom and told me to start changing my clothes if I was going to get to the meal in time. I said I wasn't going. Miettinen couldn't bring himself to believe me. He went to the minibar and poured himself a whisky and soda; then he sat in my armchair, and looked me straight in the face, but not quite in the eyes, I noticed.

'Listen – do you think it's easy for me?' he said.

'No, that I don't think, at all,' I said.

'Have you considered that we'll be laying off two hundred people if we don't collect enough orders from this fair?' he asked.

'All the time,' I said.

'Oh no you don't,' he said. I claimed I put in a lot of hard thinking about sales and the factory's output.

'What you're thinking about, listen, are your own little troubles,' he said. He was asking me one more time: was I or was I not going to this meal? And when I said no, he tossed the whisky into his mouth, got onto his feet and set about leaving. He said he wouldn't forget this, no way, and he regarded my hanging about in the hotel as rank disobedience to a boss's order. I said we weren't in the army now.

He didn't like that: he was a former cadet-school trained officer who, on his wife's orders, had relinquished his lieutenancy, transferred to a School of Business Studies and qualified as an economist.

'Listen, you could learn a thing or two from army discipline,' he said.

I promised I'd try. Miettinen left the room, and said he'd be round in the morning at half past eight to take me to the fair. I said it'd he worth a try.

Later in the evening I ordered food from room-service, but when the waiter brought the dish and the wine, I couldn't bring myself to eat it; and I didn't feel like wine either now. I rang and asked the waiter to take it all away. The small room was stinking with the condiments and meat, and the stale, yeasty smell of the opened wine bottle. The waiter asked if I was sick, and when I said no, but not hungry, he told me he'd have to charge me for the whole service nevertheless. He was glad when I didn't resist, took a clean folded bill out of his pocket, and I signed it with my name and room number. I opened the door for him, and he thanked me. He was young man; he spoke English so well you could only infer his foreign accent.

I rang home, but there was no answer.

II

I woke at six with the telephone ringing. It was the desk clerk, telling me it was six o'clock. I thanked him, put the receiver down and went into the bathroom. As I was shaving, the telephone rang again. It was Miettinen, telling me he'd ordered the early morning call for me, to make sure I wouldn't be late for the fair, and was checking I'd been woken by the call. I said I was just shaving and my face was still half-plastered with lather. Miettinen was surprised to hear

I was still stuck with old-fashioned shaving gear like that. The Italians had missed me last evening, he said; and he suggested we should meet up for breakfast at seven in the hotel restaurant. I said I wouldn't be there to meet him.

'And, listen, don't begin that same game again,' he said.

'What game?' I asked.

Miettinen rang off, and I went back into the bathroom.

I dressed and sat down in the armchair by the window. I rang for room-service, and the waiter brought continental breakfast in on a large metal tray: coffee, hot milk, marmalade, butter and croissants. I sat there and ate everything the waiter had brought. I glanced at the clock and worked out it was going on eight o'clock at home: I knew it was no good ringing there just now.

Miettinen came after eight. I was lying on the unmade bed, fully dressed; I got up to open the door for him, and he came in, with a black briefcase in one hand and a raincoat neatly folded over the other arm. I asked if he thought I ought to air my room a little. He made no reply, just gave me a look, and then I bypassed him round the end of the bed and opened the window. He said the hotel staff would of course air the room, make the bed and put clean towels in the bathroom. As for me, all I needed to do was get my hat and coat, and my documents, and come with him to the fair, to do the job of work that, as far as he was aware at least, I was paid to do.

'No need to pay,' I said.

'Tell that to the. . .,' Miettinen said.

I sat down. Miettinen said he wasn't going to waste much time cajoling me, and when I made no reply, he put his raincoat on.

'This is my last word now. I'm not making any unreasonable demands. All I'm asking is for you to get on with your job.'

I couldn't even begin to explain, and he left. Soon, the doorbell rang again, and when I went to open the door, there was Riitta, the exhibition secretary, or, as Miettinen liked to call her, Miettinen's secretary. I asked her to come in. She began questioning me, even before she came in, about what on earth was upsetting me.

'*I* don't know,' I said

'Of course, Miettinen's such a shit, I'm not at all surprised at you,' Riitta said.

'No, that's not it,' I said.

'What is it then?' Riitta asked.

'*I* don't know,' I said.

Had something happened at home? she asked. I said no. Wasn't I intending to come to the fair today either? Many people I knew, she said, had been enquiring about me, and foreign customers – people Riitta knew I liked. I said I'd not be coming to the fair today, probably not all week either.

Riitta left. Later in the morning the waiter and the cleaners came into my room. When the waiter had gone, the cleaners both set to work together, and the cleaning was soon over.

A little before twelve, Miettinen rang. He said he'd arranged a lunch with some customers: it was in the town centre, near the Opera: himself, he could easily get from the fair by metro, and he'd promised that I'd be along too. I said I wasn't able to come just now. Miettinen flew into a rage and began shouting. I put the receiver back. He rang again immediately and asked me to speak to Riitta. Riitta told me the address of the restaurant Miettinen was going to. I said I wasn't hungry: couldn't she see how silly it'd be to go and eat lunch without being hungry, full up in fact?

'This is a working lunch,' Riitta said.

I said it amounted to the same thing. Miettinen took the receiver from Riitta and bawled:

'Listen, you be there at twelve, or it's the boot for you!'

'I can't make it,' I said

'And why not?' Miettinen asked.

'It's a completely personal matter, you see. I simply can't tell you about it,' I said.

'Personal? There's no such thing,' Miettinen shouted.

I said there was certainly still room in the world for personal matters. Even Miettinen might come to realise that. Miettinen said the stand was milling with people, and customers were beginning to turn up as well. I congratulated him: sewing machines could still keep spinning a bit longer in the home country. Miettinen rang off.

At five I tried to order food from room-service, but the waiter said the kitchen was not open yet. Riitta rang at half past six, said she'd heard in the afternoon from Miettinen that I hadn't come to the lunch. I said I hadn't been hungry then, but I was planning to eat now in the hotel, at seven, when the kitchen staff were back at work. Riitta said she was accompanying Miettinen and some Germans to an evening meal on the left bank. Miettinen knew of a superb eating-place there. I said I'd already eaten in all the superb eating-places Miettinen knew, and wished her a pleasant evening. Riitta promised to come and see me before leaving, and she did turn up sometime before eight. I was eating. Riitta, dolled up, in makeup, and wearing evening clothes, snatched an asparagus from the tray, and told me what Miettinen had said about me during the day.

Later that evening I stood and looked out of the window. In the courtyard the same dark curly-haired man as yesterday was speaking, a white kitchen apron tied round his waist. In the windows of the building opposite lights were on, and I was able to see into quite a few rooms; evening meals were being eaten, an old lady came back home, a lonely man was watching television, children went round kissing men and women on the cheek. I rang home, and when my wife replied I told her the fair was going well: orders had been coming in and deals were being clinched. She said she believed everything would still work out for the best, and told me I mustn't lose my faith in that either.

III

In the morning I woke up so late the hotel dining room was no longer serving breakfast, but room service brought me sandwiches and coffee at my order.

Riitta rang from the fair in the middle of the day, and said Miettinen was lunching with customers. In the evening she'd been convinced I'd be fired as soon as we got back to Finland: the firm might be large, and part of a large combine, but a blind eye couldn't be turned to absolutely everything; and an ordinary salesman like me couldn't continually oppose the orders of his immediate superior.

'Give my regards to Miettinen,' I said.

'Right, I will,' Riitta said.

She also told me she'd made for the hotel when Miettinen and the Germans had booked a table in a Pigalle nightclub: she'd got here just after midnight but decided not to wake me so late.

'Were you in your room?' she asked.

'Certainly,' I said.

'I really don't get it,' Riitta said. I said she didn't have to. She would have gone on chatting a long time, but people were coming to the stand, and she had to go and be with them. She complained about not having time enough at lunchtime to get to the corner bar and grab a hot dog, as Miettinen was taking protracted lunches with customers, and I was moping in my hotel room. I said I'd not been moping, she that she had to go.

In the afternoon I watched television cartoons intended for children and nature-programmes where the animals mated, parturated, cared for their offspring and went after food. I looked out of the window: a lorry drove into the courtyard, and boxes of vegetables were unloaded from it; then a closed van drove in, and linen was carried into the hotel. I saw from the side of the vehicle that it was a laundry van.

In the evening the the waiter brought me a letter from Riitta and Miettinen, evidently written in a drunken mood. Could they help me in some way, they asked, and, if not, they urged me to resort to some institution for the care of mental health problems. They'd underlined the words *mental health* with red and blue ink, and the felt tips had stuck through the paper and spread on the back something like a broad, vaguely-outlined treble clef.

IV

The following morning I had a call from the unit manager in Finland. He asked what I was up to, travelling to a fair and then just hanging about in a hotel room all week.

I said I wasn't up to anything.

'Well, surely there's something behind it?' he said.

'No,' I said.

'Come on, let's have a sensible explanation,' he said.

When he had no reply, he went on 'Have you had a row with Miettinen?' I said there'd been no row between Miettinen and me. Miettinen was a splendid fellow and a businesslike boss. He said he was acquainted with Miettinen himself, so I didn't need to start any fairy tales: Miettinen had his faults, of course, but so had we all. I said he'd got it right there. I promised to come and see him for a talk when I was back in Finland. Miettinen, he told me, had rung early the previous evening: orders and invitations to submit tenders had been coming in fast enough, so perhaps we were out of the woods again; now it was time for me to make a pitch for new customers, so output-levels could be maintained until the summer holidays. I made no promise to go to the fair, but he didn't push me on that again.

Riitta came round about mid-day, saying she'd left to nurse her hangover in the hotel. Miettinen had promised to watch the stand during the afternoon. She told me Miettinen had said that if I came to the stand this afternoon and took up my duties like a man, he'd let bygones be bygones and not tell them back home that I'd spent the bulk of the week in my hotel-room. I said the unit manager had rung from Finland and had already heard everything from Miettinen. Riitta complained about her stomach pains, headache and exhaustion, and I got her a cold beer out of the minibar. When she'd drunk it she went to her room to sleep.

I spent the afternoon lying on my bed and looking at the room walls, the ceiling, and the frieze of wallpaper running round it in an unbroken pattern. Riitta looked in about six. She said I ought at least to get out of my room for a bit: she reckoned I'd been stuck in the hotel now for four days. I promised to think about it. Riitta asked if I'd be coming tomorrow to help dismantle the fair stand, or would she be left to do that on her own too. Whatever happened, Miettinen was going to be off on the day-flight to Finland. I promised to come.

'Wonders'll never cease,' Riitta said.

'There's a lot you've still not understood about this world,' I said. Miettinen had rung her in the afternoon and said it would be all right for me to come along to the final celebration-dinner with the rest of their crowd. I said it was nice to hear that Miettinen considered me part of his crowd.

'I'm not going,' I added.

'Why not?'

'I'm not hungry.'

'You should come anyway,' Riitta said.

When Riitta had gone, I stood by the window and looked out into the courtyard and in the windows of the building across. The telephone box was illuminated, but no one had come from the kitchen to telephone all evening.

About elevenish I went out. The air was dry and sharp, and there was still quite a bit of traffic about on these streets. In front of the hotel there was a little square, and I walked across it and sat down at a street café. I ordered a beer and sat with it for a while, looking at the traffic and the sky: a bit of sky was visible above the square, black and broken by stars. Finishing my beer, I left the money on the table and walked back across the square to the hotel. Two young girls were standing by the hotel entrance, and as I was passing them one of them asked me in English:

'Do you want to make love?'

'Don't think I know how,' I said. They both looked at me, and some words passed between them in French.

'Are you sick?' asked the girl who had asked me about love.

'Don't know,' I said.

I went into the hotel and took the lift to my room. Miettinen rang at two o'clock in the morning. He seemed drunk and asked if he could come round for a while and have a chat. I said yes, I wasn't asleep yet. He came and helped himself to a whisky and soda out of my minibar; he urged me to have one, but I said no.

Miettinen took a seat and told me his life hadn't always been a bed of roses either. I said I could well believe it. He said he'd still got a yen to go back into the army: he'd been a fool ever to leave: he'd loved its straightforward hierarchy and the overall simple style of life, and knowing where you were.

'But do you know how to make love?' I asked. At first he was thrown by the question, and then he said yes, he knew quite a few good places: we could go somewhere right away.

About fourish I managed to get Miettinen to see that it was time for him to be off to bed. He'd drunk all the stuff in the minibar, apart from the champagne and the wine. He stood by the door a long time and beseeched me not to leave the firm: he'd sort everything out for the best back home.

'It'll be all alright with us yet, you'll see,' he said many times. When Miettinen had gone, I closed the door and went over to the window. In the building opposite there were no lights any longer; the telephone box in the yard was still illuminated and empty.

Looking at the clock, I realised it was after five in Finland: already it was getting light there. I worked out which way I'd have to go never to see morning, and how fast I'd have to go.

1983

Erno Paasilinna

THE ADVANCE OF OUR TROOPS

I

When dark came they set down their loads and built a campfire in the shelter of the forest. The sound of a distant shot came from behind. It was brief, like a question, as if asking where the fugitives were hidden.

It began to rain again, like the previous evening, which they had spent by a river. The water had washed away the Black Major's sleeping blanket. The rain hissed down vertically and drenched everything.

They ate the last scraps of food and the Padre read a short prayer in which he requested the blessing of the Most High on the remaining troops. The Black Major nevertheless ordered a scout to reconnoitre southwards. He commanded him to return at dawn. After the scout had set off they went to bed. When another shot was heard they knew he would not return.

The Black Major said that everything would be all right when morning came and they could shoot some game. They were very tired and there was no longer a tactical objective.

Before he went to sleep the Black Major took out the map, as was his wont, and spread it out over some spruce branches. He examined it carefully, as if he was looking for holes. Water spattered on the paper. He folded the map up and put it under his head.

They knew that it was useless. In any case it was the enemy that controlled the retreat.

II

The uninterrupted rain made them dejected; the Black Major was apathetic. The Padre had fed him heather tea, but now the season was changing it, too, was in short supply. They waited for the weather to brighten and snow to fall.

The Black Major had thick, black eyebrows, like thatch; you could tell his mood from their position. In summer they attracted raindrops, in winter frost and ice. Generally they hung downwards, and he looked as if he was asleep. At such times he did not speak; he turned over on his bed of spruce twigs and lay awake. Clouds lay among the branches of the spruces, and the fog swirled. The smoke from the campfire hung here and there over the recumbent men. The watchman, wrapped up in his greatcoat, leaned against a tree and listened.

So many officers had died; there were only four left – in addition to the Black Major, there were only the Padre, Education and the Lieutenant. The Padre had followed the troops since the beginning; he had grown old, and lame in one leg. He had committed more than half the men to their final resting place, and said he would do his best with the rest. Education had begun in the educational corps, but with the current turn of events he had left his regular job, and generally kept himself to himself. The Lieutenant had really been discovered by mistake. He had been lying face down on the ground, apparently unconscious, and had been added to the baggage at the order of the Black Major. He still had a complete uniform, and a Sam Browne belt.

The front line had turned northwards, and there had been occasions when the men had been in danger of being surrounded. The worst thing was when, from time to time, they got lost, wandered in some direction, and pitched camp for the night. It was slightly safer in the vicinity of the enemy; there was some human contact, at least, and life did not seem completely pointless. They boiled water, and cooked hares and fish. In the evenings they generally gathered by the waterside, mended their fishing tackle and patched their battle-dress. There was no other maintenance. At the beginning of the retreat, the Black Major had kept up contact with the neighbouring division, but the day came when the radio transmitter could no longer reach them. It had remained unclear to them what had happened to the other division. Perhaps it had slipped out of the main area of operations and was now wandering in some unknown place without directions or contacts. The radio message had been answered by the enemy, and since then conversation had been carried on exclusively with the other side. The radio operator had been exhorted to make threats; it had been decided to try to lower the enemy's morale. The enemy's radio operator had answered that the time for words was over. Radio communication had been intense, even aggressive. When the rains started, there had been mention of an engagement which would hopefully be the final one.

But one day the radio no longer roused the enemy. An ominous silence descended around the campfire. Everyone followed, uncomfortably, the fruitless attempts of the radio operator. The enemy's telegraphist was silent; the wires strewn on the branches quivered uselessly. Finally the radio operator took the headphones from his ears and said it was no longer worth trying.

They ate in silence. Education raked the fire and said he considered the situation grave. The rain trickled on as usual; from time to time the clouds drew back and a ragged grey strip appeared in the sky. Drops of water fell from pine needles, the soldiers' greatcoats steamed and gave off a sweaty smell which brought to mind a rotting heap of rubbish. Some of the men had hung their footrags up under the pines; the indefinite, black impressions of their toes could be seen. Eighteen horses remained after the others had been slaughtered for meat. The horses were generally left untethered: in the thick forest it did not occur to them to try to escape. They spent the night close to the camp like wild animals, standing in circles, tails touching. Sometimes when exhaustion among the men was so great that no one could keep their eyes open, the watch was left to the horses. The dormant mind was sensitive to their sounds: before the horses began to circle the campfire most of the men were wide-awake and ready to begin defence.

At the beginning of the retreat, the Black Major had believed it essential to engage in active fighting, surprise attacks and counterattacks. The loss of life had been great, however, and once they had lost radio contact with their own forces the customary encircling manoeuvres and groupings became meaningless. Twice the Black Major had tried to break through to their own side, only to discover that they were surrounded by the enemy. Fourteen men died in the ensuing fighting, and had to be left on the battlefield. They no longer had their own field hospital; the nearest was now under enemy control.

After the failed battle, the exhausted troops gathered by the mountain wall, where they could hear the enemy commands and see the lights of the flares. After that a plane took off and dropped leaflets; they were quite new and told of their hopeless plight. They fell to the ground like autumn leaves and the men stared at them as they landed by their feet; one or two picked one up. The rest of the evening passed in discussion of the matter. Then the Black Major called the men together and issued an order, the only possible course of action, to proceed to the area on the map that had not yet seen action.

After that there began a period of rain, long, apparently eternal, and no one could really remember any more what sunny or bright days were like, the kind when you can see the horizon, a forest or lake close up, where the patterns of the waves form a living surface.

Although it was not completely dark, the air was so grey, dense and foggy that trees often had to be identified by bayonet, and boots by hand. The campfire shone like a candle-flame, and the horses' flanks, glistening in the rain, could have been a metre or a hundred metres away.

The men marched in a formation dictated by the terrain and by individual preference. When they stopped they sat or lay down for the allotted time, and started off again when the Black Major got up, each of them following the sounds and movement, and making his own decision as to direction and pace.

The horses carried the baggage in the midst of the men, with the horsemen helping to push the carts until mud and obstacles made it necessary for everyone to get behind the carts and push. As the horses struggled onwards the men were equally stricken with tiredness, but abandoning the baggage was unthinkable. Only when a horse was shot and butchered was a cart left behind. The wooden parts of the cart were chopped up for firewood and other uses. The metal parts of the harness were placed in a box containing various requirements for life in the forest, such as fish hooks and string, empty cartridge cases and ammunition belts. The remains of the horse were carefully gathered together, including its hide, its hair, and bones that could be boiled to make glue. Then they continued on their journey.

III

The scout's continued absence caused a degree of regret that could be considered normal, and to which a number of memories were attached. Because of earlier battle groupings and the deceased's position in his unit, some of the men hardly knew him at all. He was fair-haired man of medium height who often spoke of a woman named Laura with whom he had visited the seaside at Pietarsaari. The story was highly embroidered and the acquaintance had been a short one, but in these circumstances it had swelled to embrace a whole lifetime – it was assumed that the scout would be one of those who would die. He was given tasks which presupposed his coming fate; he had, with his story, made a reality of his approaching departure. When the shot was heard, the men looked first at one another, then at the Padre.

The Padre was troubled, because deaths were his business. It was no wonder that each time he carried out his duty he feared for those whose turn would soon come. . . Often he stopped to think of those who were still alive, prompted for example by the sight of a man sitting at the campfire: mentally he groped for words of condolence, tried to characterise this particular individual. He thought of the men with warmth, hoping that he would not have to bury them, but nevertheless he found himself composing funeral speeches for the man sitting opposite him, and as they apparently conversed, the Padre, through his own words, imagined him dead. He was greatly troubled by this unpleasant habit, but try as he might the result was always the same. He had already buried the Black Major two or three times, once using the long form of service. When news of the actual death of one of the men reached him, his tension eased, but at the same time he was filled with a terrible sense of guilt.

The scout's body was in the forest where he had died, and had to be consigned to eternal rest in the same way as a drowning at sea. Experience had shown that it was not worth searching for bodies, and it was certainly impossible even to think of transporting them until a proper funeral could be held. The Padre held his modest ceremony by the campfire, where the men usually gathered; if there was more than one campfire, the funeral was held by the fire where the deceased's closest comrades in arms were. Thus the ceremony acquired a certain intimacy, and it often happened that men from other campfires gathered to listen to the speech.

The Padre took as his starting point the biblical story of David and Goliath. He quoted phrases from the Bible in the order he remembered them, developing an interesting portrait of the struggle between David and Goliath. He went into extensive detail about the Philistines, a nation to whom he accorded a significance in keeping with the current situation. All the time he wove the scout in and out of the narrative, attempting to build a picture of him alongside the the Bible story. Understandably, it was not possible for him to stick dogmatically to David and Goliath, and the narrative, dependent on his faulty memory of the texts, began to wander freely in the Bible lands. His story soon had the men leaning up on their elbows. To sketch in some historical background, the Padre explained the natural conditions of the Sinai desert, its geographical position and the technology of the period. Aware that he had captured the attention of his listeners, he abandoned the scout at some point of the story and, without himself noticing it, began to weave his way skilfully and enthusiastically among kings and centurions. He lowered his voice to narrate long episodes, which were charged with a peculiar, obscure atmosphere.

At length the Padre shifted. He threw the men a startled glance and lowered his head. Noticing Education shifting his feet, he quickly recited the routine words of remembrance. He beseeched God to take the scout to His bosom. He said it so fast that it communicated despair. Then he sang a hymn. Some of the men joined in, and for a moment the hymn floated with the smoke into the spruce forest.

When he had finished the hymn he rose and stepped out of the circle of light. He turned his back and did not take part in conversation.

Education had followed the funeral service from a distance. He was not easily moved, for his former career as an officer in the educational corps had emptied him of his once comparatively abundant spiritual resources. He felt that the atmosphere had changed and that the only fruitful topic of conversation was the opening positions of the war. That could still be a point of conversation. He felt that he should say something. The embers of the fire were burying themselves in the ground; grey ash was building up in layers around them. The Black Major was lying on his side, his face toward the forest. He had not turned round at all during the Padre's speech. He looked as though he had been asleep, but experience suggested that this was not the case.

Education felt the situation was becoming melancholy, empty and gloomy. A number of unconnected thoughts crossed his mind. He remembered the riding breeches of a certain short general, which had hung on the wall of the staff officers' barracks. They had been used by the younger officers for target practice. Where had the breeches come from, and where was the general who had owned them? It was on account of the general that the breeches had been shot. Perhaps the general himself would have been shot, too, if he had happened to be in his breeches; the atmosphere had been unusually relaxed. When one remembered those events they seemed a bit mad. It was all a long time ago.

At last, the Padre's talk came to an end. The Padre could be seen as an indefinite shape at the edge of the circle of light; it was impossible to tell whether he was doing something, or whether he had sunk into a daze. Education asked whether the assembled gentlemen wished to hear his customary lecture. He began by saying that when the war began the enemy had 449 tanks. The figure was from his first survey of the war situation, and he still had the relevant circulars. He referred to official communiqués every time he needed to demonstrate the truth of a fact. Against the 449 tanks deployed by the enemy in front-line positions, our own forces had 332 tanks, of which some were TU-type heavy models, which corresponded to the enemy's lighter, although more agile, tanks. In terms of manpower, the enemy had fourteen divisions supported by aircraft and special divisions of infantry. Our own forces consisted of fifteen divisions, although three of them were made up of older home reservists. Those were the figures. The weather at the beginning of the war had not been favourable. Clearly not everyone knew what was going on.

Education said that the task of examining front-line divisions was interesting in terms of morale: nervousness and slight unease were observed. After the first wave of attacks, a degree of hesitation was noted among the leading troops, and some special forces thrown into the fire at critical moments lost their striking power in the face of the ferocity of the enemy's defence. This, however, was not of long duration: when the forces were withdrawn and, after a day of hard battle, received their battlefield rations, a complacent mood returned. The front sector commanders visited the forward positions to speak with their troops once the results of the day's fighting were clear. Checkpoint and guard duties were carried out cheerfully, sometimes jovially. Not counting a few outbreaks of fighting, this trench warfare phase lasted until the evening of the fourth day.

Education spoke in a thin, colourless voice, as if he were reading from operational instructions. This he did, in fact, from time to time at appropriate moments, omitting personal opinions and avoiding ideological questions. He said he had tried only to sketch a general picture. This was how the war had gone. These were the results.

The Lieutenant sat in front of the campfire leaning his arms on his knees, without raising his head, throughout the entire duration of Education's speech. At the end of the oration he rose suddenly and, with harsh words, attacked the general in charge of the fighting: it was his incompetence that had broken the front lane in the attack; that negligent commander might have planned the attack, but he hadn't carried it through. The Lieutenant warmed to his subject and criticised the errors made during the fighting, scourging the general's incompetence and complaining that it was a crime to put an idiot like that in charge of tactics. War has only one objective, and that is victory, the Lieutenant said, and began to poke the logs on the fire. Some of the men shifted, raised their heads for a moment and looked up at him. Education remained silent. He folded up his circular and placed it carefully in his suitcase. He had no rucksack. The suitcase had been in his hand when he had wandered out of the burning staff headquarters.

IV

During the night the scout returned to the camp, exhausted and quite unable to answer the numerous questions addressed to him. He was tended with melted resin, and attempts were made to dry damp sleeping blankets to warm him. The Black Major rose and asked whether the scout had seen anything. In these circumstances, the commanding officer's interest was taken as a sign of hope, and many of the soldiers tried harder than usual to help the scout recover so that he would be capable of answering the Black Major's questions. He was fed boiled water, his head held upright so that it would not spill on to his jacket. The Padre was particularly attentive: he felt the scout's pulse and spoke optimistically of the situation, which he affirmed was taking a turn for the better. At the same time he kept an eye on the Black Major and tried to ascertain whether his interest was really a sign of something.

The squally rain continued and the wind murmured in the trees, sometimes fanning the campfire's flames higher, sometimes blowing them along the ground. Sparks flew into the dark night and the soldiers' greatcoats smelled and steamed; the horses shifted at the edge of the circle of firelight and their ears flickered as they listened to the sounds of the wind.

When, the next day, the scout died of fever, camp was struck dispiritedly, the horses were harnessed to the carts and the company set off once more. A memorial service was considered unnecessary, since the words had been recited once already, and because Education felt they had been heard by the Almighty.

V

Later, perhaps in October, to judge by the weather, they reached a hill overlooking a valley. The landscape looked bare. On the hill was a monument to some earlier war. It had evidently been forgotten for a long, long while.

The estimated march for the day had been completed, and it was decided to stop and set up camp. The flagpole was erected beside the monument, and a tent was improvised from the blankets of slaughtered horses in an attempt to keep the rain off. While the water boiled Education and the Padre tried to solve the riddle of the monument. The inscription was strange and partially illegible, and they could not make out who had fought the war or which side had won.

As they drank tea, Education examined the map, which they still looked at from time to time, partly out of habit, partly because it was the only clue to their whereabouts they had. He said that it might be that he was not reading the map right, but it didn't seem to correspond to reality. There was a hill where there ought to have been marsh, and where there should have been a hill there was in fact a river. He showed the map to the Padre. We're off the map, Education said, in some unknown direction, perhaps north-east; a long way off, at any rate. The Padre thought they had wandered off to the south-east. Education said that was possible. The Lieutenant did not take part in these deliberations, but lay in the shelter of the tent canvas with the Black Major. The Black Major sometimes talked to himself, but when questioned declined to continue the conversation.

Education invited the Padre to consider how much the nature of the war had changed now that it had proved so overwhelmingly difficult to engage the enemy. The Padre suggested that they could attempt to gather together the remaining ammunition and fire signal shots; perhaps the enemy would hear them and respond. He remembered the existence of some law that said that such shots should be fired in emergencies, and that the enemy was supposed to respond to them and try to contact the distressed troops.

Education admitted that he had heard of such a procedure, but could not say whether it would have results in their case. A rifle shot's range is very short, Education said, perhaps a couple of kilometres at most, although from a high spot, and in clear weather, it might be more. But he considered the initial idea of trying to contact the enemy a good one.

Education said the onset of winter made such contact desirable. As rations dwindled and material requirements could no longer be met, morale would inevitably decline. Perhaps there was no guarantee of finding the way back without the enemy's help.

VI

With the arrival of winter they reached a strange place covered in thick forest, full of trees they did not recognise. The radio operator tried once more to make contact with the enemy, but after the battery failed hope faded. Sometimes there were strange rustlings, but on closer examination they always turned out to be illusory. There were also attempts to light a beacon on a mountain peak whenever they succeeded in scaling one; but the fires did not achieve the desired results. Perhaps the enemy had gone in the other direction and was now seeking them somewhere completely different, in the south-east or perhaps the south; perhaps the enemy had given up the operation, perhaps even the war.

Two men had disappeared, although it was not clear who they were. Roll call was still taken regularly, but the exhaustion and indifference of the men made it unreliable. After the coming of snow more and more of them began to long for skis.

Nothing much happened, except that the Black Major hanged himself.

There were discussions about orientation. Some of the group believed that the bearing should be changed to south-west, but as the journey progressed they changed their mind. Before midwinter, the majority believed it would be best to head south, until others began to criticise this decision and suggest that the bearing should be south-east. North, too, had its supporters, despite the falling temperature; the enemy had originally attacked from the north, so perhaps they could still encounter it there.

VII

Fortunately spring came early that year, and they were able to consider stopping and setting up a longer-term camp. The Padre surveyed the landscape ahead through binoculars and said he wished he could see a sign of permanent habitation. He asked Education if he felt the same. Education said he didn't know who owned this land, but perhaps they had finally arrived at land that was not owned by anyone.

The two officers were speaking in private; the men were holding a meeting under a nearby tree. They decided to go on alone. Snatches of conversation carried on the wind: the officers had betrayed the men; it was time for the rank and file to take the reins in their own hands. They demanded for themselves one of the two remaining horses.

Education asked the Padre to lead the animal to the meeting place. The Padre did so, and begged permission to bless the men's leader, to lay his hands on the head of the chosen soldier. The reply came that there were no leaders any more. In that case, the Padre asked, could he talk to them all.

In order to have something to do, Education began to distribute the circulars. He said that he did not want to remind them of the past, but if they would permit him he would carry out certain formalities. At this stage of the campaign, his chances of influencing the course of events were slim. He shook each man by the hand and asked them if they had any questions. He himself had none.

The men shook their heads. They began to gather together the remains of their equipment and disperse into the forest, to drift away, climb the green hummocks, call out to each other. Soon their voices could no longer be heard.

The Lieutenant's body drifted in the stream, for he had wished to keep his word.

The Padre and Education sat and waited for lightning so that they could kindle a fire. In quiet voices they discussed the events. It looked as if the sky was clouding over. The horse was restless.

1977

Intimacy

Intimacy

When the one that gave you life
has left in pain
it's as if a swing stopped, or
the world crashed mute.
You see a quiet house in a country landscape,
children there, in front, tall as hay,
someone opens a garret window,
the rowan sprouts a berry.
You approach it slowly
from the lake
and every rustle,
scent, sough
rips open the channels
into all the summers of childhood.

1971 **Helena Anhava**

Our friendship was sealed
before he learned to speak,
when he chuntered chaffinch-talk.
Only then did my world turn real.
One needs a likeness to be able to live,

but friendship is friendlier than likeness:
our laughter is unanimous:
        I hear his voice in all I'm saying,
I hear my saying in his voice:
life is only all there when all the generations are.
This language of candles lighting candles is unforgettable.
Friendship alters like a child
        into what I do not know.
His thoughts were worldsized
        till he was seven.

1958 **Maila Pylkkönen**

LOVE SONG
TO THE SMALLEST BIT OF PARADISE

It was easier to love at that time,
It was the smallest bit of paradise, no more than a
drop of rain that fell as we fished.
The ant with her straw did not give up, she is always the same.
She gleamed in the sun, she was on her way somewhere
with a secret she is still full of
and on the jetty where we lay on our stomachs we saw
the sea's fluted bottom: the one who
slept down there with skin shining
did not forget us,
we were in love with the world then: there is

the beach where I poured sand over you,
the fear too is there, that glittering sense
of not really understanding, of being outside,
a part of it remains, a part
one shares with others

when one loses what one loves,
when one recreates it

when the smallest bit of paradise goes on glittering
among the days that we live.

1980 **Inga-Britt Wik**

ARCTIC JOURNEY

Fog only makes this emptiness vaster.
What I see is the window, my own face,
cold that congeals my eyes is what I see.
I remember believing, when I was a child,
the world ended at Hammerfest,
the earth came to an abyss
and there was just fog beyond;
that's what I believed.
I've come north because something
in me was finished, I'm dead weary,
compass gone, its needle constantly
wandered, it's been lost in the snow.
If only I could hear a ship's horn hooting
in the fog out there, I'd find my way.

1980 **Kirsti Simonsuuri**

The music has died away, leaving
on people's faces
the look of a distant mountain
or a seagull over a lake.
A tree, bent by the wind, that doesn't move, doesn't straighten.
The wave doesn't come to the shore.

1973 **Kai Nieminen**

My old dad
says he's on bad terms with the sun.
Mornings he draws the curtains tight-closed with his stick
and sits down on the edge of the bed.
There he rolls back his sleeves
and strokes his damp arms
in the day's longest moments
and speaks his soft muffled tones:
'These shoddy modern clothes, too soft they are:
stick to your skin.'
His room's on the other side of the kitchen.
My old ma opens and closes his door,
to let now the colder now the warmer air in,
and often gives long sighs
when my dad can't hear.

Born from this love,
I remember my ma's bright glad eyes,
remember my dad's pittance in his poorly-paid job,
his absences in the forest,
those draughty kipdowns in forest bunkhouses,
and his bad back and his bent walk –
how well I remember his way!
Now, a few times daily, he toils
with his stick across the bedroom floor,
slow as a worm, and waits for winter.

My old ma's tough and nippy:
she bears the burdens of her days
and occasionally sits herself down on the sunny steps.
She tells about God in her letters like a little child,
about her weariness and her stamina,
and always signs off brightly.

Always they're back before my eyes.
Born from their love, I know
how intimately they tread the narrow road,

and I've no reason, either, to tread otherwise.
We love the sun:
it *is* bright
on summer's leaves, and on autumn's,
from end to end of the road.

1969

Year by year the summers shorten:
        morning, a green day, birdsong above the window.
The words seem abortive as the forest
        that grows to be hacked by the axe.

1969

Niilo Rauhala

Come home from the dark waters
Come home from out of the gale
Like a first-former with your red
schoolbag on your back, come
home. Confusing what
was, confusing you.
The days look like one another.
Rows of jars filled with blood and mucus.
It's a question of not remembering
It's a question of not remembering that morning
dawn by the smooth water, real
as an imagining!
Once upon a time there was innocence and delight
Once upon a time there was a reckless purity
One is a moment
One is a sandy floor in the market tent
One ferries ice-skates and small children
to and fro along icy winter roads in one's yearning
for the cool light, come home

1987

Tua Forsström

THE BOAT

I took the boat and rowed out into the bay. I stowed the oars and lay down on the boards between the seats, leaning my head against the stern thwart. The stem rose and traced a wide arc across the blue sky until the boat settled in the direction of the wind. With burning hot fingers on my eyelids, the sun closed my eyes, and on the calm sea the waves gently rocked me.

At that moment I was like a happy child. Not hungry, wanting nothing, remembering nothing, I had no future. Every one of life's distinctive features ceased to exist, there was nothing but life and a perfect pleasure. I thought: this is what it must be like before birth and after death. Once I'd thought that thought the moment was gone, for in such a moment there is no room for thoughts.

And yet I still felt happy and held up my hand and pointed toward the sky and then to my joy I discovered that all the heavens rested upon my outstretched finger like a blue parasol. A white gull sailed in under my parasol and it was my gull for, after all, I was the whole world and my finger propped up the universe.

1959 **Henrik Tikkanen**

AND THEN

And finally he came to
reality. He grew afraid
of his courage, for here
there was no possibility
of defence. He was
his own body. And knowledge
proved to be his own
ignorance, but clearer
and greater. It embraced
atoms and galaxies, but not

reality, that place
in the soul. All he finally
found was goodness, a kind
of residence in knowledge, and then
stayed put in the dark,
bleeding ranks.

1990

CIRCLE

All is as before. The clock
glows in the morning darkness. But
every answer diminishes the question,
every legend must be told
at last. You have moved
in your sparse constellation
of years; you have waited.
Nothing is as before, for
nothing has happened. You never dared
to receive, and your gifts
were only a protective wall.
It is growing light; in the east
red organ music is rising. My friend,
you have misunderstood everything.
Life is not the goods, it is
the price. Empty-handed you turn round,
but it doesn't matter. Everything
is as before; soon
you will be home again.

1990

AT HOME

He remembered setting up house with Seija for the first time. When they moved into the flat, their only bit of furniture was Seija's portable radio, blaring out. The rooms echoed emptily, like a church. Seija stood in the middle of the floor, glaring round in a rage: the previous tenants had left without tidying up their remnants. Seija began shouting and tossing newspapers out of the cupboards and all over the floor: 'It's only good manners: you don't just clear off, leaving all the cupboards stuffed with junk and newspapers.'

'Never mind,' he said: 'I'll sort it out; anyway it's actually easier to put it all into a bigger pile for carting out into the yard.'

But Seija went on ranting and raving, and bottles went rolling across the floor. He began gathering some of the stuff up into cardboard boxes – bottles, dirty cloths, newspapers – and carrying them down. The windows were open, the radio was blaring out, and over the sound of the radio you could hear Seija's voice, shouting that there could have been a little bit of redecoration here before they moved in, some clean wallpaper at least, when it was clear what sort of tenants the former occupants had been. Letting the flat, the agent had said it was in good shape – less than a year since the previous redecoration.

'And you, nitwit that you are, you didn't even come and take a look,' Seija burst out: 'I've never come across a tenant like that in all my life.' How could he take a look, he asked, when the previous tenants had left no key, and, at that time, the caretaker didn't have one, either.

Seija insisted on summoning the agent to come and have a look. He did come – came at the same time as the removal men. He dodged round the cupboards and tables, looked over the rooms and admitted he'd had no inkling what they were like.

'It stinks: it's absolutely putrid in here,' Seija said. 'Even though the windows have been wide open since morning.'

The agent lifted his nose, took a turn round the apartment, and said that actually the fresh air was beginning to have some effect: he couldn't smell anything particularly bad now. Seija blew her top again and said they had a right to have the flat redecorated, for it was a pigsty.

'At this particular juncture it'll be difficult to get the painters,' the agent said. 'You see, madam, it's spring, the best season for all painters: and the men we employ in this particular building have to be booked well in advance. If we contact them now, we'll be talking about sometime in the autumn – if indeed you'd find it convenient to have them in then, with the days getting cold and rainy. The ideal thing, madam, would be to wait till next spring.'

'That'd be the ideal thing for you,' Seija said and began demonstrating her feelings by pushing cupboards and beds about. There was no method in her madness: when Antti tried to help her by grabbing the other ends, she let go and went to look out of the window.

'By no means, not ideal for us at all,' the agent said, beginning to lose his temper himself. 'Doing up one set-up in a building like this is no great shakes, whether we do it now or a bit later.'

'Do it now then, if that's so,' Seija hurled over her shoulder.

'I've told you, haven't I, why it can't be done now. And look, here are your personal belongings coming in, madam, as we see: for you, decorating'll be just as much a nuisance now as when the furniture's in place next spring.'

'That's our business,' Seija said aggressively. 'And besides, what, I'd like to know, is the general set-up here? Isn't it part of the caretaker's duties to see to the tenants? Just see this cleaning-up job. Look what kind of a midden your new tenants have had to move into. I came here expecting to do a normal cleaning job, and instead the whole thing's like the aftermath of an earthquake – bathroom full of old rags, cupboards stuffed with bottles and papers. The management should certainly see to it: new tenants shouldn't have to find that their first job is cleaning up other people's muck.'

'It is distressing it's turned out like this,' the agent said. 'I do offer my apologies on behalf of the owners, and I'll tell Lahtinen to come up at once and see what he can do.'

'We've already shifted a lorryload of junk at least into the yard,' Seija said. 'What'll Lahtinen find to do now: the work's been done for him.'

Seija went into the kitchen and broke off her exchange with the agent. She could be heard starting to take crockery out of baskets, putting cups on the table, running water from the tap and putting the kettle on. In spite of and in the middle of everything, she was going to make some coffee.

Antti accompanied the agent to the passageway outside the flat. Speaking in a low voice, so that Seija wouldn't hear, he said his wife was tired through lack of sleep: it had upset her, coming into a filthy flat, and, being so tired, it had made her lose her composure. The agent gave Antti a pat on the shoulder and said the things that went with this job were inconceivable, and of course he knew how it was with women: they had those times of theirs. It took Antti a moment to realise what the agent was implying, and then the man was already on his way down in the lift.

When Antti went back in, Seija was standing at the kitchen door and asking what he'd been going on about with the agent outside.

'Going on about? What was there to go on about?' he said. 'I couldn't say nothing at all, and there wasn't time to say much.'

'You were talking about me, weren't you?' Seija said.

He sidled past Seija into the kitchen, saying: 'You've made the coffee, why not forgot all this junk for a bit: drink your coffee and have a stare out of the window.'

'You were talking about me, weren't you?' Seija said.

'Well, I had to say something – had to try and explain why you were so upset.'

'So wasn't the reason plain enough already then?' Seija exploded. 'I know these agents: this one's a friend of that judge, that Asikainen, the one who owns the "Three Towers" – the building firm. And I know what sort Asikainen is – I've heard what they say. When he builds those condominiums – this was his job too, you know, though it's rented – when he builds those condominiums, he does all he can to cheat the folk he's selling them to. For example, the rooms are supposed to be a certain size, but there's a kind of dodge – I forget what it's called, but I've heard what they say – and with it he can manage to build those flats just that bit smaller than the designs show.'

'He simply can't do that,' Antti said.

'Oh yes he can.' Seija threw her cleaning-apron off and began pouring coffee. 'Oh yes he can. I've heard what they say: and when people buy into their condominium, they think they're buying a flat of such and such a size, as the designs show, but in reality the flat's just that couple of square yards smaller: they don't know that, and they don't see it, for those square yards have gone west in the wall-space, and the cupboards, and the hallway. But they say these other architects are onto his games now. And then again, when he sells these flats, and the folk, in all good faith, think the building and its holdings, like the garages for instance, are in the control of the condominium it comes out no: it's the builder who owns them himself.'

'Well, that's the purchasers' own stupidity, isn't it, if they let themselves be diddled like that?'

'So you think that sort of dishonesty is all right, do you? Completely justified? You can cheat people as much as you like, provided they don't find out?'

'That's not what I meant either.'

'So what did you mean then?' Seija pushed the window open, stretched her hand out and waved it back and forwards in the air. 'And you yourself'd be an easy one to fool. They could whip the clothes off your back, and you'd not notice a thing. Like now, for instance: if I'd managed to get here, I'd have raised such a commotion, I can tell you, the decoration'd've been done and the place cleaned up.'

They began to place things in their positions. The relish had gone out of the move. Seija circled round complaining about everything: she lined the cupboards with paper and sent him out to buy white paint and smarten up the worst places; but then the smell of the paint brought their arranging to a stop: dishes and linen lay all around on the sofas and tables. Seija claimed the removal men had banged the table-legs and damaged them.

Hannu was brought round from Seija's home, and the boy sat in the middle of the floor at first; but then he went to a drawer and started digging his things out. That infuriated Seija too, and she put the lad to bed before his usual time.

'We're not getting anywhere with this,' Antti said after he'd been mopping the floors and Seija had scrubbed them all over again with a hard brush. He couldn't bring himself to do a thing more: he sat on the sofa, seeing Seija rampaging, picking things up, moving them round, spreading cloths on tables and taking them off. Completely done-in, he finally got up, took his cap from the hall and went out. Seija shouted after him, but he went off as if he hadn't heard. He took the main road up the hill and turned off it onto the ridge.

There was a sandpit there, unused for decades, its edges growing willowherb and a stunted birch; behind it were some wooden houses, abandoned by their inhabitants, the windows boarded up. He stared at yards overgrown with weeds, and porches with their windows broken. The ridge was growing heather and lingonberries, with grass and strawberry leaves in the more open places; brown paths of pine-needles criss-crossed, and in some places the whole hillside seemed a single large maze of a footpath. The wartime entrenchments had collapsed and were almost completely overgrown. He recalled his mother saying there had been anti-aircraft guns in them. The bottoms of the entrenchments were covered with excrement, bits of paper and bottles; but on the sunny side there were large patches of white and pink cat's-foot. He stopped at a clump and began to pick them systematically: he picked a thick bunch and when he'd finished one clump moved on to another, and he continued his picking until he was holding a large rustling bouquet of pastel-coloured flowers.

He remembered taking them home and giving them to Seija, and how they hardly said a thing, and not a single word about their daytime quarrel.

Seija made the beds and laid them with linen sheets with broad lace panels on; the window was open to air the room, and the bedside table had a white cloth, edged with embroidered blue bellflowers. And Seija brought the vase of cat's-foot in and put it on the bedside table. They took a bath and went to bed, and he could still remember seeing the flowers against the window and the night sky visible through it.

They lay close together. Later, in the middle of the night, Antti woke up to find Seija's warm skin against his own skin, and she began talking as if she hadn't been asleep yet. She talked about her father and mother and brother, and then about some cousin and the cousin's wife. This cousin got sick with cancer; the woman, the cousin's wife, had been tormenting the man all her life, and all their married life together, and now, when the man was in the hospital and on the point of death, the wife rushed into the hospital and fell on to her husband's bosom. He lay there helpless, with God knows how many tubes in his nose, and his wife threw herself on to him, shouting and praying that he mustn't die. The nurses and the doctors hustled the woman out of the hospital and forbade her to come back, so that the poor man could at least give up the ghost in peace.

When she'd told all that, Seija lay quiet for a bit and then said, in an almost inaudible whisper, that she was like that herself: she was the same sort of person as that cousin's wife, just as awful. She sat up in the bed, moaning how terrible it was, and beginning to weep bitterly. Antti remembered pulling her back to lie down beside him and saying it wasn't like that: if they did have to search out some guilt in their relationship, then he was the guilty one.

And when she still went on weeping, not getting over it, he began to speak to her as if she were a little child, gently stroking her tearful face.

1974 **Kerttu-Kaarina Suosalmi**

A FAMILY REUNION

By dinner-time, everyone was in celebratory mood; even Lauri had changed his blue tie for a grey one. No one had seen Rafael since afternoon coffee, but he appeared from somewhere in the labyrinth of the house at exactly seven o'clock, the appointed time, in the dining room, where the others were waiting silently. A three-branch candelabrum burned on the table, and all the china belonged to the same Meissen set. The table-cloths were of homewoven linen.

The repast was made up of four courses: the hors d'oeuvres; asparagus soup; a roast with a cream sauce; and fruit ice-cream. The appropriate drinks were served – beer and schnapps, sherry, red wine and madeira – by a corpulent waiter, borrowed for the occasion from the town's assembly rooms, whose pale eyes never appeared to focus on a particular spot, but who nevertheless seemed to notice everything. Maire followed his calm and purposeful movements warily, as if this newcomer had threatened her supremacy in the kitchen. Nevertheless, Maire had herself prepared the food that was to be served.

Evidently Rafael had given the order that the boys were to be treated as equals tonight. At all events, they were offered the same drinks as the adults, with the exception only of the schnapps: they were given mineral water instead. Astrid and Mikko sustained an official conversation with Rafael at such volume that the trio at the other end of the table, Maire, Lauri and Katri, were able to take the opportunity to whisper to each other, led by the last-mentioned. The boys did not speak at all, but by the time the soup was served their cheeks were glowing, and they exchanged furtive glances with slightly moistened eyes.

Astrid attempted to begin a conversation with Rafael about his new book which, according to Mikko, was a real masterwork, but since the subject appeared not to interest Rafael, she changed the subject to the charm of old wooden buildings, the advantages of small towns compared with cities, cookery and the children's education. Nothing perturbed Rafael's silence, however; he spoke only as much as was necessary in order not to seem downright rude. In the end Astrid and Mikko had to content themselves with talking to each other, reminiscing about their last trip to Rome, where they had unexpectedly met a group of Finnish scholars and the whole journey had turned into a drinking bout. They seemed to have many happy memories of their time there. Even Astrid had been so daring that she had stolen from a night-club table a silver bell intended to help customers attract the attention of the waiter. It was a really charming object, and real silver, with an ivory handle: she had sought expert opinion once back in Finland. She had just slipped the bell into her handbag and no one had noticed, that's how simple it is to commit a crime. It's strange, isn't it, how skilful thieves are half admired: their profession really isn't very difficult. All good stories have a moral, and this one's no exception. Astrid laughed.

A supercilious smile played around Rafael's lips: until now it was his only expression of feeling throughout the whole dinner.

'You really did steal it?' he asked.

Rafael used the formal 'you', and Astrid was so surprised that she was unable to answer; but luckily the roast was brought in at that moment and created a welcome diversion.

During the roast, Mikko clinked glasses and gave a speech in honour of his 50-year-old brother, saying that in the broader perspective Rafael was still a young man, but that on the other hand his life work was already extensive and diverse. Mikko cited Rafael's merits as a banker and writer, or rather thinker, and then turned to childhood memories. It was difficult to believe that the kid who had so often encouraged Mikko to raid the neighbours' apple orchard had grown into a man respected by the entire Finnish intelligentsia. It was not inappropriate to speak of Rafael's fame, for it was not many days since a selection of Rafael's aphorisms had been read on the radio. Mikko had been told of this by friends. Mikko would have liked to have gone on reminiscing about the childhood shared by Rafael, Lauri and himself; but he was aware that they would hear more that very evening, told by Rafael himself in his own incomparable way. They would also hear about J. Arponen, their father, whom Rafael has so solemnly wished to honour on his own special day. Mikko extended to Rafael the birthday greetings of the entire family, and raised a glass in his honour.

– –

After dinner Rafael and Mikko went out for a walk, for the older brother wanted to show his visitor something of his current home town. They visited the bank, where the staff, on overtime, were clearly startled: it was not difficult to see that the mice were at play while the cat was away. The real reason for the overtime was a coffee party that had been arranged in the back room, and his staff's guilty faces revealed the whole story to Rafael before he had even noticed the festive table. He did not consider it appropriate, in his brother's presence, to reprimand his subordinates, and decided to leave the matter until later. In his work-room Rafael explained to his brother the work he did in service of the bank and the principles that governed his financial decisions. As the manager of the largest bank in the area, he bore a heavy responsibility for the industrial and economic development of the entire region, and in addition he was naturally forced to intervene in the economic affairs of many individuals. In a way you could say that his cultural philosophy and his concept of economics came together in the principle by which he believed it was his duty to support traditional and well-established businesses and to be wary of newcomers, of whom thesc days the majority were profiteers and who, what's more, were easily misled into ill-considered experiments.

After this serious exposition Rafael gave a short laugh, commenting that he had probably overtired his dear visitor with such explanations, when he ought to have been concerning himself with Mikko's comfort. And so he continued with a lighter programme. The brothers set off on a walk along the town's main street, with Rafael enthusiastically showing off the goods displayed in the shop windows. Finally they stopped for a cup of coffee at a small, really very charming café which just happened to be empty. Sitting there by the window they could enjoy watching the passing townsfolk, all of whom Rafael seemed to know and whom he enthusiastically described to his borther. Mikko could not help but be amused by the fact that a universal soul such as Rafael turned out to be a real provincial, and he said as much to his brother. They both laughed merrily at the thought, for the human aspects of greatness often seem very liberating.

On leaving the café, the brothers turned toward home, but decided before going in to take a small walk along the lakeshore road. The tranquil beauty of the countryside silenced them, and they walked along lost in their own thoughts.

1961 **Pentti Holappa**

VANUMÄKI

The monetary trinity of
commerce, corporation and church
constructed cramped quarters
for the people expelled from
light, space and liberty.

I

Vanumäki's slumdwellings
are called terrace houses, their precast walls
are plastered with gravel from Myllykylä heath –
with nightjars' nests, fox's holes,
and vipers' rocks: concrete's a natural product.

Chipboard furniture –
that's wood:
                                        a mock-wood plastic face,
on natural-wood cardboard doors.

II

A scrapheap of rusting sheet-iron, petrol flares,
fumes of burning gum
          and sulphur everywhere.
Hell is – hell:
a lifelong debt,
a yard four yards square,
a playground
for those I hear have a future.

III

Death reaps the happy,
no one the unhappy.
          Mercy, mercy on those

who have to survive
those who've nothing but
the chance-begotten
chance-preserved life
from the birthpang to the new pang:
the interminable journey to death.

IV

No acid mouth,
no dry ash of a look,
no monoxide embers of thought
can communicate
the iciness of the alchemy
someone makes gold with
out of someone else's suffering.

1986 **Pertti Nieminen**

THE DAYS

What day is it today?
Are the days in the right order?
Did our calendar start at the right time?
In the sky there's a passing-by
of gloomy and white clouds.
No stir in the branches.
Where to look, how to see?
The landscape under the clouds
is gloomy and bright.
In the yard a removal van is being loaded
and another unloaded.
Everyone

who notices
what others want from him
has to become different.
In the old window you can see
the new inhabitants.

1986

Hannu Salakka

Unlived life gloomed
the young forest
my lived infancy had grown.
Some dark-blue shade
I imagined I loved
filled my mind so often,
its blue flicker nurtured umbrage
and birdcalls of backlash
on everything.

Now the table burns with an oil-lamp
that smokes a little, a sound of surging
sweeps round the house.
We sit late, and towards dawn
I watch my vengeance fading
into children's eyes, into
bluely luminous shades.
I can make another
choice of myself, be reconciled.

In the soul, still, a pad of paw,
a growl, the lick
of a rough tongue

1979

Little children, they come
diving through warm
dark water
to the sky's delta, rise
and widen our edges,
they come into the world
as if they know,
with a rose-stem in their fist,
and they bustle about,
pounding each other and us,
without hurting
or stopping,
like a heart.

1982 **Pentti Saaritsa**

Right in the center of a low-pressure area
long spells of rain on all sides
the storm clouds pile up beyond the forest
the rain waits to start pouring down

Just like in the middle of a drinking bout
long wet days on every side
so far, you can sleep once you've fallen asleep

Never is our house so quiet

1978 **Märta Tikkanen**

AN EXTRA CHRISTMAS GIFT

Juhani Tiikka, profession unknown. Easy case, no notes after 27.2.1979. Nature kind, playful.

Tiikka wanted to be Santa Claus. I didn't want to spoil Kaarina's Christmas, so I joined in. Tiikka rushed out to the kiosk, he wanted to buy orangeade, at eight o'clock on Christmas Eve! There were four bottles of it in the fridge, and all the kiosks were shut, but what did that matter. The doorbell rang and in stepped a man in a ridiculous false beard, wellington boots, a pointed red hat and a grey sweater that smelt of Tiikka, bent double. He asked: 'Are there any good children here?' I swallowed a lot to stop myself laughing, and tried to say something, but couldn't. Kaarina's hands clapped together and, in a voice I hadn't heard before, she crowed: 'There are, there are!' After that the man disappeared back into the corridor, and dragged in a bundle wrapped up in the white sheet which had been on Kaarina's bed in the morning. Then I had to sit on Tiikka's lap. That was almost the most embarrassing thing. According to Kaarina and Tiikka, all good children sing, and the songs name was 'Putting out the Torches'. I stared at the brightly coloured heap of parcels and tried to guess where the binoculars were, a tool I would need to expel unpleasant human material from our home. But first I had to sing. Then Tiikka was thanked, I couldn't work out why, so I declined to join in. Kaarina said I was shy. Tiikka tickled my ear with his fusty hemp beard, but it didn't make me laugh. He told us the news from Santa Claus' home in Korvatunturi, where there are also apparently little boys like me, real little rascals who are called elves. The elves help Santa Claus before Christmas: without them, he wouldn't be able to make all the presents that the children of the world want. Had I written to Santa in Korvatunturi? I started; my thoughts were miles away. Tiikka asked again. There was a warm smile on Kaarina's face, and I nodded; how long was I going to have to put up with this clowning?

I refused to sing, so Kaarina and Tiikka sang. They danced round the pile of presents, tripped along on tip-toe, tip tap, tip tap, and raised and lowered their index fingers in time to the song.

Kaarina was wearing my elf's cap. They put their hands over their eyes like a visor when that point in the song came. Tip tap tip tap again. It went on for a terribly long time. I sat in my armchair and looked at them and felt that I was with two complete strangers who would do anything to please me, and to whom I had to be grateful. But loneliness was what I really felt, complete and absolute loneliness. I wasn't unhappy, quite the opposite, in fact I was grateful, it almost seemed as if that too was a present, an extra Christmas gift for me. I remember I smiled at Kaarina. She stopped, fingers raised, ended the song, came up to me, lifted me from the chair and, for some reason I couldn't understand, pressed me to her, kissed my cheek and stroked my hair and said, mummy's little darling, mummy's Antti, mummy's little elf.

I was so moved that tears came to my eyes. Tiikka went on dancing by himself; we laughed. Tiikka laughed back, and then we opened our Christmas presents. In the last package were the binoculars, continuous zoom, enlargement factor 10–30, non-reflecting objective.

Gradually I began to have had enough of him. He was artificial, like most people whom I had met during the course of my short life. He became boisterous every time he saw me: without taking his outdoor clothes off he would throw himself on me like an animal, toss my spindly body into the air, and grab my ankles so that my hair swept the floor and the blood was forced into my head. Once I looked at the clock in the midst of it all: it lasted almost four and a half minutes. He walked to the balcony, and I feared he would throw me over the railing and beat me like a rug. Kaarina laughed. She looked at me and, with her laughter, begged: laugh too, Antti, laugh!

I decided to put my plan into action, not for my own sake, but for Kaarina's. I was five years old, and I went to bed at ten. Kaarina went to bed an hour later. What on earth was the man waiting for, sitting on the sofa and doing a crossword although it was almost eleven o'clock at night? Kaarina lay beside me and tried to coax me to sleep, but it turned out that I lulled her. It was exhausting. Whenever she stirred, I made it clear that I was awake; I coughed, whimpered, or let out a sigh. She sighed back, whispered, go to sleep now, Antti, go to sleep. Each time her voice was more agonised.

A couple of times I caught her creeping, slippers in hand, towards the door, and then I let out a pitiless scream. She dived back under my quilt: go to sleep now, go to sleep, she almost wept. I pitied her, but did not give in. I knew from three months' experience, starting with Tiikka's first visit, that after an hour relief would come and Kaarina would fall asleep. Then it was my turn to creep from the room, stand in front of Tiikka, cough, look at the clock, take him to the front door and, without a word, watch as, pale and sleepy, the man gropes for his overcoat and disappears.

Not all cases were as easy as this one. Among Kaarina's women friends were a couple of difficult individuals whose stubbornness and persistence it was impossible not to admire. Marketta Halmetoja, record card 1980. Profession: kindergarten teacher. Expert in educational questions. Angular, clattering, reminiscent of a camel. Brown-rimmed square glasses and a constantly smiling mouth which, without reason, flies open to reveal large, yellowing, chisel-like teeth and strong, muscular gums. Once when I was sitting under the dining table colouring one of her leather boots yellow with chalk, she said she could see right through me. I raised my eyebrows and smiled; after all, I was sitting under the table. Kaarina should take me in hand, set me limits, say clearly and definitely NO! Apparently I nipulated Kaarina. It sounded strange, but that was certainly because I didn't understand the word. Later I realised that she meant manipulate.

30.11.1980: Halmetoja disappeared temporarily from our lives. After a week the telephone rang: Halmetoja said I should visit a psychologist. Kaarina didn't understand why. I've never had any difficulty with Antti, she said, and it was true. The difficulties were elsewhere, they lay with other people. Anyone would get a shock if they met a camel like Halmetoja.

I am a little ashamed of myself when I think of that period. But I also enjoyed it, I cannot deny it. I learned from others sometimes at the birthday parties in which I was forced, from time to time, to participate. I didn't receive invitations from my acquaintances, they generally came from friends of Kaarina whose children were celebrating their birthdays. On these occasions you had to feel behind a quilt for rubbers, ends of pencils, used pencil-sharpeners, bitter-tasting licorice sticks or exercise books so ridiculously small that they wouldn't hold any decent notes. Then you had to play hide and seek, or, with your hands tied behind your back, bite at an apple which hung on a string above your head and which always slipped away from your mouth. That was really fun. Everyone laughed. But the best was when someone had a tantrum: that's what I was waiting for, and that's why I went to these parties. With bated breath I followed every detail. The reaction of the adults was every bit as important. I learned a lot. An uncontrolled racket nearly always resulted in a favourable result for the child. I understood that it is necessary to lower oneself, however humiliating it might seem, and descend to the adults' level. There is no other way. Ear-splitting screams or nerve-racking, monotonous crying are coercive means that lead to the exhaustion of the adversary, and thus to surrender. I should like to say that Kaarina is an exception, but this is not the case. She is 34, an age which would make me cry if I were in a similar position. But reaching such an age demands blindness to certain matters, otherwise one cannot bear what one sees. Life is merciful, they say. Life numbs!

Kaarina arranged a party, and I wearied my guests by showing them all my drawings over a period of four years. After that it was their turn to draw. Each of them was given crayons and paper, they had to keep to the subject and no one was allowed to talk, otherwise I interrupted them immediately. Sometimes I went out on to the balcony in October in my swimming trunks, locked the door from the outside, and howled, sometimes I threw myself on the floor and stopped breathing, or peed in the bed until I got what I wanted. Babysitters I drove away at the door, I'm a child, after all, and out of the mouths of babes. . . so I said what I thought of them. Almost always I commented on their appearance; the girls were at a tender age, and sensitive about it.

Our life changed. The telephone, the doorbell, no longer rang. Matters were in order. I read a lot, there was plenty of time. I didn't visit the windowsill for a long time, I even forgot my binoculars and card index. In the dark of the autumn evening there was no sound in our living room apart from the click of Kaarina's knitting needles or the rasp of a pen, the gentle rustle of paper as I turned a page.

Kaarina had become very quiet, and that pleased me. Her sleepiness, on the other hand, concerned me. She would fall asleep in the middle of a meal, fork in hand, or slip under the water in the bathtub. I rescued her many times. Often it seemed that she was afraid of me. She coughed up water, gulped in air and looked at me as if I were the guilty party. She no longer loved me, I could see it in her eyes, I had become repugnant to her. She quickly took a towel and wrapped it around her body. She said nothing, but I understood that I had best leave the room.

Perhaps I sometimes did wrong, perhaps I was a little selfish, sometimes unfair, I don't know. But in her inner self she know that I wanted the best for her, and I believe that she approved my plans in her own quiet way. One evening I received confirmation: she thanked me. It was a great moment. We were sitting together, Kaarina in her armchair, I in mine turning the pages of a book, when she raised her moist eyes and smiled at me. I read in them humility and deep gratitude. I thought: now she will forgive me and love me again. Deeply moved, I was unable to do anything but go to the record player, select from our collection Mozart's Piano Concerto no. 20, and begin to play the romance. Then we lacked nothing.

1985 **Annika Idström**

My child, my mourning dress,
shadow-eyed house,
I'm a crossroads where innumerable paths
twist and turn towards you.

Like a cuttlefish
I conceal myself
so you can't find me.

Listen,
mothers live in a gingerbread house
and stir a witches' brew.

Mothers charm their children
into visions of love's blinding flowers.

You flutter in the warm garden
like a serious glance
till it's evening and the lights go on.

Then you're a house, a ship with lights,
and oh how I'm terrified
someone in the garden will tumble on a scythe.

Up from the depths I've thrust you
into the ranks of the dying.
And now, my five-year-old,
I'm terrified of your grief
when you demand the impossible:
that I'll never die.

If I were good at deceiving, I'd think up
diamonds with battleships inside.
If I were the moon, I'd lift
the sea up and look at the ocean floor.
If I were the sea, I'd freeze
a glass lid over the top of me for ever.

1983 **Eira Stenberg**

EAT THIS MESSAGE

Streetcar drivers!
At nights Helsingfors is the city of the birds,
Building project seagulls, noisy & rank,
of mysterious blue electricity, a solitary wild duck

where the finally used-up sway to and fro eyes melancholy &
bluntly they tell in a hurry a few small sparrows sometimes
of loneliness, chaffinches and pigeons stupidly
chewed-up lips softly, glass clear jerky throws
who the night is, and where grey asphalt, speed
without you believing laughter
for one single second that they have found it
around their worn-down shoes, knee-high
in bloody bandages, used up
they give you their hands and whisper
that the truth exists, right
here, in between your hat & their hopes
of a better-world & this
unpleasantly real one where the ladies sit the pastry tables fat
presses sweat & flesh, twitter
that they all wished it had-never happened,
hissing:
'No, don't look at them, children,
they're awake,
they live quite shamelessly,
naked.'

1980 **Thomas Wulff**

MIDSUMMER EVE

A middle-aged civil servant on his way home in the bus, sits with a briefcase over his knees, looks straight ahead, notices the bus stopping and starting again, people getting on and others getting off. It is hot at last, and the people look bothered, for they have forgotten that it was cold. Where he is passing there used to be grey façades, wooden houses. Now the façades are white, the wooden houses are gone, the new bridges over the water are larger, broader and smoother than ever before. Yet the journey from his home to his place of work has not grown shorter.

It is two o'clock in the afternoon. His family has gone off to the country, as people usually do, to the summer cottage by the lakes. He thinks about the long journey and already knows that he does not want to go. He wants to remain in his wooden villa, near his berry bushes and his apple trees. He wants to remain in the silence, even though it has vanished, for right next to his house passes the wide new road, and for several years now he has had to get used to explosions.

When he came to the city over thirty years ago in order to study, this villa idyll existed outside the city like an oasis of silence, spreading trees and in the autumn bright red and yellow walks, falling leaves and the congenial silence from well-heated houses. It was a city outside the city. He dreamed of being able to live there, but never thought it could be a reality. He wanted to complete his studies, get an interesting job, make a career. His thoughts did not go so far as marriage. Now when he was alone he saw his life as turned grey, shrunken and finished, he himself old, the children fully grown.

When he moved into the house the suburb had already begun to decline, and its romantic splendour was gone. The shady walkways were no longer silent, and the bold villas had been replaced by others, built for people who had new requirements. Since the house was old he got it cheap.

In those days he would have bought birch saplings and taken them home for Midsummer Eve, stuck them in the earth by the doorstep. Within a week they began to wither. While the children were little they had mostly stayed at home, but later in the evening they drove somewhere to watch a midsummer bonfire.

During later years he had most often driven over to the summer cottage, which they had built with the help of a carpenter. He had also experienced midsummer in wartime. The blue-and-white flag on a tall pole in a courtyard, dirty grey tents and soldiers who had managed to get spirits from somewhere. But no bonfires, for they might guide the ferocious enemy. Now it was all curiously far away, like youth itself, all of it lost in the romanticism of the past, a picture book of which he could turn the pages and dream about, but which never came back. Somewhere in his body, like a soreness or a sorrow, memory lay waiting for a moment when it might master him. Here and now was the reality.

The reality was his work, the documents that each morning were shovelled to his table, the conversations with colleagues at work, and then the view across the square, the vegetable stalls, the fishing boats, the water and the cranes. Reality was his vacation that would begin on the first of July. Reality was the bushes he had planted, the garden that was flowering, in red and yellow and blue, and a little in white. He loved strong colours, but was too old to hear crickets. The children were no longer reality. They would leave home, they were fully grown and had their own opinions. He had done his bit. He did not need to worry about them, but they gave no happiness either. They would not choose his life, and it was so much easier for them to get started. Each day that they lived he moved one day closer to his death.

On summer evenings he sat in a garden chair, and looked at the water of the lake, or at the new road, and waited for sunset. On Sundays he hoisted the flag in the morning. Sometimes he thought that his wife did not understand what he loved, but that feeling too disappeared when he realised that it was a matter of indifference whether anyone else loved what he loved, a scent and an evening.

He sometimes thought about death. Did it come perhaps like a colour or a coldness, or in one's sleep at night. His life was not insured, his wife had often asked him to take her into consideration. If he had a heart attack, a cerebral haemorrhage or something else, was there really any point in thinking of others? They had the villa, after all, and a little money. They did not have him, but he was merely someone who came and went.

Now it was summer, and to it belonged his rites. He admired youth, the light movements and springy steps of young women. In August he usually ate crayfish with close friends, and during all the months of summer he was alone. When he was in the country he tried to get outside, and in the city the floorboards creaked with his footsteps. Everything grew, and the warm scent of ripe berries and flowers came to him. He dreamed of plants which like arctic brambles needed many hours of sun, and every year he planted something new. When he came home there was no more work, in spite of the briefcase on the writing desk.

He goes up the sand path to the house and already knows what he is going to do. He opens the door, picks up some newspapers from the floor, then changes his trousers and goes out to water flowers. On the expressway the traffic is growing and from the water there is a sound of motor boats. Only much later in the day, when he has performed those tasks that give him peace, is he roused to the awareness that he ought to make a telephone call. He calls his wife and wishes her a pleasant holiday, he has no time to come now, he says, and in any case his vacation begins in a week's time. Deep inside he feels relieved.

He has no plans when he goes outside again. The light has attained its greatest strength, the plants the most of their energy. Now the bonfires will burn, and on large dance floors that smell of birch and sweat people dance the night away. The days grow shorter and shorter, and time cannot be stopped. He sits down in the half-dark living room, where the curtains are drawn and the dust rests. He sits and closes his eyes, and does not want to go out.

1961 **Jörn Donner**

A town,
a broad childhood street, a rippling smell of asphalt,
sleep curled up in a ball against a wall.
Under its courtyard there was the overwhelming
stale warm smell of a black cellar.
In the windows of its house familiar faces were reflected, in the serials
the sounds of radios, from the roof views in every direction
over the whole breathing town. There, on the roof,
it was easy to decide, standing in rubber shoes:
if I get down alive, I'll live!
From the depth of its courtyard balloons rose
towards the eye of the sky,

the swords of Christmas trees wounded many hands and minds,
beside its rubbish chutes a great stream of love awoke
for a girl with a pointed cap and a flat chest,
a longed-for Russian ice-cream. In its gateways
a scent of leather jackets lingered, dusk softened
by cheap alcohol soap hairgrease, a loneliness that read many books,
an ego that wanted to be itself for ever.
Childhood, all childhood in the same stony language,
soil into which the foundations of houses have sunk their teeth.
Kallio, hewn with big ugly hands
from a rock that's stronger than the sky,
hewn with curses in a language only wild men speak,
a language that at school was washed out of our mouth with soap;
this language, the stroke of its every knife, the crash of a bottle
is in me, it rows through my veins its own rotten boat,
it rises into a fist against every command,
it longs for the freedom of a broken tree, for an engine's exhaust,
the inviting expression in the glass eyes of cars.
Kallio, every day I rebuild you
on the ruins where you're second already,
I climb on to your stone bear as I swore I would when a child,
I build my own cabin in a stack of firewood that can't be burnt,
to be part of the never-stopping train of memories.
Kallio, on your tin roofs
the name, deed, purpose of all your people
has been written in tar. It's always on your side, is truth,
ever distrustful of others and unique:
the ever indissoluble bond
between man's noise, stone and iron!

1980

I'm drinking tea,
watching a storm clear up through the window,
leaning carefully against a rickety table.
I'm happy and alone. Here on the hill

I'm now, at last,
the Old Man, the Wise Man of the Mountain;
always a kind word for others,
advice on every problem.
The river flows through the valley below,
the wind blows, and the aspens
I've been constantly cutting down
are still making a noise
on the other side of the loose windowpanes.
The river flows against the wind, lazily,
and I'm drinking old
stale tea, with a smile.
I came here, for that's how it once was.

1985

On every side there are junipers,
old, massive,
reminders that
this rocky hill too
was once an island
defying the sea.
Here now I sail,
ever more safely
than as a son of the sea.
The sea disappeared, a lake came;
the lake was drained, but no field emerged;
mere alluvium, all right for birds.
They're the fittest inhabitants, after all.
And when a snipe creaks,
and then bleats with its tail feathers,
I shout mute encouragements at it.
Fly, fly, defend your territory,
guard it alertly!
Don't ever let anyone on it!

1985

Hannu Mäkelä

When I was born, Helsinki was a medium-sized
town with cobblestone streets
A few years later the war broke out
I had just learned to keep my mouth shut
Old ladies lay strewn about the streets
after the bombs fell   They were trying to kill us all
All order was gone   One furious night
that came rushing down, blacking everything out,
Mother carried me down to the cellar
Then she vanished, she had no eyes
It got cold and wet and dark
You felt it in your lungs
There was an iron door you were not to open
When I screwed my eyes tight the house was composed
of swinging cobwebs, and they strung all
the dead from long ropes in the cellar passage
Just when a bomb dropped quite close by, Mother
and Father embraced for one last time
as in a film adults alone may view
The sirens had gone wild, they invaded
my ears through my earflaps
Father was away all the time, though this slipped my mind
I carried my white cat into the cellar   We sat there
so long it went blind, ran away
Someone found it with its head blown off in a box
marked NEWSPAPERS
I recognized it all right, I understood you
couldn't trust anyone
I did not cry, I was all dried out
I seemed to take off, rise out of myself, saw
myself lying there below without a head
I held my breath until my cat was whole again
It never worked
My lungs were useless, soon I would die
We lived in the water under a crust of ice
I was a quiet child, I shot the heads
off rats with my BB gun

It was far too difficult to breathe
Something moved back and forth like a pendulum
along the bottom under the water
It looked like the remains of a little boy
in knickers frozen solid under the ice

1984

When a person goes to pieces
        like freezing sparrows her thoughts depart
The seeds run out of her and she's hollow
        It happens so slowly, her own mother
fails to notice
        You can't hear her cry anymore, the tears
have frozen solid in her past
        and she is no one
We first take notice when her eyes
        are gone, her gaze coagulated
For a little while yet she keeps going
        as if propelled by motion itself
When she stops
        it grows quiet around her
This was she, this was she who once
        hoarded joy's love's belonging's
every possibility

1970

Claes Andersson

DEEP SOUTH NIGHTS

The flood is up: cold water is already
        licking round the steeples, strong men are groin-deep
in the high street, and the Moon, looking

down on a village in the middle of a pine swamp,
is a dad with DTs
staring at his sixteen-year-old daughter. . .
bleary and bloodshot as that
is its one eye!
Moon over the Delta, Dixie Moon.

I was born here, in the Deep South,
and I'm home again when the frog quintet
swings it in the pool among the pale waterlilies,
the Ku Klux Klan sheets stream out,
the marsh marigolds rage
in wet soil on a night silvering with rain,
and we inherit the glory and shame
of our fathers fallen in the Battle of Gettysburg –
their bloodstained Confederate-coloured tunics
in the damp dark of the attic. . .
our only inheritance we passed on to the attic,
to the quietly swinging clothes-hanger. . .
we hitched along Highway 742, through the
dark-gold-glowing crops. . . we left our mothers
to sob, to croon a Pietistic gospel
among the wall hangings and a life cut up
to make rag carpets. . .
but in the spring you have to go back
by the same route, competing
with the snow-patches broadening in the sun,
and your cheek bones
ring to the invitation of the waking pine swamp,
with spring's moonlight-pierced wings
over the flooding Delta, a paddle steamer
gliding majestically down the river Kyrönjoki. . .
and Jim, the old nigger, clops to Kauhava station
in the go-cart to meet the prodigal son!

I was born here, in the Deep South,
and I hate this territory – night

full of exploding sun in a shattering glass
and sunflower seedcases crushed into the soil,
I was born here, and at that moment
Jerry Lee Lewis's grand piano
surfaced out of the marsh, covered with mud and fluff,
he himself tapdancing on its lid, on the captain's bridge,
                    in his crapesoled shoes. . .
                                        the singers! one of them was a frog
turned into a prince, Elvis Presley, I remember
those violet-lit draughty dancehall vestibules,
                frozen pissholes in the snow,
the taste of kümmel coagulated with cold. . . that quilt-jacketed
Queen of Sheba's promises of love
behind the dance hall while the back-teeth-afloat band
played Putti Putti. . . I remember the summers!
the dim lime-dusty earth closet where
I read Nietzsche with my trousers down!
                I'm at home again when the frog quintet
                    swings it in the pond
                        among the pale water lilies,
the marsh marigolds rage in the wet soil,
and the Ku Klux Klan's sheets stream across the plain. . .
                        This road goes to New Orleans,
                                via Kaustinen,
and on the Deep South horizon
the lights of the village of Kälviä are going out.

1982

Arto Melleri

EUROPE'S ANTECHAMBER

I met him at the beginning of January, during some empty weeks of rain. He had been playing billiards alone four nights running when I offered to join him.

'Do you particularly want to play alone?'

He raised his eyes slowly to my face, stared at me suspiciously for a moment:

'Not particularly.'

We played, hour after hour, without speaking, hardly even looking at each other.

After midnight I hung the cue up on its hook and left. He came after me, although I hadn't asked him. First we walked along the verge of the motorway, then turned left. He stepped into my attic room and his head brushed the roof. He had come to stay. We never spoke about it.

At that time I was a photographer for a mediocre Danish arts magazine, that's how I made my living. He went to the social security office once a month and picked up the minimum allowance, that's what he lived on. We never needed to talk about money.

We spent the daytime sitting at home, listening to cassettes over and over, reading, dozing, or just existing. In the afternoons we used to go for long walks among the fields and conifer plantations on the other side of the motorway. Evenings, we propped up the café billiard table or, if finances permitted, went to the cinema. We both liked the claustrophobic movies of the Forties. Often after the film we went to the cake shop in the marketplace and ordered marzipan pastries.

He never lost his cool. Morning and evening, the same before and after sex. He wasn't particularly interested in his own body, or in mine. He preferred lying still and staring at the ceiling to busying himself in the antechambers of love. He slept in a little pair of blue briefs, I in a T-shirt.

I slept soundly all night long, he stayed awake. He lay on his back and smoked one cigarette after another. Often I woke at night and found him staring at me like he was insane. Sometimes I was really afraid that one night he would strangle me and chop my body up for firewood. In the morning, when I was ready for a new day, he entered his dream world.

In those first weeks I sometimes asked him what he spent his nights thinking about. He didn't answer, just shrugged irritably and was silent. Conversation really wasn't one of his strong points. He would give you brief answers to specific questions, but if you tried anything more general he would reply: 'That's private.'

I got to know his abrupt movements and tense body, but I didn't have any business inside his head. His cool never let him down. His self-control was even more perfect than the round spheres of the billiard table. You couldn't get a grip on him. If he was in a particularly good mood, he would sometimes stroke my hair and say, in a low voice, 'A-ah.'

After four months of living together I knew a few facts about him. I never got an overall view of his personal history, but I did learn to interpret, to lay out and put together the pieces of the puzzle.

He had spent his first 14 years in the African savannah, on the borders of Kenya and the Sudan, run away to Nairobi and there learnt to speculate with money from the dollar tourists, to live in the streets and the bars, to sleep in the sweaty arms of syphilitic prostitutes and to swallow, easily, little white pills. His parents were Danish missionaries or commercial agents or (most likely) both. At some point he had done time, either in Nairobi or Denmark. Why, and for how long, I've only the smallest inkling.

He didn't really drink, or show the slightest interest in drugs. On his 19th birthday he swallowed a bottle of 45 proof, but it had no effect. Perhaps he smiled just a little bit more.

One night he went out for a crap as usual. He covered his thin body with a sweater and a pair of black trousers, took his cigarettes and lighter from the night table, and closed the door without looking back. I went on with my technicolor dreams.

He never came back from that trip.

Rosa Liksom

1985

Very possible that once I thought
it was the 'great' simplicity I sought.
After all, when the road stretched through narrow
forests, entirely ugly cottages lay thrown out on the fields,
it was beautiful to see how sea and sky
there by the shore reflected one another.

When now from the window I idly consider
some bit of forest with snow-slush under grey clouds,
the slope's bare bushes, forgotten summer tools,
birches and firs, scrubby wild vines
I find the 'great' simplicity complicated.
There is far too much that is unseen between trunks,
shadows of unease, and a magpie
flies violently up and is with ugly wingbeats
soon gone. Icy winter stands at the door.
This hesitancy everywhere, even in the mind:
where then is the simple in the simple?
Was the secure certainty that fields and heavens open
when a forest, a curve in the road suddenly lead
away, past, and are swiftly lost
in their own darkness? And it begins to blow.
But what winds sweep away is often pure rubbish.

1989

When I was younger I sought answers to questions.
Silence was an answer, if I listened
I heard the wind moving, a door banging.
People came and went, I looked forward
to the unknown, forgot it quickly,
both the joy and the surprise, at home.
Now I have begun to talk to myself
as though I wanted to know this person who talks
and listens so badly, inside my thoughts.
A few words found their way close up to me
as though they sought protection from something
that was too hard to see. I wrote down.
This they taught me, the words that came:
farewells are parts of everything that lives
and, when I have dreamt most intensely,
a homecoming.

1989

WINTER

For the first time, I enjoy winter.
There's so little light to it
and almost as little darkness.
Against the white backdrop of snow
I see each tree and house.
The air is cold champagne.
All the time I keep taking off my mittens
so I can be bare-handed
just as we go barefoot
in summer. Night starts as early as four
and lasts till nine in the morning.
The long nights are for staying awake
and watching the reels of your own life.
Whenever you stay awake when you could be sleeping,
the film rolls on. You can't see it, you just feel it.
You can see in the dream what has
eluded sight: summer's winter.

1980

BIRTH AND DEATH

Birth is a tough one, to pass through
a tight, bony gate, your head bloody,
mouth, eyes full of blood, mucus, piss, to suffocate,
artificial respiration, to hang upside down
in empty hollow air, noise, stench,
glowing light bulb, tortured
unconscious woman, knife bright as a blow-torch,
Ku-Klux-Klan of doctors and nurses.

Death is a tough one, to go through all this again,
to shove yourself out, all of you bit by bit,
to suffer, crush life, spirit, body,

resistance of flesh, bones, sinews, veins,
to let cut, burn,
smash through the elements: water, fire, air,
through friction, human relationships, fate, hope,
expectation,
through compression into a universe so vast that
nothing reaches, fits, agrees, invites, rejects.

That's why life is repugnant, because people are always
passing through doorways, coming in, going out,
saying this or that for someone to answer, for still another
to ask, letting needle, thread, bullet, letter, priest,
God, morning, evening, spring, autumn come and go.

1980

Veijo Meri

DANIEL KATZ
RAIJA SIEKKINEN
JONI SKIFTESVIK
JOHAN BARGUM

Daniel Katz

A LITTLE NIGHT MUSIC

Rantanen sat on a swivel-seat office chair in the loft of his cowshed, playing the old blue piano. The piano belonged to his wife who was sitting with The Log Man and The Log Man's woman in the big living room of the house, drinking the liquor and beer The Log Man had brought. They had been at if for five hours. There was no space for the piano in the living room, and it wouldn't have looked right there; as for the parlor, it hadn't been fixed yet – a crater of sand gaped where the floor should have been. The bottom logs of the parlor walls and the entire floor, each one of the three-inch-thick, wide, handsome floorboards, had rotted out. That parlor hadn't been heated for fifteen years before the Rantanens bought the house. Twenty years ago, someone had tricked an old widow who was then the mistress of the house into letting him pour a fake base around the bottom logs. He had left only minimal vents in it, and before she passed away the widow had decided and managed to block up the ones below the parlor. The floorboards had started rotting just as fast as that widow. While contemplating the purchase of the house, Rantanen had noticed that the floorboards had a certain amount of give in them, and even the seller had admitted that, so they knew that the house might need some work but did not anticipate any catastrophes. After the springiest boards had been pried up with handspike and crowbar, the horror became evident: in the whole fifty square meters of the floor, there wasn't single board that was still sound. A powerful, sweet-and-sour smell of rot and decay rose from the hole and spread into the room, and when Rantanen turned the boards over, he was thunderstruck: the undersides of the boards were completely covered with multicolored mycelial threads, ranging in color from white to indigo. There was a teeming jungle below his parlor.

Rantanen wandered around his yard like a sleepwalker, kicking rocks and toys and pets that crossed his path, his wife took care not to speak to him, the children whispered among themselves in the upstairs nursery. The following day Rantanen spent from dawn to dark on a wooded slope of his property, measuring pine trunks with a somber stare. On the third day, he took a piece of rotten floorboard to a governmental research laboratory in the nation's capital, returned, nailed the parlor door shut and tried to forget the fifty square meters that lay beyond it. He began to build a study for himself in the old log-built granary. First he cleared out a ton of junk, then he raised and insulated the floor, used a chainsaw to cut two windows in the walls. . . After reaching this point, he rested on the seventh day, leaned on his axe, looked at his handiwork and was well content with it. At that very moment, his wife and dog returned from the mailbox. She handed him an official-looking letter: in a cheerful tone, the governmental research laboratory people told him they had analyzed his piece of floorboard and had discovered that it was afflicted with a fungus, a true killer fungus with a Latin name, officer's rank, and decorations from two world wars. The laboratory enclosed a grim ten-page set of instructions on how one might try to eliminate this fungus, or at least neutralize for a moment, along with a bill for three hundred marks.

That was almost three weeks ago. Rantanen sat in the loft of the cowshed and played the blue piano. He played angrily, relentlessly, a cigarette between his lips, smoke rising into his eyes; the smoke bothered him but he didn't feel like interrupting his playing – he had decided to play the piece all the way through without a single mistake. Above the piano, at his eye level, swung the end of a thick rope whose other end was tied to a roofbeam of the shed. There were several ropes hanging here and there: assisted by his buddies, his son had managed to hoist a brown metal bedstead onto the rafters. How they had achieved this surpassed Rantanen's understanding. The boy had boasted he'd sleep on that bed anytime – or at least on a bet – but hadn't done it yet. Rantanen looked up at the bed, gauged the height, imagined himself sleeping in it; the thought made him dizzy, and he struck two false notes in a row. He clenched his jaw and started the piece from the beginning. In the village, dogs were howling and barking. His own dog replied from under the living room table – Rantanen didn't need to hear him to know that. The moon was full.

On the evening on the day of the bad news from the lab, Rantanen rode his moped to the nearest small town in eastern Uusimaa province and entered a smoky basement bar to have a few drinks. Finnish-speaking clients sat at the tables on the bar side, Swedish-speakers on the other. There were more tables in the middle, and these filled up slowly with bi-lingual growlers. One of the center tables was taken by a group of men from the nuclear power station. They drank briskly but gloomily and looked around with defiant stares: the Chernobyl disaster was still fresh in people's memory, and the nuclear workers felt they had been much maligned. Now they wouldn't sit still for one more inappropriate remark from uninformed creeps. They were determined to defend their honor along with that of their power station, and, while they were at it, they'd also defend the memory of Marie Curie, Max Planck, Einstein, and Oppenheimer, with their bare knuckles if need be; they were the nuclear boys, and their civilizing task was to pound some sense into the heads of uninformed creeps.

Glumly, Rantanen considered his own Chernobyl. He was on his fifth beer and none the merrier. The nuclear gang interpreted his glumness as a demonstrative gesture, one specifically directed at them, and proceeded to launch verbal trial balloons in his direction. Rantanen caught them and sent them back. The atom smashers were delighted. They got to their feet – hand-to-hand fighting was about to begin, for Rantanen's sense of proportion had fallen into some crack of his rotten floor. But at that exact moment, an small, nondescript, unfamiliar man sat down at Rantanen's table and in a monotone began to relate a life story so pathetic that Rantanen calmed down. The colors of the mycelial threadwork faded from his mind's eye. After uttering a few more insults, the offended nukers sat down again, looked disappointed, and aimed their glares at other targets.

The small man had had a business – but he had lost it, and that's why he was drinking. He had also had a wife and a child – but he had lost them as well, and that was another reason to drink. Now he had a new woman – but she had an alcohol problem, so that was yet another reason. Rantanen nodded. He understood. The man asked if Rantanen, too, was drinking because his wife was an alkie. Rantanen thought this over for a minute. Then told the man, from beginning to end, how the floor had collapsed under his feet. The man expressed his sympathy. Rantanen announced bitterly that it wasn't sympathy he needed: he just needed some old logs to replace the two bottom layers of the parlor walls – old, sturdy, trimmed logs. The man looked offended and said that if life, Rantanen's life, depended on such trivia, that was a sign of spiritual impoverishment. If a person didn't require anything but logs to be happy. . . 'I sure don't,' Rantanen said pointedly. . . then he just happened to have some: he had bought an old log-built threshing barn and granary, for the lumber. 'You want to make a deal?' the man asked, gloomily. 'I'll let them go cheap, money is the root of all evil. . .' He told Rantanen that he had become a boozer the moment he was old enough to earn his own money. Then things had just gone on like that, first he had spent his wages on drink, later the money from his business. . . The mention of logs cheered Rantanen visibly; he instantly nicknamed the man The Log Man, made a verbal deal with him, and got up to leave. The Log Man asked for a loan of a hundred marks, earnest money, as it were, it so happened that he was flat broke, that was one reason he was drinking, the lack of money made a man feel so vulnerable.

That evening had given Rantanen a second wind. With the help of his unemployed neighbor he had taken up the entire parlor floor, sawed and hammered loose the bottom logs, massive floorbeams and joists and braces, all of them rotten and slimy and colorful. They had carried them out into the yard, burned some, sawed and split some for firewood. They had shoveled tons of fungus-infested soil into a wheelbarrow, dumped the stuff behind the cowshed, and replaced it with fresh sand. Rantanen's wife had lent them a hand, she was energetic and strong and didn't tire easily. As the odor of rot dispersed, their moods had improved. A spirit of co-operation and pioneerdom had spread over the Swedish-speaking lands of eastern Uusimaa. Neighbors had come to gawk, shake their square heads, and utter slow words of belated advice. Then Rantanen had settled down, impatiently, to await the arrival of The Log Man.

Rantanen sat in the loft of the cowshed from which the last bales of hay had been carried out more than years ago – nevertheless, dry throat-tickling hay and straw still pushed through the cracks between the boards. Rantanen played the piano the way he did everything else: energetically, without much feeling, swearing. . . He was a rank amateur in almost every respect, his wife had taught him the rudiments of piano, and over the years he had acquired basic skills, perhaps a little more. Now he was playing, stiffly and loudly, the nocturne Chopin had dedicated to Mlle Laura Duperré, struggling manfully with those lush chords and managing to get the better of them. The notes rang out in the shed with a curious resonance; there were large cracks between the boards of its walls, a couple of windows were broken, and the tin ceiling was too high – nevertheless, the sound wandered around the sturdy struts and supports, bounced off the ceiling, and somehow came out pretty impressive.

A rumbling sound was heard from beyond the woods on the other side of the field where there were railroad tracks that had once been used to transport passengers. Now, at night, and only at night, waste materials from the nuclear plant were carried back to their great homeland for temporary disposal – since no one knew what their final resting place would be. It had taken many years to repair the tracks for this purpose, and now they bore concrete-hulled, specially constructed carriages that proceeded slowly through the moonlit night in a light *andantino* rhythm, secure in their statistical freedom from risk, and the village dogs howled lugubriously.

At last, The Log Man had appeared with his automobile, trailer, and woman. He also brought a shopping bag full of liquor and beer and smelled of alcohol on his arrival. The woman with the alcohol problem had done the driving, and thus The Log Man had been forced to drink. 'Let's relax a little,' he suggested. 'Those logs can wait.'

Rantanen had opposed this idea, but not forcefully enough. His wife, on the other hand, had been delighted with it. After only two hours of bullshit, Rantanen's wife had tried to start an argument with him, but he hadn't fallen for it. The Log Man's woman who called herself Reiska – 'just call me Reiska' – had succumbed to her vice; now she poured out cross-eyed sympathy to the mistress of the house, specifically in the name of 'womens's solidarity'. She had nothing personal against Rantanen, how could she, she admitted that readily, but it was more than obvious that Rantanen was a real shit, a typical male who did not deserve such a wife since he didn't know enough how to appreciate her. This got The Log Man going, and he proceeded to denigrate the entire female race and to praise Rantanen, whom he didn't know, for characteristics Rantanen did not possess. Rantanen's wife derided her husband for such unearned praise. Rantanen tried, in vain, to get The Log Man to shut up. Call-Me-Reiska insisted tearfully that Rantanen was unqualified, unqualified to say anything at all. Then she tried to embrace Rantanen's wife, just in a purely sisterly fashion, and announced that she had no demands to make on Rantanen, nor did she want to express any wishes in his regard, she was simply disgusted by a man with such an inflated view of himself.

Rantanen left the room, followed by The Log Man. They inspected the log-grid of the parlor that now rested on short blocks; a gentle wind blew through the room. Seen from outside, the parlor wing of the house looked like an old lady who'd pulled the hem of her skirt up to her knees to show ten skinny legs.

The Log Man clicked his tongue as he scrutinized Rantanen's handiwork. He shook his head, slapped Rantanen on the shoulder in an encouraging fashion, and said that optimism was always a laudable character trait. However, he said, a basic rule to be observed in the repair of rotten log buildings was that if the rot could be noticed up to a certain spot with the bare eye, it was surely active more than a meter farther on, but hidden from sight. 'They just keep on breeding there, those little spore devils,' said The Log Man. 'But not to worry. I've got plenty of them logs.' Then he pulled out a bottle he had saved from the women, took a long swig, and offered the bottle to Rantanen. Rantanen shook his head. All of a sudden he felt strangely nauseous. He left The Log Man to smack his lips, ran behind the cowshed, and vomited.

When Rantanen had succeeded in wading through the Chopin nocturne up to its restrained *forte fortissimo*, the cigarette in his mouth began, without any outwardly visible reason, to turn upward in the direction of the tip of his nose. His hands were glued to the piano keys, fingers spread apart in the broken chord, he was unable to detach them, and he could predict what would happen; at the same time, an image from his childhood flashed through his mind: little Rantanen learning to walk on stilts – with the bare eye his feet seem to be glued to the footrests, he is unable to detach himself from them and, soon enough, falls flat on his face, his hands still clutching the poles. . . Thus, the glowing tip of the cigarette approached the tip of Rantanen's nose until it made contact and caused a painful burn.

Rantanen roared and jumped up, spat the cigarette out of his mouth, stomped on it, slammed the lid shut of over the keyboard, kicked the office chair over and marched outside. The dog had been let loose in the yard. It ran to him, holding its head low, its cylindrical body wiggling in an ingratiating manner. Rantanen suppressed the urge to kick it, shooed it away, walked over to his car and decided to go for a drive. He fumbled in his pocket for his car keys, then remembered he'd left them in his coat pocket, and that coat was hanging in the living room where Rantanen wasn't missed if even remembered. He sat in the driver's seat in the dark garage but took care not to touch the steering wheel so that no one could accuse him of drunken driving. There always were informers lurking in the dark who would snap on the lights and there'd he be, caught in his own garage.

Before long he had to get out of the car and walk into the yard to relieve his bladder. Rocking back and forth on heels and toes, he stared up at the sky. The moon's violet light shone through the trees in the woods. He tried to look at the whole sky at once: if he got lucky, this was the time of year he might catch a glimpse of the Perseid shower, see a whole swarm of falling stars that all seemed to appear out of the same point.

He didn't see a single one, but a friendly light shone from the living room windows of the old log house. Slowly, the glow of fireflies inside his head dimmed; their buzzing had already subsided. Rantanen buttoned his fly and went into his house.

1989

Raija Siekkinen

THE MEAL

In the trap was a pike.

Hanna had put the trap out purely from habit: during the whole summer they had not got a single fish that they had not thrown back into the sea. There had been roach, which left just the memory of a swift glint as they fell through the open mouth of the trap and slipped swiftly, invisibly, into the depths. There had been green tench, which made a sound that brought to mind the dull plop of air bubbles rising through mud. Most often the trap was empty, and a green slime hung from its net with a smell like the sea floor at low tide when the water has fled and the damp green and brown beach, as if covered in lichens, is exposed. A motor boat mooring had been built on the opposite shore, and behind it, in the forest, a sludge basin into which a pump constantly sucked the mud of the sea bottom. At night its whine could be heard clearly on this side too. Fish were no longer comfortable here. All the same, every time she came, Hanna rowed out to set the trap among the reeds, without thinking why.

The pike lay motionless at the bottom of the trap. It was a big pike; its stomach glistened gold, its back was dark and hard and narrow, its yellow eyes stared expressionlessly. That's what it looks like when it lies motionless against the green sea-bed, lying in wait for smaller fish, Hanna thought. She opened the trap, and the pike slithered along its base and fell into the boat, jumping and thumping against the side for the whole journey back to the shore. Hanna looked at its body, bouncing, taut as a bow. No fear now that it would succeed in getting over the side of the boat and into the water. All morning, and throughout the preceding night, she had had an empty, hungry feeling; as if the July heat had burned her, charred her like the parts of the garden where the sun shone from dawn to dusk.

She had left home in the early hours of morning, cycled through the forest, and the sky had been covered with a glowing haze which had told her that the day would be another hot one. No one had noticed her departure; no one had come after her. Hanna had slept on the upstairs bed, loose-springed and so short that her feet stuck out beyond the end, smoked, listened and then lain with her eyes closed, in her mind odd words and half-phrases which now felt like too many cigarettes on a hung-over morning. As she lay there, it felt as if there was no one whom she would have wanted to see, and it had been as easy and empty and hopeless as old age. She could not remember having felt like this ever before. She fell asleep, and her dreams were as black and echoing and splashy as drains.

As Hanna walked up the shore carrying the struggling pike in her hands, her brother arrived. He stood next to the steps and smiled at Hanna.

'Hello,' he said.

'I knew it was here you'd be,' he said.

Beneath his eyes were blue-red shadows, and the blue of his eyes had faded, transparent as water.

'A fine pike,' he said.

Hanna looked at the pike. Now it opened and closed its mouth, and she saw its bony jaws and the big, square mouth which could gulp small fish down whole.

'It needs killing,' said Hanna.

'Give it here.'

Her brother took the pike and carried it towards the sauna. Hanna followed. In front of the sauna was a chopping block, some uncut logs piled up on top of bilberry twigs, and an axe struck into a block of wood. On the ground were splinters of wood, bark and sticks from many years, all of them already blackened and composted, making the surface black and soft; after rain, it stayed wet for days. Hanna's brother put the pike on the chopping block, held it still with one hand and chopped its head off. The fish jerked and twitched, the tail flailed against the block, thrashing vehemently; blood flowed on to the block and the axe's blade was red.

'It's alive,' Hanna said.

She watched as the fish's severed head opened its mouth and the gills opened and shut and, a little lower down, the heart beat.

'They're only reflexes,' said her brother.

All the while as her brother opened the fish and gutted it, its head continued to open its mouth. The heart went on beating.

'Kill it,' said Hanna.

'It's dead already, really it is,' said her brother.

Hanna turned and crossed the courtyard, went inside, took a bag of potatoes from the cupboard, poured them into a saucepan, covered them with water and went out on to the steps to wash them. The potatoes were as white and round as balls, the skins as fine as human skin peeling after sun. She took the pot to the stove, lit a fire, and laid the table with plates and glasses and forks and knives, butter and tomatoes from the cellar, and bread from the cupboard. She did everything as she had always done.

She fetched water from the well. The early summer had been wet: it had rained constantly, the local papers had sympathised with holiday-makers and the weather forecast promised good weather which never came. Hanna had enjoyed the rain and the fog, which closed in around life and made people and houses invisible and deadened sound. Then the hot weather began. The newspapers and television showed half-naked, well-toasted people, the radio seemed to play non-stop folk music. Hanna sought shady streets. Here the lupins and willowherbs and cow parsley had grown taller than her. Going to the well, Hanna could not see ahead, the heavy lupin flowers brushed her face, the sky was empty and open, and she was afraid.

When the wood had burnt to embers, Hanna put the fish, stuffed with spices and butter and wrapped in aluminium foil, in the oven. Soon she was able to bring it to the table in its partly burned covering, sizzling and fragrant. They began to eat. Hanna toyed with the potatoes on her plate, pulled fish-bones away from the flesh with her knife. She remembered the pike's head, its eyes.

'Why aren't you eating?' asked her brother.

'I'm not hungry.'

'This is good,' her brother said.

Hanna took small bites from her bread and chewed them for a long time.

'Nothing happened,' said her brother. He was sitting opposite Hanna, his wrists against the edge of the table, holding his knife and fork, and looking at Hanna. 'Do you hear. Nothing happened.'

'Mmm,' said Hanna.

Her brother went on eating.

Nothing had happened. Everything was as before, as always. Everything would always be like this. Hanna sat motionless and thought about it. In her mouth was a piece of bread, it was difficult to swallow. She remembered how she had gone outside to eat, by herself, sat at a table covered with a white cloth and chewed meat which gradually lost its taste, tried to swallow, chewed again and then swallowed the meat and washed it down her throat, which seemed too narrow, with mineral water. She had begun to pull at another piece of meat, small enough to swallow, and it had all seemed like a task which she would not be able to complete, this eating of good meat and gravy and salad and potatoes, for which she had paid forty marks. Walking home along the Second Line she had seen the street and houses and people floating around her, and everything had been bright and sharp and come towards her as fast as a bottle that flies through the air, smashes against the wall beside you and shatters on the floor. In front of a hairdresser's she had often visited she began to feel sick. That was the end of the good meal she had treated herself to. As she walked on, she saw a woman with a little girl with a black eye. She saw Dimitri, carrying an abacus, a shepherd's crook in his hand, making his way towards the dole office. The world swayed and swam and its colours were garish, tasteless. Thc sky glowed so brightly that she thought an atom bomb had exploded somewhere and all living things would soon be charred and dead. The rumble she heard came from the number ten tram, which left people carrying briefcases and plastic bags at the stop. The wind blew sawdust into her eyes from the wooden houses that were under demolition.

'I wish you'd eat,' said her brother.

At home she had stood in front of the mirror and looked at her face, which was completely naked and devoid of any expression. It was like a completely unknown face, as if the mirror was warped, or as if she had seen her reflection in a glass along which water ran.

'No,' said Hanna.

She had slept like a log and, in the mornings, been awoken by everything coming back into her mind with a bang. She never knew where she would find herself: she woke in the kitchen, in the bathroom, surprised herself staring at the underside of the dining table, on which the glue had made brown marks as if in a language she could not read, or washing that hung, crinkled, above the bathtub, having dried in too constricted a space.

'Everything's fine,' said her brother. 'It's all over, believe me.'

One night, Hanna remembered, the furniture from the top floor of the block of flats next door came tumbling down through the glass on to the street below. People gathered to look. A young man stood on the window-sill, clinging to the window frame, and threatened to jump. On the tarmac lay glass that crunched underfoot, and splintered wood and crippled furniture. The police came.

'He won't jump,' people said.

'He won't dare.'

Some began to drift away. A policeman's hands pulled the man inside from behind, and quickly brought him down through the courtyard and into a black maria. That same autumn, a wooden house in the neighbourhood burned, whose conservation had been the subject of argument. A little while later Hanna's brother bought a car. They had spent the evenings driving along the motorways that led out of Helsinki, stopping from time to time to listen to the knocking that came from the engine, and always they had to turn back at some point, to return to the city, to go home. The autumn had been warm, and it had lasted, on and on, as if they had been granted a reprieve, but Hanna had already lost her long, slow mornings, her dreams were empty and white and she woke panic-stricken, feeling as if she was late for work. She already knew that the world was ending, bit by bit until there was nothing left, and she woke only to see how much had already gone.

'I wish you'd say something,' said her brother.

Hanna remembered the night when all the winter snows had melted. Water had come from the eaves, it had flowed down the streets, water-drops had hung from the trees and glistened in the light of the street-lamps, and all around was the sound of sliding, falling drops and running water and ice melting on the roofs, there was not a moment of silence. She had spent that night standing on the balcony, and in the morning her brother had come.

'I'm tired,' said Hanna, 'tired.'

Her brother cornered the last remnants of fish and potato on his plate. On Hanna's plate was an untouched portion that already smelled of cold, uneaten food; a fly circled, landed on a potato, rubbed its front legs together and walked along the hard, grey-red flesh of the fish. Hanna watched it.

One cannot be lonelier than this, she thought. She got up, went out through the door, and sat down on the steps. The sun shone so brightly that it seemed as if all colour had been leached away and the trees and the earth and the sky were glowing a shimmering white. Through the window she watched as her brother buttered more bread for himself, took a bite, ate. From the rubbish heap she heard a rustling; she saw the piece of paper in which the fish's head had been carried there, and which had now been opened, and she saw the gills, which were still moving. Suddenly she felt happy, with the sort of well-being that comes in the moment after a hard blow to the head and before the nausea and pain, and she remembered the dream which she had had when she had come here in the morning.

In the dream they had been locked into the porch. Both the doors, inside and outside, had been locked, and through the window they had watched the winter like a play.

'When will they let us out of here,' her brother had asked from time to time, and Hanna had answered:

'When winter is over.'

The forest had been full of snow, little animals had slipped from crevice to crevice, and all of them had a bite taken out of them, from tail or paw; the snow was full of bloody tracks.

'When will they let us out,' her brother had asked.

'Winter's nearly over.'

Hanna got up, opened the porch door, and went inside.

In the evening she was alone again. She lay in the garden swing until late at night, and watched as the darkness rose from the ground, reached the tops of the trees, turned the buildings and the trees and the ground black and left the air grey. Then she saw the bat. It soared over her, black against the sky, and soon returned. It was soundless and black as a secret thought, beautiful as a beast of prey. They had been here for eight summers without once seeing a bat, and now: here they were. Hanna lay in the swing, which stirred slightly in time with her breathing. She lay with her eyes open, and saw the black branches and sharp black pine needles against the grey sky; and the bats, making swift curves above her, were as if her own thoughts had for the first time taken form.

1983

Joni Skiftesvik

THE BLACK GULL

Heikki and me were standing in the warm cabin – looking out onto the trawler deck where dad and Lemetti were hauling in the trawl out of the sea.

It was drizzly, and there were gusty squalls coming from the southwest. Further out to sea, round the Artunmatala shallows, a low-lying fogbank had settled. Heikki had been out on deck several times to warn dad about it, but in his hurry dad had snapped at him not to come out there and get frozen: 'Keep back in with Markku. Have a thermos of coffee. We're not scared of fogbanks: we've got radar aboard, and automatic pilot. It'll not get too thick for us to get home.'

Heikki felt somewhat put down.

'Who does the lad got this bragging from?' he said. 'You can't go mucking about with the sea. I know it, but the lad doesn't seem to. The black seagull's not flown close enough to him yet.'

I felt sure Heikki had some old yarn in mind about a black seagull. Before I could ask more, he'd started. As he spoke he wiped the rimed cabin window with his sleeve and looked out at the approaching fog.

*

This goes back to the prohibition days.

Outside the territorial water limit there were bootleggers' ships swinging round on their anchors. And motor-boats used to come alongside and collect the cargo. Took it back to the mainland. Got rid of it there at a huge markup. The hooch from the ships in these waters went as far afield as Kuusamo. And the same stuff was sold many times over before ending up in someone's belly. Those who broke the law hit it rich. The lawabiding stayed broke. That's the way it's always been.

The fortunes of a lot of the wealthy families round here were founded in those days. A certain pile of bricks and mortar was put up with bootlegging money. I'll name no names, but I'll say this much: the local councils and Rotary Clubs are well-stocked with bootleggers and their offspring – ranting on about law and order and horrified at kids irresponsibly drinking lager and riding their mopeds with no lights.

And there were other things, too, besides smuggling hooch. A fair number of men fell in the sea in those days. And hardly any of those cases were ever so much as investigated. They were after each others' cargoes. All they needed was a bullet in the head, chains on the legs, and over the side with the bastard.

I was doing a lot of fishing in those days. Money and food were tight with us. The children were still little. Lemetti, Erkki. . . your dad wasn't even born then. We were living in the old part of Vahtola.

I've never seen an autumn like that before or since. It was rain, rain, storm, storm for weeks on end: not a day's respite in between. I did my fishing off the outer islands and lived in those fishing huts, wherever I could light on one and get a roof over my head. Storm was ripping the nets apart. Lord, how I froze, mending them and sorting out the tangles. That's how I got this heart trouble, you see. Nowadays, without my pills, I'd not get about at all. Heart can hardly keep turning over, and half my arteries at least are gummed up. Blood's too thick, I'm always cold, and I need longjohns even in the summer.

To begin with the fish were on the increase. I was salting them by the firkin. It was because of that haul that I was still hanging about there – otherwise I'd have taken off for the mainland. I could have managed it before the worst of the storm hit me.

Then suddenly the fish stopped coming, and I was down with a bad fever. Hell, I was in bad shape. I lay there on one of the fishing-hut bunks, I was shaking so much you could have heard my teeth rattling outside. I forced myself up onto my pins – enough to make myself some fish soup and warm up some sea water: there's so little salt in it you can certainly manage to drink the stuff. I swallowed it down just as it was, for there was no coffee or tea around, and I wasn't up to picking any raspberry leaves. I'd got worms, I was bleeding at both ends.

Three days I lay there in that hut before the fever began to quieten down enough for me to totter down to the shore and take a look at the boat. The sea-level had risen, and it'd tossed the boat onto the rocks sideways on. It was holed in one side. I got so down, I slumped on the rock there and cried like a kid. I went back into the hut, and there was a coil of cord on the wall. I took it down, and I thought to myself, now the time's come: it's your turn, Heikki, to swing.

You've no idea what that means, and there's no reason why you should. But those were hard times, and there was many a one who decided to pack it in and take a one-way ticket out. I stood for a long time holding that cord in my hands. Inside my head, a voice kept saying over and over again suicides are a feeble lot, you're not one of them yourself, and remember, you've got a wife and two lads.

I threw the cord into a corner, and never again have I thought like that, with a rope in my hand. I gathered up my tools and went back to the shore, and I started banging away at the hole in the boat side.

Then, from God knows where, there was a seagull – stepping along there on the rocks nearby. The thing was pitch-black. It gave me a hell of a shock. Now, I thought, things are really getting bad for you, Heikki, if the Devil sends his bird along. A thought drove through my head – comical enough it seems now: they must have coal-firing in Hell, if this bird's smothered in coal-dust. The ships were coal-fired in those days, you see. The stokers and engineers were as black as that seagull.

I threw a bit of herring for it. It snapped it up in its beak and flew out to sea. I felt a bit better. I began to think I might get out of this yet.

I managed to patch up the boat and get it into some sort of shape, and I swapped islands. I kept the nets on the west side of the island, for there was a promising-looking rock there for whitefish. But I got nothing, save the odd bullhead. It began sleeting down. The water was doing funny things. Alternately rising and falling. The wind kept swinging round, changing direction and knocking great pine trees flat on the island-tops.

I can tell you straight: I've spent my whole life at sea and on the islands, but I've never been as scared as I was then. I began to get the feeling that nothing was right. Nature'd gone topsy-turvy, and the weirdest sounds were coming from all sides – from the sea, the storm, the squalls. First it was like an old man's death-snoring when he's on his way out, then, all at once, it was a young girl's shrieking.

I stood on one of the knolls where the pines had been knocked flat and stared at the sky. Not a thing in sight, save some stormy black rainclouds. Suddenly I realised I was shouting. Stop that wind, I bellowed – long enough at least for me to get back to Helmi and the lads! But no use, God damn it. Only got worse. I wasn't getting any more fish, and I wasn't even trying. If I'd let the nets down, even on the lee side, the storm'd have had them away.

Days went by, a week at least. The hut I slept in, and kept a fire going in, was a ramshackle old thing. Food was running out, and my fever was worsening again. I lay on the bunk and I went into some sort of drowse. Couldn't even distinguish night from day any more. Whenever I opened an eye, it was still raging round the hut, exactly the same. I began to believe death was on me. I've never been a mocker of the Lord. I called on him now for help. I was aching all over, pain in my head and in my hands and in my legs and in my belly. I prayed God, take away these pains and this fever, and bring me home.

I woke out of my doze when there was a knock at the door. I rolled myself round onto the floor and crawled on all fours to open up. Outside the door stood the black seagull. Good God! Talk about a shock! I thought, now it's come to get me. I'm not dying, be off! I shouted, as far as I was capable of shouting at that time, and slammed the door shut. It knocked again. I opened up and tried to tell it it was wasting its time: I wasn't bad enough to be changing parishes yet. When it just went on staring at me with that devilish eye, I bellowed that I wasn't one of the Devil's own anyway! Robbery and whoring and worse – they'd been the sports of others in our village, not me! Of course, I've always liked a drink when I got one, but that's no sin. If it is, then Paul and the whole New Testament lot are sinners – for they drank wine now and then, you know.

When the seagull knocked a third time, I wasn't up to shouting any more. I just said, 'Coaly, *you* save me: bring me some help'.

How long I slept on the floor, there by the door, I've no idea. When I did wake, there was a strange fellow standing there beside me, wearing dark patched clothes. He dragged me onto the bunk, got a fire going in the fireplace and made me something hot to drink. He gave me that and fed me some sort of fish soup or something, as if I were a tiny tot. He put his hand there behind my neck and raised my head, and he had a spoon in his other hand, to feed me with. I tried to tell him where it hurt, but he said never a word. I noticed the black gull was standing near the fireplace. I wasn't afraid of it any more. The fellow muttered something to the bird.

I dropped off to sleep again and when I woke, the fellow was holding out a cup to me. It reeked of medicine. I drank it. It tasted bad. Again I dropped off. I went through some muddled dreams about the sea, and birds, but all through the dream I knew the sickness was starting to get better, and the pain and fever were going away. I was sweating like a pig.

When I woke, I stared at the ceiling, expecting the fellow to be bringing a cup to my lips again, and the gull to be peering from the floor. But there was no sign of man or gull. I felt as if there was a bit of strength in my legs. Carefully I got up and tried them out. At first they tended to give a bit, but soon they began carrying me. I staggered round the hut and outside. I couldn't see the man or the gull.

The weather was fine. Even though it was cold, the sun was shining, and the visibility was good. The wind was coming in from the west. I touched up the boat and got it into a bit better shape, put my few things in it and sailed for the mainland.

I did let on to people about the black seagull, and the strange man. But of course no one took me seriously. They laughed and said, Heikki, what you're telling us about is your delirium. Glad you came through all that alive, though.

I couldn't be bothered to argue with them particularly, even though I knew that gull and that man were anything but hallucinations.

*

When Heikki had finished, I asked him if he'd ever come across the strange man again. To my surprise, he replied, You bet! Many's the time.

'Always he's got different clothes on, but he can't fool me. I'd pick him out among a thousand.'

'How do you know it's him?'

'I know him by the eyes. When you've seen those eyes, you'll never forget them.'

'How if he was one of those hooch-merchants,' I suggested. 'You know, you said it was that time. Supposing he'd gone out onto that island to lie low for a bit?'

'Those were no hooch-merchant's eyes,' Heikki laughed. 'I've taken a drop myself and had a look in the mirror. I've a fair notion what a hooch-merchant's eyes look like.'

1988

Johan Bargum

CANBERRA, CAN YOU HEAR ME?

Lena called again Sunday morning. I had just gotten up and was annoyed that as usual Hannele hadn't gone home but was still lying in my bed snoring like a pig. The connection was good, but there was a curious little echo, as if I could hear not only Lena's voice but also my own in the receiver.

The first thing she said was, 'How is Hamlet doing?'

She'd started speaking in that affected way even before they'd moved, as if to show us that she'd seen completely through us.

'Fine,' I said. 'How are you?'

'What is he doing?'

'Nothing special.'

'Oh.'

Then she was quiet. She didn't say anything for a long while.

'Lena? Hello? Are you there?'

No answer. Suddenly I couldn't stand it any longer.

'Okay, you can have him. I'll bring him.'

There was a shriek, then a whole string of happy exclamations and lots of Oh, thank you, Daddy's – while I sat there wondering exactly what I'd committed myself to.

How the hell do you transport a hamster to Paris?

During the following Saturday's rehearsal, Stina and I had three long scenes together, so of course Sigge blew up when I told him that I had to be in Paris that day. He's the stubbornest person I know, which more or less accounts for his success as a director; we also went to school together, and he knows me inside and out. He rushed back and forth between the rows of seats, working himself into a sweat with a series of impressive little outbursts while I tried to look guilty and Stina stood giggling in the wings; every director has a repressed desire to be on stage, so instead they do their acting during rehearsals.

When I got home after that evening's performance, Hannele had washed the dishes, tidied up, made the bed, thrown out the pile of old newspapers and bought an azalea – but hadn't gone home. It was a bit embarrassing because I'd brought Stina along with me, but the ladies pretended that nothing was wrong and sat down at the dinner table, which Hannele had set for two with candles and a dark red linen tablecloth. They had a high old time chatting and gossiping about colleagues while I had to get my own plate, light the candles and pour the wine in their glasses as well as take the two warm mussel sandwiches out of the oven. They were getting along famously until the sandwiches were on the table, but then everybody got so nauseatingly overpolite that I excused myself and slipped into the hall and out the front door without looking back and headed for the bar at Socis, where I sat staring at the wall without coming up with the vaguest plan of how to do it.

When I got home, the women had finished off the sandwiches and wine, and decamped; Hannele had left the key on the dresser in the hall. I went to bed, and right after midnight when the telephone rang, I was tossing and turning – and still had no idea of how one gets a hamster to Paris.

Susann didn't either.

'What the hell is this all about?' she said. The line was as clear as the last time; I could hear her short, intense breathing – the way she always breathes when she's excited.

'I thought I'd come down to see my daughter.'

'Oh you did, did you? Without asking me first it was convenient?'

'Not at all. Is it?'

'And what's this nonsense about Hamlet?'

'What nonsense?'

'Lena thinks you're going to bring him with you.'

'Mmmhmm.'

'You shouldn't tell her things like that. She and I have already discussed it. Don't you see how disappointed she'll be?'

'Why?'

'When you show up without him!'

'Calm down. I'll bring him.'

She paused, and then said something incomprehensible in French; I heard André's voice in the background.

'How the hell are you going to do that?'

'I'll manage.'

'Listen,' she said, sounding a bit tired. 'you know you just can't behave like this.'

'Like what?'

'I have nothing against your coming to see Lena. But I want us to plan it together. You and I.'

'Isn't that what we're doing?'

She sighed.

'And this business with Hamlet. It's sheer blackmail. By the way, she doesn't need him anymore. She forgot him a long time ago.'

'It didn't sound that way to me.'

Again she sighed and fell silent. There was just a faint breath of wind in the receiver, and far away someone was shouting in English: 'Canberra, do you hear me? Canberra, do you hear me? Do you hear me?'

Then she said: 'So when are you coming? And where are you planning to stay?'

The lady in the travel bureau where I got my ticket asked me the same question – as if it were any of her business; but I was pissed off at myself when I realized that I hadn't given it a thought. I'd simply assumed that I'd stay with Susann and André, something which I actually had no desire to do. It turned out that in the center of Paris there was a cheap Hôtel de Finlande.

At the SPCA they referred me to the veterinary division of the Ministry of Agriculture and Forestry, which in turn referred me to the French Embassy, where an official started speaking in broken English about forms and proof of profession (Hamlet's?); in other words, it was just the way I'd expected it to be.

There was only one chance.

At the bottom of Susann's closet – which was still an incredible tangle of everything imaginable – I found a piece of sturdy canvas that I sewed into a small pouch. Onto the upper corners I fastened a pair of shoelaces. Then I stuffed Hamlet into the pouch and closed it at the top with a couple of safety pins. I tied the shoelaces around my neck, put on an undershirt that held the pouch close against my body, and over that a shirt and a big, baggy sweater. It was perfect: Hamlet lay quietly in his pouch, but even if he moved around a little, it wouldn't show under the sweater.

I seemed so simple. Just a few hours on a plane with the hamster on my stomach. What could possibly go wrong?

Just to be absolutely sure, I sat in the aisle seat with a newspaper in my lap. The seat next to me was empty. By the window a lady was sitting bolt upright, her body as rigid as if someone were holding a gun on her. Hamlet was peaceful; I'd gotten through the security check without any problems, done my dutyfree shopping, had a beer and flirted a bit with a ground hotess who insisted that we knew each other, and all the while Hamlet had been so quiet that I'd almost forgotten about him.

The lady in the window seat leaned forward, holding her nose.

'Forgive me,' she said. 'It's my ears. . .'

Endless streams of French gibberish poured out of the loudspeakers, as well as something garbled that was supposed to be English. The engines roared, the plane lurched forward heavily, almost reluctantly – and Hamlet launched his first attack.

It came so suddenly that I jumped. He scratched upward with his front paws, trying to work his way out of the pouch; he was going at it so hard that it felt as though he were trying to dig a pit in my mid-section.

'Sure makes your stomach feel funny,' said the woman by the window.

'What?'

'To fly in the air. You know, they don't have time to get out of each other's way. . .'

She looked anxiously out the window and began a long, involved harangue about planes on collision courses. The flight attendants were struggling with their food trays and drinks, I managed to slip a hand under my sweater to pat Hamlet. But it didn't do any good – it merely made him more furious. The woman leaned across the empty seat as if to hold my hand. I tried to flash a nonchalant smile as Hamlet scratched away. The woman's eyes bulged: she explained that even if the pilots sighted each other at a distance of two kilometers, there wouldn't he more than four seconds before the crash. I couldn't follow it all; all I knew was that Hamlet was poking around with his nose, trying to bite me through the fabric.

His sharp teeth jabbed into me.

Now the lady had lined up a whole battery of small bottles before her. She proceeded to gulp them down one by one.

'I work at the Bureau of Statistics,' she said, smiling apologetically. 'Statistically speaking, I know that the risk is negligible, but what good does that do?'

A little while later, as we were coming in for a landing in Stockholm, she leaned forward and held her nose again. Hamlet's forepaws scratched and dug. If he managed to make a hole in the pouch, I thought to myself, what would I do then?

In the Arlanda transit hall I locked myself in the bathroom and took Hamlet out of the pouch. He'd calmed down as soon as we touched ground. Now he sat quietly in my hand, looking at me with his peppercorn eyes. His whole body shivered, as if he was freezing,

He wasn't interested in the lettuce leaf I'd brought along. 'I don't think you like flying either,' I said.

The plane filled up with Swedish and French businessmen on their way to Paris; sitting between the woman at the window and me was a garlic-smelling tub who spoke French to me for a long while without my understanding a word, and then fell asleep. While we taxied out to the runway, Hamlet was peaceful, as though he too was sleeping. The woman looked enviously at her neighbor and stopped up her nostrils, the plane accelerated, rose, and dived in along the clouds. And Hamlet went into action.

He seemed to have a definite objective: his claws kept digging and digging in the same spot.

Again, the flight attendants came running with their carts. The garlic-smelling Frenchman didn't stir, and the woman in the window seat lined up another supply of little bottles. Hamlet was indefatigable. Before long I realized that now it was about to happen: he had almost made a hole in the pouch.

I felt his sharp, eager claws against my skin.

It hurt.

The woman by the window knocked back half a glass of cognac, and looked at me with bleary eyes.

'You're not feeling well, are you?' she said.

And suddenly, as if by magic, Hamlet calmed down.

I didn't answer. Sweat was pouring out of my armpits. While Hamlet remained quiet, I didn't dare speak. Then I understood why he was quiet: something else was running down my body, down my stomach toward my groin.

'Relax,' the woman said encouragingly. 'Statistically speaking, flying's much safer than driving.'

Hamlet started up again with renewed strength. The hole seemed to be growing larger and larger. He ripped and tore at it with his teeth, and his paws kept scraping away.

There was only one thing to do: I stuck my hand under my sweater and grabbed him.

He went crazy. Already halfway out of the pouch, he started digging and rooting and biting so hard that I had to squeeze him tight to keep him quiet.

It hurt like hell.

'Look, there's Paris!' the lady said thickly. 'Hello down there!' I closed my eyes, clenched my teeth, and squeezed even tighter, pressing him against my stomach to prevent him from getting loose.

'It'll be over soon,' she said, trying to comfort me.

As if he'd understood her, Hamlet began to calm down. While signs lit up and seatbelts clicked and the lady squeezed her nose, I could feel him relax, stop biting and rooting with his forepaws until finally he was lying still with his damp little nose against my stomach, as calm and quiet as if he'd fallen asleep.

While I went through passport control and customs (as usual, they opened my hand luggage) and took the bus to Port Maillot and managed to find a taxi, wondering in passing why there was so much damn traffic on Rue St Denis right in front of my hotel, Hamlet didn't move once. 'He just doesn't like to fly,' I thought as I changed out of my bloody, smelly clothes and took him out of the pouch. It was only then that I realized why he'd suddenly gotten so quiet.

I flushed him down the toilet. Then I washed the scratches and bites on my stomach, and called them.

'Hi, Daddy,' said Lena. 'Are you here now?'

'Yes, I'm here.'

I was standing by the window. The street was still crowded; the sidewalks were black with people, and there were long lines of honking French cars.

'Did you bring him?'

'Sure.'

From time to time women disappeared into doorways with solitary pedestrians. Suddenly I understood what the crowds were all about.

'Where are you?'

'In a hotel.'

'Mama says she'll come and get you in the car.'

'Not tonight.'

'Yes, Daddy! You have to!'

'No, Lena. It's a little late and I don't feel so great.'

'Why?'

'I just got a little airsick. I'll come tomorrow morning.'

One of the women had noticed me in the window. She waved cheerfully.

'Daddy,' said Lena, 'give Hamlet a goodnight kiss for me. Right on his nose!'

The next morning I found an English-speaking taxi driver uho was kind enough not to laugh at me as he took me across the river to St Germain. It was a clear, cold day; Parisians were sitting in their café with fur coats over their shoulders. In one of the narrow streets behind Odéon, we found a petshop. The taxi driver went inside with me and started a spirited discussion with the shopkeeper. Oddly enough, he didn't laugh at me either, but helped pick out the hamster that looked most like Hamlet, put him in a shoebox, and wrote 'Hamlet' on the lid: it cost practically nothing. As I sat in the taxi with the shoebox in my arms, the driver turned around and looked at me worriedly. 'Good luck,' he said. Parisians were rushing by, hunched over, hands deep in their pockets, newspapers or baguettes as long as baseball bats under their arms. 'I'll need it,' I said.

But of course it was completely hopeless; how could I possibly get away with it?

Lena tore the lid off with a shriek of joy and picked up the hamster, pressing it against her chest, while I, who should have been relieved, felt curiously disappointed instead.

'Hey, be careful!' I said.

'What for?'

'Don't squeeze it like that. You'll hurt it!'

They lived in a giant apartment behind Champs-Elysées, with high-ceilinged rooms, whitewashed walls wlth narrow friezes near the ceiling, mirrors everywhere, pale leather sofas and armchairs, glass tables and track lighting; it was like walking into a design show.

Susann had cut her hair and started to smoke Gauloises; she gave me a friendly hug and a little smile and said, 'Nice to have you here. How the hell did you manage with the hamster?'

'Nothing to it.'

André was filming – some scene that could only be shot on a weekend.

'But that's nothing new,' she said with a small laugh.

She was dressed in something pastel-colored and a little wrinkled, which made her look girlish. She looked at me with a slightly amused expression, and suddenly I felt insecure: had I forgotten to button my fly?

'So how did you do it?'

At that moment I noticed the cat, a Siamese, stretched out languidly in an armchair, staring with shining eyes at the hamster in Lena's arms.

'Isn't he great?' said Lena. 'Guess what his name is!'

'I'll go put up the coffee,' Susann said, and disappeared into the kitchen.

'Hamlet,' I said, feeling tired. I sat down.

The cuts on my chest were stinging.

'Isn't that cool, Daddy?' Lena chirped. 'Now I have two Hamlets!'

The cat slowly raised its head, never losing sight of the hamster.

They hadn't even gotten a cage for it. After a few hours I was the only one who gave it a thought – I and the cat who lingered around the hamster with feigned indifference. By the time André got home that afternoon. I'd put the animal back in the shoebox and set it on one of the shelves in Lena's closet. The cat had settled down on Lena's bed, and alternated between looking at the closet door and at me with a slightly contemptuous expression on its narrow cat face. André was tired and preoccupied. Susann laughed and said that he was exactly like me: when he was filming, he was always somewhere else – only his body came home at night.

Maybe that's not so bad either, I stopped myself from saying. But I didn't need to: it showed all over her.

Lena had learned perfect French; she called him Papa. Susann insisted that they were best friends. During dinner Lena did most of the talking, French and Swedish mixed. I drank a good deal of wine to dull the stinging pain in my chest. Later I put Lena to bed and sat next to her with my hand on her cheek just like in the old days. In the closet the hamster rooted in its box, while the Siamese, who'd stationed itself outside the door, sat with pricked-up ears.

I explained that I wanted to walk to the hotel to see Paris by night, but after a half hour I'd had enough. On Champs-Elysées I found a Drugstore in which the only thing English was the name. I know something about mime, but mimicking 'antiseptic scab softener' was beyond my powers. So I grabbed a taxi and almost got bitten in the foot by a fox terrier lying on the floor in front – where clearly I wasn't supposed to be. The driver got furious and muttered to himself all the way back to the hotel, where I changed the bandages. For lack of anything better, I poured whiskey into the wound, which hurt so much that I sat there panting for quite a while. Later that evening the same girl appeared in the street. She waved at me again with a smile of recognition. She knew a little English: when we'd come back to the room, she told me that if I wanted to, I could take my clothes off. But I kept my shirt on.

The next day I took Lena out on the town. We went to a café where with great expertise she ordered cocoa with whipped cream and two giant waffles with jam, which didn't go down easily because my stomach was still feeling somewhat shaky in spite of the fact that most of the whiskey had been poured into the scratches. Lena was in her contemplative mood, quiet and sort of distant, and she ate my waffle and then dragged me to a playground where we played our old swinging game that she never seemed to tire of – until Susann came to get her.

Susann seemed contemplative, too. We sat down on a park bench while Lena continued swinging.

'Has she talked to you about the hamster?' Susann said.

'No, what about it?'

She bit her lip.

'The cat got it?'

She nodded.

'It wasn't my fault,' she said angrily. 'I can't be everywhere at once!'

'What did Lena say. Was she unhappy?'

'Not because of the hamster. But she wondered what you would say.'

Lena wasn't pumping; she let the swing take her up and down, up and down, and looked at us as though she'd heard every word.

'Well,' I said, 'what do you think I should say?'

'Nothing. It's better simply not to talk about it.'

I didn't reply.

'You have to understand,' she went on, 'she's so crazy about that cat. Actually, she'd completely forgotten about the hamster. That's what I was trying to tell you.'

Susann offered to take me to the hotel, but I excused myself by saying that I wanted to go straight to the airport. Lena hopped into the back seat of Susann's little Renault, and they drove off. After ten meters they stopped for a red light. It had started to rain, and Susann turned on the windshield wiper in the back window as if they wanted to wave to me. Lena pressed her face against the glass, and I smiled and waved as though to tell her that Susann had been right: how, after all, could you compare a hamster to a cat?

It seemed like an eternity before the light finally turned green, and they disappeared around the corner.

On Monday I had to stop in at a clinic because of my chest and consequently managed to be late for the rehearsal, which brought forth all the usual nasty little remarks: I hope you'll forgive us for starting without you. . . Oh, we're so honored that you graced us with your presence today. . . I hope you don't mind if we work on Finnish time, not French. Sigge had scheduled Scene Three, which meant that Stina had to chase me around the stage five times, and I had to stumble over furniture and slip on rugs, and finally get slapped by her. She put everything she had into it, especially the slap, but when Sigge finally noticed that I was walking through it he bawled me out, and when that didn't help he looked worried, told the others to take a break, came up to me and said, 'so what's up?'

'Nothing,' I said.

1986

Beyond reality

Beyond reality

I speak and listen, but my soul is in its casket as if I were formally receiving someone with my glove on: in the backlands of my words are my own footsteps and departure; two years I've been this way in alien rooms loose from time and speech has lost its significance, impoverished into commonplaces, as if I were a cleaning woman new to the house, banging herself on all the things and sloppy.

1972

Call these rooms your home and peep from the window! It's summer, the time of smiling footsteps, and the trees so thick with green the shadows fall like black tar. Call this summer the last, and let winters be forgotten, time of flowers in gardens, fragrances. Where are these sudden jasmines from as if one were off to a ball?

1976

Keeping silence
in an I greater than I:
shadowlike it throws itself ahead of me
down from higher.

1987

Here I am
my shoulders burdened with yesterday
and now the sun is setting
my eyes are wings carrying it
                    into your eternity, gods.

1987 **Tyyne Saastamoinen**

I think of a beech-tree, centuries-old, with a radiant body set beside its trunk. The mise-en-scène speeds the pulses of a photographer, an ad-man, and a moralist. The photographer sees contrasting values and substances; he snaps away and is happy. The ad-man sees with occult depth and puts a clock in the girl's hand and is happy. The moralist sees the flesh withering as the beech drops its leaves and again renews its green; he is happy. I too want to be happy. I want to snap and advertise and I am in fact a moralist; besides, I like big trees and young women. And so I went for a walk among the beech trees: photographers, ad-men and moralists were swarming all over the place, but no sign of the girl.

1964

When the Heavenly Host and the legions of Lucifer were first seen in empty space between Aries and Leo, all traffic and business stopped for almost two weeks. Newsmen and talking heads crowded the observatories: the world's TV flashed newsflashes at first six times nightly. But when they discovered the vanguard angel's sword moved much slower than light and was approximately six hundred thousand light-years long, calculations suggested the first stroke would take at least two hundred and fifty thousand years. The public's interest flagged, business and traffic again started apace, and when the astronomers showed that what was now visible on earth had occurred millions of years ago, everyone settled down: only the parson was left wondering.

1964 **Pertti Nieminen**

To the union's member country I wrote a memorandum on
two-syllable words
and simple thoughts: our M. Lautrec-Lautréamont
is a hundred years old, and in his honor will be issued a
commemorative postage stamp
printed on human skin.

Afternoon.
Now that my voluptuous belovéd has died, I
put a sweater on her, because it was always cold.
Always someone was writing about wages and dashed hopes,
in favor of sales tax, mileage allowance for stinking automobiles,
or women's pensions and subsidies for brassieres.
It is always cold when you think about words, and
(When she thinks, I grow pale)
(When courageous strangers, beyond the seas. . .)
(When I write 'Bytå', I travel)
it is cold when she is stone dead; to her memory, I publish
a two-stroke Eastern poem, consumption: five liters,
fingers, cold, Swedish steel attached to plastic, cold,
she is gone, a big bull weaves a wreath on her grave,
in her church, a red piano plays, her bones
and small head sadden me until I no longer exist,
since she is not, and no one thinks about their sheets:
not a stain in the world that I am to blame for, not a night
to make me warm. Winter comes, the coachman dies inside the horse.
The restaurant opens its clothes and is erected again.
When she is dead, nothing is again.

1965 **Pekka Suhonen**

If a lady's hat comes flying one May day
we catch it and eat it
if on the other hand it is a man's hat bought in London

we tread on it if we can otherwise
we run about and are good
we catch children's hats in both hands
upturned as in prayer or as in order
to fondle skirt-linings when the sun shines
caps do not matter so much except when
they belong to babies their small hats
we hoist on flagpoles and play
something nice on a comb it is always
memorable as when military headdresses
glide through the air and we stand there with
a net as to catch death's-head moths
at strict attention and with blood under our boots
heroes without haloes but with the lustre
of everyday in their eyes shadowed by heavy eyelashes we do not say no to tall hats
or those little skull-caps the Caucasians
carry eggs in those we go bounding after as in the
fields when it is spring and unstable lung-
patients give up we open the gate and
say farewell some time in worldtime if such
a word does not frighten it probably does frighten
one must busy oneself with small bright-red words good
if a hat comes flying.

1967

The crow has an oval face
and an interesting profile
I have trouble understanding the dialect
but we see eye to eye
the important thing is not what one says
nor how one does it
the important thing is to get along
the sense of belonging together
means more than verbal communication;

when I am together with the crow
I have this life-warm feeling
we often sit close to each other
each on a branch of the big tree
the crow winks one eye now and again
now and again I wink back
more is not required
our agreement is perfect
neither of us feels lonely
after all we have each other
and we have the big tree to sit in.

1967 **Per-Hakon Påwals**

A time's coming when this house too must crash
        and no one now can say
who will lie beneath and who will be left
        all times roll by and none recur
                it changes, all,
so slowly and yet we must persist

        A time's coming of no Gallup Polls
when all the cars will have done their mileage
and the time's been already, been many times
been as close as air on the skin
        when you're cold

and the first cry is a crash of metal –
        I've heard it
but I continue like the days and nights
I now speak with no line between dream and day
        for what should I fear here,
here I was born, not to be alone
but like the world, not into completion

but into motion without end
        and therefore I say:

I, a frantically flashing forming image, of the world
I, a space between two temples, a duplicate
I whose incomprehensibility is only that
there's this speech, I must make do in this falling house
        without falling

for I'm earth grown out of earth
I tell what's coming what's gone and all the times
I'm all cardinal points, the lands and the seas
        I'm a man, and I've a woman in me

I'm a child that never cries
I'm the eyes that never close
all the birds have come from my body,
        the birds land at my feet.

I'm a moon no one touches
I'm a light no one puts out
for my memory knows no abstractions –
        only mathematics,
        no Time –
        only times,
        a rhythm.
                fug it ive

and here there's no loneliness
there's the touch of total death, a light kiss
        is always going on,
        has always gone on.

1969

As light on a rock.
Or as a ball arcs in flight
        and drops
on a girl's hovering hand.

1985

Caj Westerberg

EVERYTHING, EVERYTHING!

A continual shouting is going on: Clear out your house!
Scrub out your room, clear out your house,
open your windows and doors, everything's coming!

1984

SWIMMING INSTRUCTIONS

Look at this swimmer, he fears the ocean, the high seas!
Barefoot he steps to the sea's edge, does a pair of air-strokes,
then is forgotten.

And this hunter? Not caught a thing,
a mere hunter's feathered hat and a rusting gun.
Yet bears a name like a man and like
a wild beast roars.

And the mother, the mother in her cradle
rocks nothing but her dreams,
and herself into a deep dream.

Ah! the ocean is wide and deep. Drowning is good;
not too little and not too much.
Only a fool drowns altogether.

1984

Risto Ahti

THE AQUARIUM

I came across the little house in a forgotten quarter of town. I call it the Gothic House because its roof slopes so steeply and the narrowness of its sides makes it look so high that it seems like a dwarf cathedral.

I have never seen the people who live there, but I have, once, been inside the house. I went there on account of an aquarium, because a friend of mine, who knows the owners, had promised to look after the fish while they were away. One Sunday in May he rang and asked whether I wanted to go with him. I did; I would have wanted to go anywhere with him.

'Here it is,' said my friend, opening a mouldering door. It was evening, and the slanting light cut across the long grass of the garden.

We entered a room that was cool and large.

'Wait a moment,' said my friend, and disappeared somewhere.

I found myself looking at a painting on the wall, and to me it seemed strange. Someone was lying, eyes closed, in the middle of an open field. The figure was inside a low, transparent tent, perhaps a mosquito net, made out of some kind of gauze. The sleeper in the painting was surrounded by the twilight of a summer night; he lay on his back, his hands by his sides, like a dead person. But he was not dead, for the gauze, the room, and all the summer night swayed with the breath of his dreams.

In the darkest corner of the room stood the aquarium. I noticed it only when my friend returned and switched on the lamp that was attached to its inner lid. I gazed into the small, glowing, water-filled room.

'What are you going to give them?'

'Mmm.' He studied the label of the fish food jar. 'These are freeze-dried termites.'

I opened the jar and inhaled; the contents were small, dark crumbs that smelled of nothing. I was alert and light-hearted. I could see everything close up and in accurate detail.

The fish swam close to the surface as soon as the light was switched on. I sprinkled the crumbs on the water, and their ring-mouths snapped. One of the fish was particularly large, greedy and beautiful.

'What's that?' I asked.

'It's an ordinary goldfish, don't you know that?'

'Ordinary?'

Nothing was ordinary that evening. With what grace the creature moved; it had a shimmering, floating tail which fluttered slowly and skilfully, as if the fish were a dancer.

'Do you think it can see us?'

'A few movements, perhaps.'

The aerating device in the corner of the aquarium hummed unevenly: there was something in it of the wind and the sound of bells. The glow of the aquarium light struck the water and reflected from its surface into our faces as we leaned over the tank.

'Listen, about that trip,' my friend said. 'I don't think it's a good idea, after all.'

'What do you mean?' I asked. He was talking about a plan which we had been discussing for a long time: a visit to Assisi.

'I'll have to give it some more thought.'

'Don't you want to go, then, after all?'

'It's not a question of that,' he said, absentmindedly trailing his fingers in the water. The fish swam up to look at them, waving its tail, and the reflections of the water, glimmering with the movement of the fins, marbled the skin of his cheek like reflected sun, as if we were standing in a stream under a summer sky.

I wanted to ask: 'What do you mean?', to sort the matter out immediately, get right to the bottom of it. But the strain of speech was overwhelming.

He lifted his fingertips and drops fell back into the underwater landscape with its carefully placed, reddish shells and thin rushes, which bent elegantly as if before a wind.

'I'll just go and water the upstairs plants,' said my friend, and closed the lid of the aquarium.

'I'll wait here,' I said.

I watched his back as he went upstairs. Twilight poured from the small black and white painting, spreading like a ring on water.

The incipient spring spread itself in front of me with dazzling emptiness. It was a table spread with a spotless cloth, set with the empty dishes of lonely weekdays.

The fish whisked its tail, and I wanted to say to him: 'You don't know me.' How quickly I grabbed the crutch, the secret comfort of all rejected souls: 'You don't know me. If you knew me, if you knew who I really am, you'd love me forever.'

He returned carrying an empty watering can, and looked at me attentively.

'I suppose I'd better turn off the aquarium light,' he said.

1983 **Leena Krohn**

THE OLD WATER RAT

There's a quiver in the reeds,
and a rustle through the grass.
Slop-lopping through the mud,
who's that puffing past?

Who's peeping there?

A whiskery jaw
and a muddy paw.
It's old Mattie
Water Rattie.

Squeezing water from his eyes,
a dewdrop on his runny nose,
he freezes and sneezes:
A-snee, a-snee, a-snizzery.
Oh what Misery!

Snizzery: sneezing misery –
it's trouble with sneezes.

Too many sneezes always displeases.
Snizzery's the water-rat word
for the thing that's occurred:
the need for a hanky.
A-snee, a-snee, a-snizzery,
Oh what Misery!

Old Mattie Water Rattie
is a workaholic
and a slave to duty.
Duty's beauty
for this sensitive dedicated Water Rattie.
Is he batty to get so wet?
It means he'll get
coughs and colds and nasty wheezes
and sniffly noses and beastly sneezes.
Well, it's how he's made –
to suffer for his trade.

But look, poor Mattie's taking a rest.
His cure is to lie with his feet north-west.
When his nose is due south-east,
that's when he seems to sniffle the least.

It seems to soothe and heal poor Mattie.

1957 **Kirsi Kunnas**

BIRDS

Some birds
          seek the lines between the trees,
                    the outer parts of the foliage, movement
                              colour & life,

other birds
seek their way into the tops of the trees,
find labyrinths there & are quickly lost.
Some birds
fly terrifyingly close sometimes, farther
test space widely, distance with
their wings stretched,
other birds
are so tilted that they just collide and
build their prison themselves, wall by wall.
Some birds
rush out, into the bathroom when they are really in a
scrape,
lock themselves up, away from the rest
in order to build coffins quickly, but free,
other birds
just sit and mumble, completely mummified
already locked up, in themselves.
Loneliness too
is something one shares, and one chooses
with whom one will share if there is no
one one chooses to be alone.
I watch the falling lights of the evenings, comets across the sky,
there is always someone bleeding, always someone
walking harbour edges, melancholy
& sunk in thoughts, loneliness
is not a thing one chooses, it is inborn
We are born, die alone under the cupolas of the
streetlights,
slowly ever more forlorn between the lamellae of
the Venetian blinds
the darkness lingers too often, my phantoms
are quieter sometimes, sil enced
Some birds
just fly for a while with others, glide
over the lands where others are
a distraction, gone the grass is always greener

somewhere else,
other birds
remain, in colour drawing
of shadow & leaves.

1980

Thomas Wulff

OLLI JALONEN
SIRKKA TURKKA

Olli Jalonen

AN EVER-DEEPENING SLEEP

There was a great hovering and soaring, a swooping and darting under the blue, over the black mud.

A flock of large birds swarmed down onto the newly cleared ploughed land, so lazily that she moved to one side to take in the wing-beats and swirling from there. It was pleasanter standing where the plough had not been but the thresher had. The short stout stubble crackled under her shoes and didn't give easily; it certainly didn't concertina under the weight of bare feet. But once the birds were on the ground their silence ended: the whole field was full of their squawkings. She couldn't watch them any more, or at least she didn't feel like it.

Not far from the screeching flock of seagulls the houses began: first sheds, huts and shelters, then blocks of flats and other buildings. The agro-industry had completely encircled the public spaces and inhabited quarters in the town centre – the cinema, the cultural centre, and the two bars. If she hadn't been an outsider, she'd have been tempted to grab a rake, the sprinkler centre's control desk, or her schoolmistress's aluminium pointer, which could be folded back to pensize. Large double racks on the loading wharf were stacked with cucumber and tomato boxes; every cucumber was squeezed into a patterned green clingfilm tube.

Only a little of the clanking of the inspection conveyor-belts was audible in the crêche playground, where many dozens of little ones, dressed in various kinds of school gear, were playing and running and cartwheeling into piles of sawdust. One of them was trying to blow dandelion petals into the air with enormous puffs but stopped and ran to get help.

'Marileena, come here. Come and have a puff. Your turn first.'

The petals didn't move, for they were still yellow as the sun. Fed up, Jyri chucked the flower away on the ground and started running again. Clasping each others' hands, they rushed to listen to what Sirpa was going to tell them. Sirpa was the crêche lady.

Well, once upon a time there was a father whose job was in a dairy. And the mother was a shopkeeper. The man and woman next door worked in the dairy too. And there was the father's brother. And he lived in a flat in the same block. The father's brother worked in the same shop as the mother.

They always set off to work at the same time, unless it happened to be duty morning in the dairy. They all left at half past seven, and the father brought the children to the crêche, to this one in fact, or one almost like it. There was enough room for all the children in the same crêche, and there was never any need to queue. For the fathers and mothers were at work during the day, in the co-operative dairy, or the shops, or the fields. And there was a machine-servicing station as well, and a library, and a school, and everything.

This father went to his dairy and started looking after the milk machines. One machine made cream and one butter and one cheese. It was the sort of cheese that has holes in it and sweats. After they were made, the cheeses were packed into plastic bags.

Listen! All of a sudden there was a telephone ringing, and this father went to answer it. For he was near. Good morning, this is so-and-so speaking from over here. Good morning, the father replied. The weirdest thing has happened: the cheeses are turning out to be nothing but hole all the way through. That really is a weird thing, the father said. It certainly is. Should I come round and see what's the matter? the father asked. Yes? So the father went round to see what was the matter.

He got onto one of those delivery mopeds and circled round to the other side. It was time for the lunch break, and a whole crowd of people were coming in from the fields. Hello, they said. And nice weather.

The person who telephoned had some tea in the pot for him, and some slices of bread. They drank their tea then and chatted about the weather and the salmon. The father did wonder, right away, at there being nothing on the bread, but he couldn't be bothered to mention it. Then the person who had telephoned asked, Well, how does your cheese taste? What cheese? asked the father. There's no cheese here. No, there isn't, but there's a hole there. That's strange, said the father, we'd better look into it: it'll be a poor do if instead of a taste of cheese you've only got a smell, and you bite your upper lip, thinking it's a sausage.

Again the father set off to look into the matter. He went to the side of the dairy where the cheese was made and questioned everybody. But no one could explain. The father stayed there studying the way the machine was working and asked a man who had just come up why the cheese was just a big hole. The man's reply was a bit difficult to understand: what's a fault that's not a fault now but soon will be, not for me but for you, who'll leave if he remembers? The father didn't know how to reply to this. He asked and asked and asked and asked.

And finally he thought of going to the front-end of the cheese machine, where they pushed the ingredients into a chute. He went on looking for quite a while and finally saw what was happening. The man on the chute was so mean and mingy he was stuffing the cheese into his own bag and just letting the holes be packed for sale. The holes were filling up the plastic bags and no one was noticing till someone did notice.

Jyri laughed most, and Marileena. They all laughed so much, the laughter rose up into the clouds, swung, flew, cartwheeled, fell, and tossed the birds about all over the place, all of them, the white and the coloured ones: everything was wheeling about.

Even the sound, it tickled you, and all at once it was if it were going inside the Girl, growing quiet there and growing into a bulge in her lower belly. The Girl smiled under the quilt. She'd have to wait. Her belly would raise her frock still more, and instead of walking she'd waddle, legs twisting and going out all over the place. Oh my darling.

At a quarter to five she had to do her sandwiches and pour the skimmed milk into a thermos flask, where it would remain at least moderately cool until her break, around ten o'clock. The Girl made tea and collected the newspaper from the letter-slot and put it on the back of the kitchen chair. The front page had nothing sensational on it, but the printer's ink had spread and spotted the picture of the harvest.

With her coat already on, the Girl went to shout bye bye to dad and mum and wakey wakey for work.

Outside it was drizzling a little, a damp mist was coming slowly down and had wet the paving stones, making them shine like smoky quartz on a ring. In the afternoon she was supposed to go to the maternity clinic for examination. Last time they said it'd be a month, or if pains came, earlier. All had gone well that month: just a little tiredness the last few days and morning sickness a few times at work.

The Girl went by foot. The factory was in the centre, surrounded by blocks of flats: a crescent of long red-bricked ones lining the road, and some lower two-storeyed ones. At this early hour of six, most of the workers were coming from the long ones. Near the factory, extending right up to its chickenwire fence, there was first a dirty pond that narrowed into a mouth and then formed a lake. Over the narrow part between the pond and the lake you could just make out a wooden bridge through the drizzle.

You had to clock in on the ground floor and couldn't get past otherwise, as the wall of the caretaker's lodge had been completely removed on the corridor side. The cloakrooms were on the third floor. The Girl put her blue coat on and her paintspotted sneakers. She left her plastic sandwich-bag in her locker, which she locked.

Eila shouted something from too far away to be heard properly. Then she disappeared into the service channel between the conveyor-belts, carrying a short-handled brush. Couldn't she even come to say hello, the Girl wondered. Eila turned a corner, but off in another direction, and disappeared again behind the screen, perhaps to change the black water for fresh.

A couple of minutes before the beginning of her shift the Girl went to her machine. The woman on the night-shift, a person of at least 35 who had only been there a couple of weeks, looked at her from between blonde eyebrows and dark bags. Here already? she said, and something else, which the machine's clattering drowned. The woman seemed even tireder than at the beginning of the week and had given up curling her hair. Can't be bothered at that age, the Girl thought. The woman was doing the night-shift on a temporary work permit; though women were not usually allowed on night-shifts, there was little hope – or fear – of the permit being withdrawn.

The step that took the Girl up to the belt was not a big one, but it had to be synchronised with the woman's on the night-shift, otherwise there'd be a jam on the belt. It took a little concentration before the body began to think without the brain. After that her movements jolted along automatically until the break and the arrival of her stand-in.

Parcels into a pile, frayed ones set aside, the piles into cardboard boxes, the boxes clipped together and piled onto the forklifts. . . On the shopfloor not many people could be seen, as there were all sorts of platforms and other obstructions next to the belts and on top of them. Ten yards away Raija was bowing over the belt in her scarf; every hour a forklift-driver came along, and from time to time a boss, and one or the other of the maintenance men, and in the spring visiting schoolgroups that turned and stared near the guide and their teacher and tried to nick whatever they could lay their hands on.

Eila had sneaked up behind her unnoticed, and she tapped her on the shoulder. The Girl jumped and at first couldn't manage a smile, but then she smiled even more broadly than usual when Eila took her red rubber glove off her left hand and stretched her fingers out at the level of her face. The thin shining ring there was quite new. That one? the Girl shouted. Yes, him. Even Eila's back looked joyful as she bent back over the uncleaned places. The Girl had to speed up for several minutes to catch up on her half-minute pause. There was something wrong with the boxes: the flaps were too long and didn't go properly into place.

A little before ten Asta Savolainen came to relieve her for the break. The Girl went to the cloakroom for her twenty minutes. She wasn't going to waste any time going to the canteen on the lower storey: it would take her five minutes to get there.

The cupboard was warm, and the sandwiches had gone sticky, almost slimy. The Girl ate some rye bread and some yeast bread, with margarine and bologna. After she'd eaten, she was still hungry: it would have been nice to gorge herself on some potatoes and gravy, and anything at all. The little seed inside her had already grown into a green fruit and was becoming demanding: it wasn't going to be satisfied with four slices and some milk.

Then it was already time. Asta Savolainen moved on to the next person, who left for the cloakroom in her turn.

The Girl felt a little faintness coming over her; she burped and pursed her lips. Raija's back showed a change of clothes: now it was her turn to be relieved.

At half past eleven the Girl began to look around to see where the forklift driver had got to. The platforms for boxes were full and piling up even higher. The Girl was forced to raise the boxes above her head and push hard down with her legs. Every time the lifting got more strenuous, and no new platform came. Well, she'd endured this before, the Girl thought: just a little longer, she'd have to: they couldn't be piled on the floor, it'd create no end of a jam: new ones were coming all the time.

Then the pain stabbed her: it dropped her to her knees by the pile of boxes. She tried to shout, but the belt and the seamer went dinning on, making their usual invincible row. The packets of handkerchiefs continued coming and piling up on the belt and spilling over from there onto the concrete floor.

Don't come, must breathe deep, the pain's searing, help, someone. Help! The Girl was lying on her side on the concrete, her legs bent, and her hands pressing against her belly. Oh how it hurts, it musn't come. And today, just when I was supposed to go for an examination.

The forklift driver was astonished at the pile of packets on the floor, and when he got round the platforms he saw the Girl. He cut the current on his forklift and put the handbrake on.

What's up then? Hey, answer. The Girl opened her eyes, forehead wrinkled, mouth twisted, forehead covered in sweat, saliva on her lips. I'm having a miscarriage. Fetch someone.

Must ring the ambulance. Got to find a telephone. Stop that machine and give us a hand. Hell fire, stop that machine. She's there, behind that pile of boxes. I'm off to ring for an ambulance. Got to find a telephone.

The phone was in the foreman's office. They had to find the number in the directory. Neither of them could remember it.

When the ambulance men arrived, a circle had gathered round the girl. One of the older women had loosened her clothes. The Girl was lying with her eyes closed and in a swoon. Between her thighs her trousers were bright red. When the Girl was lifted on to the stretcher, a pool of dirty blood was left on the concrete floor.

On the way to the hospital the orderly tried to do something, but his help was no more than holding a kidney bowl under her groin and collecting what there was to collect.

When the Girl woke, she was on an intravenous drip: two bottles of solution were dangling from the apparatus and emptying into her veins. When the Girl moved her head, she noticed the room going round like a merry-go-round, and from somewhere behind her came a nurse. Have to be absolutely quiet now, try to sleep.

Next time it was night. A lamp was lit over the door, but covered with a towel. The towel had been put there to make the room dimmer, the Girl thought. There were three beds in the room, with a plastic tent over one. Opposite the Girl and close to the door lay a grey-haired woman, with her mouth open. Her breathing was wheezing hard, and at evey outbreath she groaned.

The nurse circled the beds, looking at each face. Thirsty, whispered the Girl.

Ah, you've woken up. I'll bring you a drop straight away.

From somewhere the nurse came back with no more than half an inch of water at the bottom of a glass. I'm still thirsty, the Girl said. Just for the moment you can't have any more: you can have little more in a while. Try to sleep till morning. What's happened? the Girl asked. The nurse turned to straighten the quilt.

Was it a miscarriage? The nurse nodded. Try to sleep now. You're still young, you've got a lot years ahead of you.

The Girl looked at the nurse. Almost the same age as herself. She took the nurse's hand and wept tears onto her fingers. The nurse sat on the corner of the bedside table and took a paper handkerchief out of her pocket; she gave it to the Girl. Dry your eyes with this and blow your nose.

Everything they take, thought the Girl. The greyhaired woman's breathing sounded bad: she wouldn't have long to live. They even took my child, my own child. I shouldn't have lifted those boxes, especially on shift work. If only I'd been able to take maternity leave, but I wasn't far enough gone. If only I'd dared to take time off, but a lot of people would be after my job. Then the Girl fell asleep, leaving a soaked handkerchief on the bedside table.

In the afternoon a social worker came. She asked about the Girl's home and work, and then delicately about the miscarriage. It was mine, the Girl said. What about the father? Does he know? He doesn't know: I'm not going to tell him anything, I haven't so far, haven't even see him. It was my child, my very own. The social worker left, nodding with a strained expression on her face and wishing her luck, squeezing her hand.

As evening came on the nurse said the Girl could leave the next day. The shortage of personnel halved the observation time. The Girl could stay the night in the intensive care unit, because there wasn't any room in the other wards. The greyhaired woman hadn't died, though the Girl heard the nurses predicting it during the night.

In the morning it was the tour of the young nurse whose hand the Girl had squeezed. She filled up the discharge papers and at the door said Bye bye. The nurse's lapel was embroidered with the name Reija Ala-Mattila. Wonder if she's got children herself? the Girl thought.

She had to walk, as there wasn't enough in her purse for a taxi, and the buses' times were not suitable: she'd have had to wait nearly an hour. It was only Friday. The Girl was astonished to see what day it was from the newspaper kiosk placards. It was Friday, at the beginning of the dog days. In the market the pigeons were brawling over fallen crumbs, and a few were waiting under the newspaper kiosk, hoping for something to fall. The girl only noticed she was still wearing her paint-spotted working shoes when she was giving way to a fat slow-moving seagull that had joined the flock of city pigeons and was only distinguishable by its lighter colour. No one had come to the hospital with her other shoes.

The Girl walked more and more slowly as she drew near to her home. Her legs began to weigh as if she'd been on overtime, and she was frightened. Should she tell the truth, just a bit of it. What use would it be to tell them everything: it'd only put them in a worse mood. But I'll tell my sister: she's so young, she ought to know the truth. I must tell her everything.

There was no one in the house. Even her little sister had already gone out to play. The Girl was very weary. It was the long walk, and she still had pains. She wrapped herself up in a red and green blanket.

Perhaps she slept an ever-deepening sleep; perhaps they were woken up by it.

1978

Sirkka Turkka

Before death itself comes,
it paints the pine boles red
around the house.
It thrusts the moon, the bright moon, into the sky
on edge, like an old dish
whose enamel of light is peeling.
Over this house that night
is now folding over.
And in the changing, embracing currents the house
gets ready, unhurriedly, all by itself
for death.
Long before death arrives
the mountains of the moon rise, set
on this little house that was a home,
that's crouching, breathing scarcely audibly.
The night-hinge turns, the moon goes,
and again returns.
I nail a cross on the door, on the wall,
on the snow and the pine bole,
I light a wax cross
for the stranger to come.
In the night, wave drives after wave,
in the night, the ebb and flow of the snow.
In the night, the pillowslips, the fragrant slips and sheets
swell into sails, into expectation,
navigating from the rib-cage to earth,

to the frosty, resounding earth.
No stop on that road,
no backward look, no
halloos to the frontier.
Let the heart unroll as little red carpets
right up to the gate, let them glow,
carnations against the skin of snow.
You too, little bush, get ready,
licking my window with black flames.
Get ready and be ready.
For death is tender
when it comes.
It hugs you to its breast.
Without a word, it teaches you the meaning of your cradle song,
which it brings you behind your stooped ghost,
behind the years, the decades.
It puts a gift into your infant fingers, a gift
you stare and stare at with dimming eyes.
It gives you the song you thought you'd forgotten.
Its breast and shoulders are garlanded with flowers.
It's hollow, to absorb a person completely.
It takes you by the edges.
It opens you:
it tries to understand you.
And then it's understood.
It nails your eyes open,
your mouth open, that the
clamour of life is escaping from.
And you look, not at me now,
through me,
behind me,
at your own death.
And at the white flowers
that have burst out
all round the tiny house.

1983

IMPROMPTU FOR MY GRANDFATHER THAT NEVER WAS

A scholar set off to meet a writer, but, iced to the eyebrows, got snowbound and never made it. Best trick round here is nip off smartly to a joiner and get yourself a nice pine overcoat. The mouth of my pinetree birdhouse is gaping, Academe is falling silent, it's high time to write an impromptu for my grandfather that never was. For arduous is my family's pilgrimage underneath the snow: watch out, all saddlers, watch out too, that vodka-still under the haypile in the loft. Watch out, and then, *reposo*, rest. So when the bombing really got under way, not a single window remained unshattered. The Academy crumbled like a matchstick house, broke like a hammer in a builder's hand, and in the bomb shelters the whisperings were dashing about like waves. Later, in peacetime, everything began thrusting out shoots again in the oddest way, even that lilac bush, where the foreman puked up his false teeth against the church wall. Actually, the fault wasn't his: I accidentally hit him with a lump of icecream I was throwing at the gardener. The grass flew up to high heaven under the lawnmowers of those days, let me tell you, up into the blue sky.

I and my tender heart, we were left to circle the island in turn. I, a direct descendent of the gloomy and rheumy tsars, and my boat, with the hole in it. Not too bad a hole: circling the island is a good enough life's work in a country where two seasons are reserved for impassable roads, one for a thaw, and one for steely ice and a resting-time for a boat, *reposo*. This is where I struggle with the wind and myself, never forgetting that my grandfather's bones lie scattered somewhere. Well, scarcely bones any more, a string of vertebrae perhaps, and a hollow spot whose stare bores a hole in the clay.

There's a juniper under my window: could be anybody's grandfather, axe on shoulder. It wears me down, this continual companionship with the deceased; winter alone's been bad enough, everlasting mist shrouding the forest; and it's not till spring, when I shed all my layers of clothes, that I notice how thin I've got. From experience I can tell you that summer's no season: nothing but death dolled up in trees and bushes. The great tit has wrinkly toes, I can forecast the spring by them: the fields'll be snow and crops, turn and turn about – all that same speechless troop. Well, best of grandfathers, here we sit, any old how, I on my green stool like a weatherbeaten crow. You tucked away there under the sod: remember to keep a tight hold on your bones when the spring floods come; they'll soon be here. When the ice goes, I'll have to melt in my boat like medieval vikings into the blue space of the lake, surrounded by the squawkings of waterfowl. There are things to be done here.

I'm the member of your family the doctor weighed in his hand and said, Heavy bones and a bad lot. Quite a few of us have gone off to join you already, unless they're sitting in some circle of hell, waiting their turn. On the other hand, I've done a lot of dropping out: I don't bang my head against stone walls any more; I don't try to poke and push my way into people's consciousnesses. Hopeless job that, miserable, but I'm packing it in. I communicate nowadays rather more with a few others. It's not long since I condescended to whack a certain obstinate lordship of a horse on the head with a spade, and three riding-crops were wasted when I was trying to surmount some hurdles mounted on a dolt of a mare, too herd-conscious. Cruelty is a form of tenderness: you can have a go at teaching brothers and sisters, you can kick a dog, but it doesn't get you anywhere. It really isn't worth wasting your precious time on people. I've sat many a while on the church steps with my dog and watched the folks coming and going: damned ants. Without being in any way devout, I may add. On the other hand, of course I do believe in God, who goes up and down in the world with his apron and carpet slippers on, I don't mind saying. He's just got a hell of a job on his hands, dragging souls up there to join him. And having to listen and witness all that dreary jawing, people explaining the good they've done, and the things they've left undone.

Revered grandfather who never was, perhaps you share my opinion that black is black, as the song has it. But not too black to prevent me, up to now at least, distinguishing truth from fantasy, though it does turn out to be tricky sometimes. On misty evenings, in particular, I'm not so certain whether I'm here where the sun's eye closes, or in the Austro-Hungarian Empire, in White Russia, the Ukraine, or maybe under a plum tree in Lithuania. Am I standing here or sitting there surrounded by dropped flowers and writing letters that all end with the word love. For once homeless always homeless. Once no grandfather, always a thousand grandfathers. But perhaps it was you who governed your family with an iron hand here in this northern country, where the dogs curl up in the snow, settling down by the roadside to sleep – these stealthy, creeping northern breeds that whelp in the snow at night with the Northern Lights flashing in the sky. And a bit further on in the same song it says: Nothing I see now, now that he's gone, that's so, that's so – gone, the sun's glow.

So on misty evenings I really think I can hear the faint creak of saddle leather, the sighs of knock-kneed nags. My God – I think – that mud-spattered family gang aren't really scrambling up the map and showing their blessed centuries-old faces, are they? But anyway, in the autumn once, it did happen this way. I'd been chopping logs; a log bit into my thumb – it wasn't the axe. At that time I was in service with a baron, working as an applepicker: I was up in the tree, and the baron was down below, telling me to be careful and not fall – accompanied by his faithful companion, a one-eyed elk-hound. Well, just as I was enjoying my well-deserved rest in the evening, lapped in the warmth of an appletree-log fire, a miracle occurred. For the first time I saw the eyes of my family: they'd all merged into one look. I swear, cross my heart, hand on Bible. Swimming towards me in the twilight were brown, queerly slanty eyes. Then I saw everything clear as daylight, right down to the thirteenth century if not further. I kept all this hidden away in my heart, all the riddles that had now been solved. I'd no need to mention a single word to a single soul. I toiled away like a mad-woman, at least in my own view: my soul was fit to burst, but all I got was a blister on my hand. The grass was tall, the hawks were stalking rabbits, the snakes were crawling about minding their own business. Everything was going on as before; the damsons were dangling from the old baroness's damson bushes.

One thing I'd like to ask of you. You know, of course, that when autumn comes anyone can see that even the sun has got legs. Well, in the autumn, with the first snow coming down, Marcus found the road to heaven opening before him. What I'm getting at is, if you can put a word or two in for him, then do it. Marcus is a horse, and I suppose there's a hoof-heaven. And a horsehair- and dingy-coat heaven. There's bean heaven, a hair-of-the-head heaven, and a sweetpea heaven, not the least being left out. No one travels alone, not even the lizard. How humbly it surrenders its tail, without being disloyal. That's it. Without being disloyal. Another thing about the autumn, I still remember how the cows drifted about in the milkwhite mist. Then I switched to my proper job: planning my coming tour round the island. This way, just as in every generation, a circle comes to completion. About those eyes again: between them, and a bit underneath, there was a nose, like a little shiny saddle.

Moon of moons, so vain, so vain, as the song goes on. And it is vain, isn't it? How on earth could you escape your fate really? This is a free country, you can go skew-whiff, if you go off your rocker, or slam up against the wall. For the flower of the psychopath is lovely and unfading. This daily-besetting stupor only deepens with every delayed heartbeat. There's a moonless period and, outside, the snowfolk sleep on, and your non-existent nose points skywards under the frosty soil. A strange weakness shakes me sometimes, the ice howls under the blows of a sky-sized whip, I row across the last strait with a thermometer and a cigarette-roller as my oars. Years since – it was the July celebrations, and the lake was ice-free – a certain colonel deigned to fall off the shore into the water. He grabbed onto a willow bush and held on, singing little evanescent songs to the rising sun. His wife was asleep, so perhaps she was my aunt. Mi esposo toca bien el piano. Before that, at the stroke of midnight he'd been dancing the trepak and conversing in Russian with a white-haired gentleman, probably of Russian birth. My father, having paid his respects, cocked his toes almost correctly. So perhaps he was your son. Or your daughter's husband. When I woke in the morning the colonel had gone already, leaving a note saying where, and how many hortensia bushes I should dig flower beds for, against the autumn. The sun was radiant, the view was uninterrupted, whether he was in the middle of some reed-bed out there or in the windy open stretches. When his time came, everything went extremely quickly: there was no time for writing notes any more. Probably you too left with your boots on, standing up – not like your supposed sister, who was my great-aunt maybe, or my cousin's.

She lay a long time in her bed before she got away; in the daytime she was reliving the sleigh rides of her youth, every now and then twitching the pelt cover a bit higher. For a long time her handwriting had been scrambling heavenwards, a sure sign, and at the end she didn't know anyone any more, and so everyone had to introduce themselves over and over again. In breaks between our studies, I and my cousin sometimes used to go and check that she hadn't fallen out of her bed. I could never concentrate on my studies properly, I couldn't keep my thoughts together. Besides, my bottom began to hurt, my legs began to ache as soon as I had to sit for any length of time. I listened close to the bed at my aunt urging the driver on, with shouts, as he sat in the front seat of the sleigh, and I made up a poem: When someone full of shrapnel slowly expires, there's no such things as swift painless death for anyone. When forgotten corpses rot in the fields and marshes, the blessed weep in consecrated ground. There's no hunger for a mere third of the people. And no shame or suffering: just one huge convulsion that the wasted limbs can no longer support. And the world spurts blood that it drowns in.

Early this morning I warmed enormous quantities of milk and drank the lot. The words of the song were going round and round in my head: You're looking for some other fathead now, my nerves are gone, time for me to rest. Revered grandfather, you must be feeling rather lonely there, in the bosom of the earth, as they say. Perhaps you used to leaf through the Bible occasionally when you were alive, as much as your piccolo-playing and boozing would allow. If you didn't, well, it's all the same: as it's the sabbath, I'll anyway send you the following sentences, like a message in a bottle: Love is everlasting. And: When that which is perfect is come, that which is imperfect shall pass away. I'm sure you think I spend my days in some kind of complete haze of inactivity. Here I must put you right. The house has got to be heated, if we want to remain alive, so logs have to be split. Half a mile off, down by the field, there's a spring of running water that I dig almost daily out of the snow. The continual rains, spring, summer and autumn, make the well in our yard overflow with water smelling of sludge. Man is as watery as a cucumber: it'd be fatal to play about with his fluid balance. The hole in the ice near the jetty has to be kept open. We fetch the paper from a mile away. At nights the Virginia creeper raps against the wall and the wicker chair creaks. I can't be bothered even to put the light on. I know without looking that one of your sort, or their sort, is honouring me with a visit.This is an out-of-the-way and quiet place, no wonder unquiet spirits yearningly direct their steps hitherwards. In the morning the birds knock on the window, the wind has built up huge snowdrifts again, and I get up. I keep the radio on while I'm getting the heating going and sorting out the dog's humble repast: sometimes he gets no more than a yesterday's left-over potato.

Then I start polishing a compass, studying maps and checking my supply of dry goods. I don't forget you, whoever you may be. Without you there wouldn't be me. In my mind's eye, I can already see waves on the lake, now free and a sparkling blue. Blue as your eyes, grandfather.

1978

Inside the trees the dead stand,
eyeing us with their eyeblossom.
Not with bomb-eyes, but rain-eyes.
When you go blessing
you go blessed.
Blessed be the glance that blesses you.
The globeflower that shone briefly,
a small northern sun.
You must live with the living
but invite the dead:
they're near us to the end.
That I have seen.
That I have said before.
And when a poet falls,
a bird falls from her hand,
takes wing and begins to sing.

1983

And I want you
        to tremble at last,
when the rain-drenched lake
        raises summer on its wings,
            its swans.
When they linger one more moment
    over the park trees, over
        all the adored gold.
When their tint is
        whiter than snow already,
whiter than the tint of parting.

1986

A history of Finland in fourteen paragraphs

One of the results of the political changes of the Napoleonic era was that, in 1809, Finland was detached from the kingdom of Sweden – of which, from the beginning of its history, it had formed a part – and became an autonomous state under Russian rule.

State organs and central institutions were developed for the grand duchy. Helsinki was constructed as an impressive capital city in which both administration and institutions were based, and the country's university was also moved there.

Finland's cultural identity began to take shape in the 1830s, when the Finnish Literature Society and the Finnish Society of Arts and Sciences were founded in Helsinki. The nationalism of the 1830s was conservative in tone. Its most important literary achievements were *Elgskyttarne* ('The elk-hunters'), a long poem written by J.L. Runeberg in praise of Finnish peasant life, and Elias Lönnrot's *Kalevala*, inspired by an equal admiration for ancient Finnish poetry.

At first institutions were described; the disciplines of linguistics, history, archaeology and folklore were developed. Later a nationalist view of history, emphasising the Finnish state and nation, came into being. During the 1840s the nationalist ideal was influenced by European social-radical ideas, mediated, in particular, by the philosopher and statesman J.V. Snellman. This phase was followed on the one hand by an emphasis on the institutional structures deriving from the period of Swedish rule and a westward-oriented national identity, and on the other by a conception of national identity resting on the interests of the countryside, the Finnish language, and Finnish history. The latter argument rested mainly on purely Finnish claims, but also drew some strength from other peoples and ethnic groups of the Russian empire with a demonstrable structural linguistic link with Finnish.

During the administration of Alexander II (1855-1881), Finland's essence as a state strengthened with the institution of its own parliament and currency. The former fostered the development of the press, the latter the country's economic life. The peasantry prospered through the sale of timber and butter, and consequently increased demand, and therefore supply, of newspapers and education in the Finnish language.

The reign of Alexander III (1881-1894) saw the development of many essential infrastructural elements, particularly the railway system. There was a corresponding growth of national societies and organisations, as well as banking and assurance institutions, factors which were of critical importance in the development of Finland's coherence as a nation, both internally and externally.

Both the economy and the country's cultural life continued to develop strongly during the reign of Nicholas II (1894-1917). The period was characterised by political debate and turbulence in which domestic social problems and the question of Finland's status within the Russian empire became intertwined. The wave of strikes and political unrest caused by the Japanese war (1904-1905) spread to Finland, and the Emperor submitted to pressure, instituting a new general suffrage parliamentary system that increased the number of voters by a factor of ten (including women), although it did not extend parliamentary power.

The outbreak of the first world war in 1914 immediately led to speculation that Finland would take the opportunity to detach itself from Russia and seek protection from Germany or Sweden. This idea gained majority support only after the October Revolution of 1917 as the Russian situation descended into chaos. In November 1917 Finland separated *de facto* from Russia; it declared its independence in December 1917, and received *de jure* recognition from Russia and other important countries in January 1918. The expulsion of Russian forces, the civil war between government troops and the socialists who had attempted revolution in Finland, and Finland's strong alignment with Germany substantiated Finland's independence; when Germany collapsed, Finland, under the leadership of the regent, General C.G. Mannerheim, turned to the western powers. In July 1919 Mannerheim signed Finland's Form of Government, a compromise between the aspirations of the republicans and the monarchists that remains in force today.

Between the world wars, Finland prospered economically and became politically more stable; the years between 1929 and 1933 were, however, a period of economic and political crisis. The Scandinavian political system was strained, but survived. An essential aspect of Finland's development was the organic continuation of the government, economic and cultural structures founded during the period as a grand duchy. The great difference was the almost complete severance of links with Russia.

Towards the end of the 1930s, as the Soviet Union recovered from its revolution, civil war and internal crises, and Germany gained strength after the losses of the first world war, the military threat in the Baltic grew. In the Soviet-German agreement on spheres of influence in 1939, Finland and the Baltic countries were accorded to the Soviet Union. In November 1939, after Finland's refusal to exchange territory and allow the establishment of a military base, the Soviet Union attacked Finland. The Finnish army, however, was able to halt the advance of the Soviet forces for a period of 100 days before the Red Army's eventual victory. In the Peace of Moscow, the Soviet Union received the territories (Karelia, including the town of Viipuri), and base (the peninsula of Hanko) it had demanded.

When Germany attacked the Soviet Union in 1941, Finland joined it, prompted by a combination of political uncertainty and the desire to win back the areas recently ceded to the Soviet Union. In 1944, again, the Finnish army succeeded in halting the advance of the Red Army. An honourable armistice without occupation could be made. A final peace treaty, respecting the borders set out in the Peace of Moscow, was signed in 1947.

After the second world war, for internal and external reasons, Finland was forced to put into effect a far-reaching social restructuring. The resettlement of a tenth of the Finnish population from the ceded areas (Karelia), and the demobilised soldiers, was an extreme effort for the country after the war, especially since a heavy war indemnity was also to be paid to the Allies (i.e. the Soviet Union). In the space of two decades, the country changed from an economy dominated by agriculture to an industrial, urban society. At the same time Finland consolidated its independent status in the 'cold war' between the superpowers. Finland's relationship with the Soviet Union relaxed from predominantly military and political to economic, the differences in cultures and political systems surviving despite the fact that the communist party periodically received significant popular support in Finland, and participated in some of the coalition governments of the 1940s, 1960s and 1970s. Finland's military relationship with the Soviet Union was defined in a treaty of 1948, which required negotiations on mutual aid if Finland were to be unable to defend itself against an attack directed through its territory at the Soviet Union. The treaty was revoked in 1991-2 without such negotiations ever having taken place.

The industrialisation and urbanisation of Finland was followed by a significant change in education and the arts. These had formerly been characterised by an emphasis on the traditions and aims of neglected demographic groups, but forces emphasising the continuity of the cultural tradition – the academic and bourgeois world – were also influential. The 1950s were very European, the 1960s American-influenced, the 1970s oriented toward the political Left. In the 1980s cultural life, along with economics and foreign policy, experienced a strong emphasis on international relations and interdependence, in which the provincialism engendered by Finland's size and internal interests was consciously rejected.

In the mid 1950s Finland joined the Nordic Council and the United Nations and, at the end of the decade, the European Free Trade Area (EFTA), and received from foreign powers recognition of its neutrality. From the 1950s onwards, approximately 80 per cent of Finland's exports went to the west, 20 per cent to the east; eastward trade declined rapidly during the latter half of the 1980s. In 1973 Finland signed an associate agreement with the European Economic Community, and in 1991, with the other EFTA countries, it negotiated the European Trade Area in association with the European Community (EC). In 1992 Finland decided to ask for membership of the EC.

Matti Klinge

Acknowledgments

Andersson, Claes
When a person...: *Swedish Book Review* 1/1989

Anhava, Tuomas
I've never made a book out of less: *Contemporary Finnish Poetry*, edited and translated by Herbert Lomas, Bloodaxe Books, Newcastle upon Tyne, 1991

Bargum, Johan
Canberra, can you hear me?: *Books from Finland* 1/1987

Carpelan, Bo
The house slowly and *The spring*: *Room without walls*, translated by Anne Born, Forest Books, London, 1987

Diktonius, Elmer
Finnish Winter Dawn: *Books from Finland* 2/1982

Enckell, Rabbe
O Bridge of Interjections...: *Ice Around Our Lips*, edited and translated by David McDuff, Bloodaxe Books, Newcastle upon Tyne, 1989

Forsström, Tua
Come home: *The Snow Leopard*, translated by David McDuff, Bloodaxe Books, Newcastle upon Tyne, 1989

Haavikko, Paavo
No forest no field, Outside, blind trees, I hear the rain wake up, Now when on some night, In praise of the tyrant, Very carefully, lingering and *Conversations with Dante*: *Paavo Haavikko: Selected Poems*, translated by Anselm Hollo; Carcanet Press, Manchester, 1991; *I like slow things*: *Books from Finland* 2/1984

Jansson, Tove
The stone: *The Sculptor's Daughter*; Ernest Benn, London, 1969 (later: A. & C. Black, London)

Kihlman, Christer
Tree of God from the novel *The Blue Mother*: University of Nebraska Press, Lincoln, 1990

Kunnas, Kirsi
The Old Water Rat: *Books from Finland* 2/1979

Nieminen, Kai
The music...: *Books from Finland* 4/1986

Parland, Oscar
In the summer of 1941: *The Enchanted Way*, Peter Owen Publishers, London, 1991

von Schoultz, Solveig
Dream and *Heart*: *Speak to Me. Swedish-language Women Poets*, translated by Lennart Bruce and Sonja Bruce, The Spirit That Moves Us Press, P.O. BOX 820, Jackson Heights, N.Y. 11372, 1989; the other poems: *Snow and Summers*,

translated by Anne Born, Forest Books, London, 1989

Simonsuuri, Kirsti
Arctic journey: *Enchanting Beasts*, edited and translated by Kirsti Simonsuuri, Forest Books, London, 1990

Stenberg, Eira
My child...: *Contemporary Finnish Poetry*

Tikkanen, Märta
Right in the center...: *The Love Story of the Century*, published by Capra Press, Santa Barbara, 1984

Turkka, Sirkka
Before death itself comes: *Contemporary Finnish Poetry*

Waltari, Mika
Aton's kingdom is an extract from the novel *Sinuhe the Egyptian*: Putnam & Co., London, in 1949; a new edition by WSOY, Helsinki, 1983

Viita, Lauri
Concrete mixer: *Books from Finland* 4/ 1988

Ågren, Gösta
And then, *Circle*: *Ice Around Our Lips*

Authors

Ahti, Risto
Born 1943. Poet; first collection 1967. Translated poems in anthologies; see *Contemporary Finnish Poetry*, edited and translated by Herbert Lomas, Bloodaxe Books, Newcastle upon Tyne, 1991.
Poems from *Loistava yksinäisyys*, 1984

Andersson, Claes
Born 1937. Finland-Swedish writer. Poems, plays, prose. First work 1962. Translations include poems in anthologies; see *Ice Around Our Lips*, translated and edited by David McDuff, Bloodaxe Books, Newcastle upon Tyne, 1989.
Poems from *Under*, 1984, and *Bli, tillsammans*, 1970

Anhava, Helena
Born 1925. Poems, prose, translations. First collection 1971.
Poems from *Hidas osa*, 1979, and *Murheellisen kuullen on puhuttava hiljaa*, 1971

Anhava, Tuomas
Born 1927. Poet, critic, translator. First collection 1953. Translated works include *In the dark move slowly*, translated by Anselm Hollo, Cape Goliard, London, 1969; anthologies: *Contemporary Finnish Poetry*.
Poems from *Runoja 1961*, and *Kuudes kirja*, 1966

Aronpuro, Kari
Born 1940. Poet; first collection 1964. Runeberg Prize, 1986.
Poem from *Peltiset enkelit*, 1964

Bargum, Johan
Born 1943. Finland-Swedish writer; prose, plays. First work 1965.
Short story from *Husdjur*, 1986

Björling, Gunnar
1887–1960. Finland-Swedish poet, first collection 1922. Translated poems in anthologies; see *Ice Around Our Lips*.
Poems from *O finns en dag*, 1944, *Ord och att ej annat*, 1945, *Luft är och ljus*, 1946, *Ohört blott*, 1948, *Vårt kattliv timmar*, 1949, *Ett blyertsstreck*, 1951, *Som alla dar*, 1953, *Du görde ord*, 1955

Carpelan, Bo
Born 1926. Finland-Swedish writer; poems, plays, books for children, prose. First collection 1946.
Nordic Literature Prize 1977.
Translated works include *The Bow Island*, translated by Sheila LaFargue, Delacorte Press, New York, 1971; *Dolphins in the City*, translated by Sheila LaFargue, Delacorte Press, 1976; *The Courtyard*, translated by Samuel Charters; Swedish Books, Göteborg, 1982; *Room without walls*, translated by Anne Born, Forest Books, London, 1987; *Voices at the*

Late Hour, translated by Irma Margareta Martin, The University of Georgia Press, Athens, Georgia, 1988; *Axel*, translated by David McDuff, Carcanet Press, Manchester, 1989 (paperback edition: Paladin, 1991); anthologies: *Ice Around Our Lips*. Poems from *Gården*, 1969, *Källan*, 1973, *År som löv*, 1989

Diktonius, Elmer
1896–1961. Finland-Swedish writer. Poems, prose; first collection 1922.
Translated poems in anthologies; see *Ice Around Our Lips*.
Poem from *Annorlunda*, 1948

Donner, Jörn
Born 1933. Finland-Swedish writer. Prose, essays; first work 1951.
Finlandia Prize 1986.
Short story from *Finlands ansikte*, 1961

Enckell, Rabbe
1903–1974. Finland-Swedish writer. Poems, plays, essays; first collection 1923.
Translated poems in anthologies; see *Ice Around Our Lips*.
Poem from *Andedräkt av koppar*, 1946

Forsström, Tua
Born 1947. Finland-Swedish poet. First collection 1972.
Translated works include *Snow leopard*, translated by David McDuff, Bloodaxe Books, Newcastle upon Tyne, 1989.
Poem from *Snöleopard*, 1987

Haanpää, Pentti
1905–1950. Prose; first work 1925.
Short story from 1946, in *Valitut teokset*, 1976

Haavikko, Paavo
Born 1931. Poems, novels, plays, essays. First collection 1951.
Neustadt Prize, 1984.
Translated works include *The Horseman* (libretto), translated by Philip Binham, Esan Kirjapaino, Lahti, 1974; *Kullervo's Story*, translated by Anselm Hollo, Art House, Helsinki, 1989; *Paavo Haavikko: Selected poems*, translated by Anselm Hollo, Carcanet Press, Manchester, 1991. Anthologies: *Contemporary Finnish Poetry*.
Poems from *Tiet etäisyyksiin*, 1951, *Tuuliöinä*, 1953, *Synnyinmaa*, 1955, *Puut, kaikki heidän vihreytensä*, 1966, *Runoja matkalta salmen ylitse*, 1973, *Viiniä, kirjoitusta*, 1976, *Toukokuu, ikuinen*, 1988

Hellaakoski, Aaro
1893–1952. Poet. First work 1921.
Poems from *Huojuvat keulat*, 1946, *Sarjoja*, 1952

Holappa, Pentti
Born 1927. Poems, novels, essays, plays; first work 1950. Translated poems in anthologies; see *Contemporary Finnish Poetry*.
Poems from *Maan poika*, 1953, *Katsokaa silmiänne*, 1959; prose extract from the novel *Tinaa*, 1961

Huldén, Lars
Born 1926. Finland-Swedish poet, scholar, novelist, dramatist; first collection in 1958.
Translated works include *The Chain Dance. Selected poems*, translated and

with an introduction by George C. Schoolfield, Camden House, South Carolina, 1991. Poem from *Herdedikter*, 1984

Huovinen, Veikko
Born 1927. Short stories, novels. First work 1950.
Short story from *Hirri*, 1950

Hyry, Antti
Born 1931. Short stories, novels, radio plays. First work 1958.
Short story from *Maantieltä hän lähti*, 1958

Idström, Annika
Born 1947. Prose; first work in 1975. Translated works include *My Brother Sebastian*, translated by Joan Tate, Forest Books, London 1991.
Extract from the novel *Veljeni Sebastian*, 1985

Jalonen, Olli
Born 1954. Prose; first work 1978. Finlandia Prize 1991.
Short story from the collection *Unien tausta*, 1978

Jansson, Tove
Born 1914. Finland-Swedish writer. Books for children, short stories, novels, plays. First work 1945.
Translated works include *Sculptor's Daughter*, translated by Kingsley Hart, Ernest Benn, London, 1969 (paperback edition: Avon Books, New York, 1976); *The Summer Book*, translated by Thomas Teal, Penguin Books, 1977; *Sun City*, translated by Thomas Teal, Pantheon Books, London, 1976; the eight Moomin stories published by Penguin/Puffin Books. Extract from the memoirs, *Bildhuggarens dotter*, 1968

Joenpelto, Eeva
Born 1921. Prose; first work 1946. Translated works include *The Maiden Walks upon the Water*, translated by Therese A. Nelson, WSOY, Helsinki, 1991.
Extract from the novel *Veljen varjo*, 1951

Joenpolvi, Martti
Born 1936. Prose; first work 1959.
Short story from *Kuparirahaa*, 1969

Juvonen, Helvi
1919–1959. Poet, translator. First collection 1949.
Poem from *Kalliopohja*, 1955

Kajava, Viljo
Born 1909. Poet. First collection 1935. Poems from *Jokainen meistä*, 1954, *Taivaan sineen*, 1959, *Vallilan rapsodia*, 1972, *Ei kukaan ole voittaja*, 1962, *Rannat, rannat*, 1977

Katz, Daniel
Born 1938. Novels, short stories, plays. First work 1968.
Short story from *Naisen torso ja muita kertomuksia*, 1989

Kihlman, Christer
Born 1930. Finland-Swedish novelist, poet, dramatist. First work 1951.
Translated works include *Sweet Prince*, translated by Joan Tate, Peter Owen, London, 1983; *All My Sons*, translated by Joan Tate, Peter Owen, London & Washington D.C., 1984; *The Downfall of Gerdt Bladh*, trans-

lated by Joan Tate; Peter Owen, London, 1989; *The Blue Mother*, translated by Joan Tate, Nebraska University Press, Lincoln, 1990.
Extract from *Den blå modern*, 1986

Kilpi, Eeva
Born 1928. Poems, novels, short stories. First work 1959.
Translated works include *Tamara*, translated by Philip Binham, Delacorte Press/Seymour Lawrence, New York, 1978
Extract from *Talvisodan aika*, 1989

Kirstinä, Väinö
Born 1936. Poems, essays, plays. First collection 1961.
Translated poems in anthologies; see *Contemporary Finnish Poetry*.
Poems from *Lakeus*, 1961

Kivikkaho, Eila
Born 1921. Poems, books for children. First collection 1942. Translated poems in anthologies; see *Contemporary Finnish Poetry*.
Poems from *Niityltä pois*, 1951, *Venelaulu*, 1952, *Parvi*, 1961, *Runoja 1961–1975*, 1975

Krohn, Leena
Born 1947. Books for children, short stories, essays, novels, poems. First work 1970.
Story from *Donna Quijote ja muita kaupunkilaisia*, 1983

Kunnas, Kirsi
Born 1924. Books for children, poems, translations. First collection 1947.
Translated poems in anthologies; see *Contemporary Finnish Poetry*.
Poem from *Tiitiäisen satupuu*, 1957

Laine, Jarkko
Born 1947. Poems, novels, short stories, translations. First collection 1967.
Translated poems in anthologies; see *Contemporary Finnish Poetry*.
Poems from *Tulen ja jään sirkus*, 1970, *Nauta lentää*, 1973, *Viidenpennin Hamlet*, 1976, *Villiintynyt puu*, 1984

Liksom, Rosa
(Anni Ylävaara) Born 1958. Prose, short stories, illustrations. First work 1985.
Short story from *Yhden yön pysäkki*, 1985

Linna, Väinö
1920-1992. Prose; first work 1947.
Extract from the novel *Tuntematon sotilas*, 1954

Manner, Eeva-Liisa
Born 1921. Poems, plays, prose. First collection 1944.
Translated poems in anthologies; see *Contemporary Finnish Poetry*.
Poems from *Tämä matka*, 1956, *Orfiset laulut*, 1960, *Niin vaihtuvat vuodenajat*, 1964, *Fahrenheit 121*, 1968, *Paetkaa purret kepein purjein*, 1971, *Kuolleet vedet*, 1977

Melleri, Arto
Born 1956. Poems, plays, novels; first collection 1978.
Finlandia Prize 1992.
Translated poems in anthologies; see *Contemporary Finnish Poetry*.
Poem from *Mau-Mau*, 1982

Meri, Veijo
Born 1928. Novels, short stories, poems, plays. First work 1954.
Translated works include *The manila rope*, translated by John McGahern and Annikki Laaksi, Knopf, New York, 1967.
Short story from 1960, in *Novellit*, 1985; poems from *Ylimpänä pieni höyhen*, 1980

Meriluoto, Aila
Born 1924. Poems, prose. First collection 1946.
Translated poems in anthologies; see *Contemporary Finnish Poetry*.
Poem from *Lasimaalaus*, 1946.

Mustapää, P.
(Martti Haavio; scholar) 1899–1973. Poet. First collection 1925.
Poems from *Jäähyväiset Arkadialle*, 1945, *Linnustaja*, 1952

Mäkelä, Hannu
Born 1943. Prose, poems, plays, books for children. First collection 1966.
Translated poems in anthologies; see *Contemporary Finnish Poetry*.
Poems from *Ikään kuin ihminen*, 1980, *Unelma onnesta no 5*, 1985

Nieminen, Kai
Born 1950. Poet, translator. First collection 1971.
Poem from *Syntymästä*, 1973

Nieminen, Pertti
Born 1929. Poet, translator. First collection 1956.
Poems from *Silmissä maailman maisemat*, 1964, *Yöt lentävä lintu lentää*, 1986

Nordgren, Ralf
Born 1936. Finland-Swedish poet and novelist. First work 1964.
Poem from *Idyll och program*, 1972

Nummi, Lassi
Born 1928. Novels, poems; first collection 1949.
Translated poems in anthologies; see *Contemporary Finnish Poetry*.
Poems from *Heti, melkein heti*, 1980, *Karu laidunrinne*, 1989

Paasilinna, Erno
Born 1935. Short stories, essays, novels. First work 1967.
Finlandia Prize 1985.
Extract from the novel *Kadonnut armeija*, 1977

Paavilainen, Matti
Born 1923. Poems, prose; first collection 1964.
Poem from *Unohduksen huvilat*, 1981

Parland, Oscar
Born 1912. Finland-Swedish writer. Novels; first work 1945.
Translated works: *The Year of the Bull*, *The Enchanted Way*, translated by Joan Tate, Peter Owen Publishers, London, 1991.
Extract from the novel *Den förtrollade vägen*, 1953

Paronen, Samuli
1917–1974. Novels, short stories, aphorisms. First work 1964.
Extract from the novel *Kuolismaantie*, 1967

Pekkanen, Toivo
1902–1957. Novels, short stories; first work 1927.
Translated works include *My childhood*, translated by Alan Blair, Uni-

versity of Wisconsin Press, Madison, 1966.
Extract from the autobiography *Lapsuuteni*, 1953

Pellinen, Jyrki
Born 1940. Poems, prose; first collection 1962.
Poems from *Näistä asioista*, 1962, *Kuuskajaskari*, 1964, *Niin päinvastoin kuin kukaan*, 1965, *Kevätpäivät*, 1970, *Kesän maa*, 1973, *Kun sinussa on joku*, 1983, *Yön kaunottaret ovat todellisia kuvitelmia*, 1987

Peltonen, Juhani
Born 1941. Prose, plays, poems; first collection 1964.
Poem from *Kesken asumisen*, 1968

Pennanen, Eila
Born 1916. Prose; translations. First work 1942.
Extract from the novel *Himmun rakkaudet*, 1971

Pylkkönen, Maila
1931–1986. Poet. First work 1957.
Poems from *Jeesuksen kylä*, 1958

Påwals, Per-Hakon
Born 1928. Finland-Swedish poet; first work 1956.
Poems from *Min salladsgröna älskarinna*, 1967

Rauhala, Niilo
Born 1936. Poet; first collection 1967.
Poems from *Joki virtaa nyt eikä liiku*, 1969

Rekola, Mirkka
Born 1931. Poet; first collection 1954.
Translated poems in anthologies; see *Contemporary Finnish Poetry*.
Poems from *Syksy muuttaa linnut*, 1961, *Ilo ja epäsymmetria*, 1965, *Anna päivän olla kaikki*, 1968, *Minä rakastan sinua, minä sanon sen kaikille*, 1972, *Kohtaamispaikka vuosi*, 1981, *Kuutamourakka*, 1981, *Puun syleilemällä*, 1983

Rintala, Paavo
Born 1930. Prose, plays. First work 1954.
Translated works include *The long distance patrol*, translated by Maurice Michael, Allen & Unwin, London, 1967.
Extract from the documentary novel *Sotilaiden äänet*, 1966

Rossi, Matti
Born 1934. Poems, prose, translations. First collection 1965.
Poem from *Näytelmän henkilöt*, 1965

Ruuth, Alpo
Born 1943. Novels, short stories, plays for the radio and television. First work 1967.
Short story, 1968, from *Suomalaisia novelleja* 1973

Saarikoski, Pentti
1937–1983. Poetry, prose, plays, translations. First collection 1958.
Translated works include *Poems 1958–1980*, translated by Anselm Hollo, published by The Toothpaste Press, Iowa, 1983; *Dances of the Obscure*, translated by Michael Cole and Karen Kimball, Logbridge-Rhodes Inc., Colorado, 1987; anthologies: *Contemporary Finnish Poetry*.

Poems from *Runot ja Hipponaksin runot*, 1959, *Hämärän tanssit*, 1983

Saaritsa, Pentti
Born 1941. Poems, plays, translations. First collection 1965.
Translated works include *Gathering Fragments*, translated by Seija Paddon, Penumbra Press, 1991; anthologies: *Contemporary Finnish Poetry.*
Poems from *Mitä näenkään*, 1979, *Takaisin lentoon*, 1982

Saastamoinen, Tyyne
Born 1924. Poems, prose. First collection 1960.
Poems from *Ehkä tämä on vain syksyä*, 1972, *Hiljaa, hyvin hiljaa teen päivistäni kirjaa*, 1976, *Ruhtinaslintu*, 1987

Salakka, Hannu
Born 1955. Poet; first collection 1974.
Poem from *Myös todellisuus on uskonto*, 1986

Sandelin, Peter
Born 1930. Finland-Swedish poet; first collection 1951.
Poems from *En vanlig solig dag*, 1965, *Tyst stiger havet*, 1971, *Var det du?*, 1973

von Schoultz, Solveig
Born 1907. Finland-Swedish poet, prose writer, dramatist. First work 1940.
Poems from *Allt sker nu*, 1952, *Nattlig äng*, 1949, *Sänk ditt ljus*, 1963, *De fyra flöjtspelarna*, 1975, *Bortom träden hörs havet*, 1980, *Ett sätt att räkna tiden*, 1989.
Translated works include *Heartwork*, translated by Marlaine Delargy and Joan Tate, Forest Books, London, 1989; *Snow and Summers*, translated by Anne Born, Forest Books, 1989; anthologies: *Ice Around Our Lips.*

Siekkinen, Raija
Born 1953. Short stories, books for children. First work 1978.
Short story from *Elämän keskipiste*, 1983

Simonsuuri, Kirsti
Born 1945. Poems, prose, essays, translations. First work 1980.
Translated poems in anthologies; see *Enchanted Beasts. An anthology of Modern Woman Poets of Finland*, edited and translated by Kirsti Simonsuuri, Forest Books, London 1990.
Poem from *Murattikaide*, 1980

Skiftesvik, Joni
Born 1948. Short stories, novels. First work 1983.
Short story from *Suolamänty*, 1988

Stenberg, Eira
Born 1943. Poems, prose. First collection 1966.
Translated poems in anthologies; see *Contemporary Finnish Poetry.*
Poem from *Parrakas madonna*, 1983

Suhonen, Pekka
Born 1938. Poems, prose, essays, translations. First collection 1965.
Poem from *Kootut runot*, 1965

Suosalmi, Kerttu-Kaarina
Born 1921. Prose, poems, books for children, plays. First work 1950.
Extract from the novel *Venematka*, 1974

Tikkanen, Henrik
1924–1984. Finland-Swedish writer, artist. Prose, plays for the stage, radio and television. First work 1946.
Translated works include *A Winter's Day*, translated by Mary Sandbach, Pantheon Books, New York, 1980; *Snob's Island*, translated by Mary Sandbach, Chatto & Windus, London, 1980; *The 30 Years' War*, translated by George Blecher & Lone Thygesen Blecher, Nebraska University Press, Lincoln, 1987.
Extract from the prose work *Över fjärden är himlen hög*, 1959

Tikkanen, Märta
Born 1935. Finland-Swedish writer. Prose, drama, poems; first work 1970.
Translated works include *The Love Story of the Century*, translated by Stina Katchadourian, Capra Press, Santa Barbara, 1984.
Poem from *Århundradets kärlekssaga*, 1978.

Turkka, Sirkka
Born 1939. Poet; first collection 1973. Finlandia Prize 1987.
Translated works include *Not You, Not the Rain*, translated by Seija Paddon, Penumbra Press, Waterloo, 1991; anthologies: see *Contemporary Finnish Poetry*.
Poems from *Yö aukeaa kuin vilja*, 1978, *Vaikka on kesä*, 1983, *Tule takaisin, pikku Sheba*, 1986

Turtiainen, Arvo
1904–1980. Poet; first collection 1936.
Poems from *Minä paljasjalkainen*, 1962

Tuuri, Antti
Born 1944. Prose, radio plays. First work 1971.
Short story from *Sammuttajat*, 1983.

Tynni, Aale
Born 1913. Poet, translator. First collection 1936.
Poem from *Lehtimaja*, 1946

Waltari, Mika
1908–1979. Novels, short stories, plays. First work 1928.
Translated works include *Sinuhe the Egyptian*, translated by Naomi Walford, 1949, new edition by WSOY, Helsinki, 1983; *The Roman*, translated by Joan Tate, Hodder & Stoughton, London, 1966.
Extract from the novel *Sinuhe egyptiläinen*, 1945

Vartio, Marja-Liisa
1924–1966. Poems, prose, plays for the radio and television. First collection 1952.
Short story from *Maan ja veden välillä*, 1955

Westerberg, Caj
Born 1946. Poet, translator. First collection 1967.
Translated poems in anthologies; see *Contemporary Finnish Poetry*.
Poems from *En minä ole ainoa kerta*, 1969, *Kirkas nimetön yö*, 1985

Viita, Lauri
1916–1965. Poems, prose. First collection 1947.
Poem from *Betonimylläri*, 1947

Wik, Inga-Britt
Born 1930. Finland-Swedish poet; first collection 1952.
Poem from *Jack's café*, 1980

Wulff, Thomas
Born 1953. Finland-Swedish poet; first collection 1973.
Poems from *Snap-shots*, 1980

Ågren, Gösta
Born 1936. Finland-Swedish poet; prose writer, dramatist.
First collection 1955.
Finlandia Prize 1989.
Translated poems in anthologies; see *Ice Around Our Lips*.
Poems from *En dal i våldet*, 1990